PUBLISHED FOR

JUDAICA RESEARCH AT YALE UNIVERSITY

on the

LOUIS M. RABINOWITZ FOUNDATION

YALE JUDAICA SERIES

EDITORS

Julian Obermann

Louis Ginzberg   Harry A. Wolfson

Volume II

THE CODE OF MAIMONIDES

(*MISHNEH TORAH*)

BOOK THIRTEEN

The Code of Maimonides

BOOK THIRTEEN

THE BOOK OF CIVIL LAWS

TRANSLATED FROM THE HEBREW BY

JACOB J. RABINOWITZ

MEMBER OF THE NEW YORK BAR

NEW HAVEN

YALE UNIVERSITY PRESS

LONDON · GEOFFREY CUMBERLEGE · OXFORD UNIVERSITY PRESS

1949

PREFATORY NOTE

With this volume, Judaica Research initiates the plan of including in the Yale Judaica Series a translation of the Code of Maimonides. When completed, this will be the first time that the entire Code has been translated into English or indeed into any language.

Of the translation projects upon which Judaica Research at Yale University has embarked since its inception in 1944, none has seemed more difficult and venturesome than that of making this work of Maimonides accessible to modern readers in its encyclopaedic totality.

The translation will comprise 14 volumes, each representing one of the 14 Books that constitute the Code. Although each volume is to be prefaced by a brief Introduction pertaining to the Book concerned, a fifteenth volume is contemplated to undertake a critical appraisal of the Code in its entirety. Most of the 14 Books are under preparation, each Book having been assigned to an individual scholar, while one is being prepared in collaboration of two scholars. It is expected that the remaining Books will be assigned for preparation in the near future. In addition to the present volume, three of the Books have already been completed, and several others are approaching completion.

From the beginning, the Editors have realized the difficulty entailed in assigning each Book to a scholar competent to cope with its particular subject. For in this work Maimonides strove to furnish an all-inclusive code of native Jewish law and mores in methodical systematization. As such, almost every one of its Books involves some branch of the social or natural sciences. Apart, therefore, from philological mastery of the vast and complex field of *Halakha,* the translation of any Book of the Code requires mastery of the sphere or spheres of science peculiarly characteristic of the Book in question, whether it be mathematics and astronomy, anatomy and physiology, law and jurisprudence, agriculture and botany, cult and ritual, ethics and metaphysics —to say nothing of the task of rendering Maimonides' incomparable style and his creative Hebrew idiom into modern English.

In the nature of things, then, no prediction could be made beforehand as to the time that might be required for the preparation and completion of any given Book of the Code. Accordingly, it has not seemed possible, or even desirable to plan for publication of the volumes comprising the translation in the order in which the Books occur in the Code. Instead, the individual volumes are to be offered in whatever order they may be completed and made ready for publication. As it is, our initial offering contains Book Thirteen, *The Book of Civil Laws*—a volume that may be expected to be of interest to modern jurists as well as to students of the legal institutions of Judaism and indeed of the Near East in general.

From all indications, it should be possible to publish the volumes of the Code at more or less regular intervals. However, owing to previous commitments the appearance of these volumes will of necessity be interspersed with the publication of other translations that have been undertaken under the aegis of Yale Judaica Research.

Those associated with the Rabinowitz Foundation at Yale are fully aware of the grave scholarly and literary responsibility they have assumed in undertaking to make one of the most outstanding works of medieval Judaism accessible to modern readers. It is their hope that they may be privileged to bring this undertaking to a successful conclusion.

J.O.

New Haven, Connecticut
  March, 1949

CONTENTS

PREFATORY NOTE   v

CONTENTS   vii

INTRODUCTION   xvii
  The Book of Civil Laws as a Whole
  The Treatises
  The Book of Civil Laws and The Mishnah
  Points of Special Interest
  The Translation

THE BOOK OF CIVIL LAWS   1

  TREATISE ONE: HIRING   3
    Chapter 1. Bailment. Types of bailee and rules applicable to each
    type. Bailment *with the owner*. Unauthorized bailment by bailee   4
    Chapter 2. Bailment. Exceptions to rules concerning bailment.
    Negligence of bailee. Things attached to the soil. Change in status
    of bailor or bailed object. Sex and age of bailor or bailee. Estab-
    lishment of bailor-bailee relationship. Stipulations between bailor
    and bailee. Conflicting allegations with respect to existence of
    bailor-bailee relationship   7
    Chapter 3. Bailment. *Force majeure*. Carriers of goods. Assess-
    ment of damages against carrier. Injury to animals entrusted to
    shepherd   11
    Chapter 4. Hirer's liability. Deviations from terms of hiring.
    Implied conditions of hiring   15
    Chapter 5. Rights and liabilities of parties to a hiring. Hired
    object rendered unusable through accident. Substitution of other
    party by hirer of ship and by lessee of real property. Destruction
    of house during term of lease   18
    Chapter 6. Letting of houses. Appurtenances. Repairs. Manure.
    Lease for definite term. Lease for indefinite term. Notice to vacate
    premises. Notice of intention to quit premises   22
    Chapter 7. Letting of houses or of other real property. Validity
    of stipulations. Duration of lease. Conflicting allegations with re-
    spect to payment of rental, date of termination, and duration of
    lease   24
    Chapter 8. Letting of fields. Letting for payment in money or in
    kind. Tenancy on shares. Local usage. Division of produce be-
    tween landlord and tenant on shares. Failure on part of tenant
    to cultivate land. Deviation from terms of tenancy   27

Chapter 9. Hiring of workers. Local usage. Wages. Breach of contract of employment. Supervening impossibility. Mistake   31
Chapter 10. The bailee by implication of law. The pledgee. The craftsman. The planter. The public scribe, teacher, planter, butcher, and bloodletter   37
Chapter 11. Employer and worker. Timely payment of worker's wage. Conflicting allegations with respect to payment and amount of wage. Worker's oath   39
Chapter 12. Employer and worker. Employer's duty to allow worker to eat of that at which he is working   44
Chapter 13. Animals at work. Prohibition of keeping animal from eating of that at which it is working   48

TREATISE TWO: BORROWING AND DEPOSITING   51
Chapter 1. The commodatary. The commodatary's liability. Injury to borrowed object during performance of task for which it was borrowed; conflicting allegations with regard thereto. Assessment of damages against commodatary. Duration of borrowing   52
Chapter 2. Borrowing *with the owner*. Exemption from liability of borrower *with the owner*. The public teacher, scribe, planter, and bloodletter. Borrowing from one's wife or from one's partner   55
Chapter 3. Commencement and termination of commodatary's liability. Sending borrowed object through messenger. Conflicting allegations with regard to time of injury or identity of injured object   58
Chapter 4. Depositing. The gratuitous bailee. The proper manner of safekeeping of various kinds of deposits. The negligent bailee. Delivery of deposit by bailee to members of his household   60
Chapter 5. Depositing. Bailee of charitable funds. Extortion of deposited money by robbers. Bailee's failure to raise hue and cry. Confusion of deposits by bailee. Commingling by bailee of deposited produce with his own. Admission of liability by bailee without admission of extent thereof   64
Chapter 6. Depositing. Election by bailee to pay rather than take bailee's oath. Stipulations with regard to manner of safekeeping. Proof by witnesses of lack of negligence on bailee's part. Deposit in presence of witnesses. Claims against bailee's heirs. Denial by bailee of continuance of bailor-bailee relationship   68
Chapter 7. Limitations upon bailee's powers. Selling deteriorating deposit. Selling by court order. Banker and depositor. Removal of deposited object from one place to another. Departure of depositor   71
Chapter 8. Bailee's election to pay. Bailee's voluntary payment or admission of liability. His right to recovery of double payment and to accretions   74

CONTENTS

TREATISE THREE: CREDITOR AND DEBTOR   77

Chapter 1. Loans and repayment. Duty of lending to the poor. Duty of repaying loans. Levy upon debtor's property. Property exempt from levy   78

Chapter 2. The insolvent debtor. The debtor's oath of insolvency. Exemptions from the oath of insolvency. Execution against debtor's debtor   81

Chapter 3. Distraint. The widow's chattels. Chattels used in the preparation of food. Prohibition of private distraint. Return of chattels taken in distraint. Judicial sale of same   85

Chapter 4. Usury. The lender, the borrower, the surety, the witnesses, and the scribe in a usurious transaction. Restitution of usury. Recovery of principal on writing containing usury   88

Chapter 5. Usury. The heathen borrower or lender. Transfer of loans. The heathen as an intermediary. The proselyte. Quasi usury. Transactions resembling usury. Evasion of the usury laws   93

Chapter 6. Usury. Pentateuchal usury. Quasi usury. Usury stipulated after making of loan. Loan on gage with forfeiture provision. Conditional conveyance of property. Gage with or without deduction. Distinction between field and house property   97

Chapter 7. Usury. Gage of field without deduction. Redemption of gage. Advance payment of rent. Lending money to tenant for cultivation. Increasing worker's wage in consideration of delayed payment   102

Chapter 8. Usury. Increasing price of purchase in consideration of delayed payment. Sharing of profits without sharing of losses by joint adventurer. Restitution of value of article given in lieu of usury   105

Chapter 9. Usury. Agreement of purchase and sale of produce to be harvested or of industrial products to be produced. Market price   109

Chapter 10. Usury. Lending produce with or without definite time fixed for repayment. Lending seed to one's tenants on shares. Converting a loan of money into a loan of produce   114

Chapter 11. Debt on a writing and oral debt; enforcement thereof. Definition of oral debt; of debt on a writing. Distinction between oral debt and debt on a writing with respect to enforcement. Enforcement of oral debt against debtor's heirs. Concealment of movables by debtors. Execution against movables in the hands of debtor's heirs   116

Chapter 12. Enforcement against debtor's heirs. Minors. Debt owed to heathen on usury. The widow's endowment. Specific instructions by deceased. Appointment of guardian *ad litem* in certain cases. Form of writ of execution against orphans' property. Proclamation of judicial sale of property levied upon; inquest and appraisal   120

Chapter 13. Enforcement against absent debtor. Notice to debtor. Necessary proofs. Loan on a pledge. Time and place of enforcement   124

Chapter 14. Oath by parties. Admission of part payment. Enforcement in absence of debtor or against property in hands of transferee. Denial of debt by debtor. Plea of forgery, usury, or other ground of invalidity of writing. Partial admission by debtor. Writing which creditor is unable to have confirmed. Claim by creditor that payment applied to debt other than that evidenced by writing. Both parties holding writing   127

Chapter 15. Stipulations with respect to proof of payment. Stipulation that payment be made in presence of witnesses. Giving creditor credence with respect to nonpayment. Empowering creditor to enforce payment without taking an oath   133

Chapter 16. Discharge of debtor's liability. Debtor's continued liability until payment reaches hands of creditor. Remittance of payment by debtor through third party. Novation. Draft on third party. Draft on shopkeeper. Suit by holder of writing other than original creditor. Writing in the hands of depository. Writing found among discharged writings   136

Chapter 17. Enforcement of creditor's heirs or against debtor's heirs. The oath of the creditor's heirs. Creditor predeceased by debtor or vice versa. Writing containing credence to debtor with respect to payment. Minors. Coin in which debt is payable   140

Chapter 18. Property liability for payment of debts. Real property. Movables. After-acquired property. Hypothecation of specific property. Property dedicated to sanctuary. Execution against real property in hands of debtor's heirs   143

Chapter 19. Execution against debtor's property. Property of best, medium, and poor quality. Free and alienated property. The tortfeasee, the lender, and the woman suing for her endowment. Successive transferees   147

Chapter 20. Priority between creditors. Successive obligations. After-acquired property. Distribution of assets between creditors having no priority   150

Chapter 21. Execution against improvements of debtor's property. Improvements through expenditures and spontaneous improvements. Produce. Improvements in hands of debtor's donee. Improvements made by debtor's orphans   154

Chapter 22. Enforcement procedure. Confirmation of writing

obligatory. Judicial extension of time. Waiting period of three court days. Writ of execution. Writ of seizure. Appraisal of property. Proclamation of sale. Formal requirements of writs of execution, seizure, and appraisal. Method of arriving at appraisal. Error. Redemption of property by debtor 158

Chapter 23. The legal document. Antedated and postdated writings obligatory. Preparation of writing obligatory in absence of creditor or of debtor. Antedated and postdated deeds of conveyance. Anticipatory declaration of duress. Writing two deeds of conveyance of same property. Writing two writings obligatory for the same debt. Substitute writing obligatory. Judicial incision of documents. Writing of acquittance. Splitting of indebtedness 163

Chapter 24. The legal document. Writings of betrothal and of marriage, of tenancy on shares, of selection of judges and of pleading. The scribe's fee. Identity of parties. Witnesses' ability to read and sign writing. Two parties with identical names. The "I owe you" writing 169

Chapter 25. Guarantee and suretyship. Guarantee after, or at the time of making of loan. Enforcement of obligation against guarantor. Insolvency of principal debtor. Guaranty and suretyship. Assumption of warranty by party other than seller of property. Conditional suretyship or guarantee. Joint debtors. Joint guarantors. Guarantor's guarantor. Guarantee for indeterminate amount. Undertaking to produce debtor 173

Chapter 26. Guarantee and suretyship. Guarantee after attestation by witnesses. Judicial extension of time to guarantor. Creditor's right of election between principal debtor and surety. Principal debtor's oath of insolvency. Guarantor's recourse against principal debtor. The bondman, the married woman, and the minor as guarantors 176

Chapter 27. Preparation of legal documents. Language of document. Heathen witnesses. Confirmation by heathen judge. Delivery in presence of Israelite witnesses. The formal requirements of legal documents. Erasures. Precautions against forgery. Inconsistency. Construction 180

TREATISE FOUR: PLEADING 189

Chapter 1. Pleas requiring affirmation by oath. Partial admission. The Pentateuchal oath plea contradicted by one witness. The quasi-Pentateuchal oath. The informal oath in affirmation of general denial. Refusal to take oath. The ban of excommunication. Shifting of oath. The claim doubtful. The oath by accumulation. Several claims by one plaintiff 190

Chapter 2. The suspect with respect to oaths. Inadmission of suspect to oath. Definition of suspect. Oath by suspect's adversary. Suspect in position of plaintiff. Suspect who is liable to informal oath. Ineffectiveness of suspect's oath. Restoration of suspect's oathworthiness 196

Chapter 3. Partial admission. Amount admitted and amount denied. Computation of amount. Utensils. Oath by plaintiff. Relation of admission to claim 199

Chapter 4. Partial admission. Things measurable, weighable, or numerable. Partial admission of liability provable by other evidence. Party's inability to swear despite liability to oath. Proof of part of claim through testimony of witnesses 203

Chapter 5. Exceptions to rules concerning oaths. Landed property, bondmen, writings obligatory, and property belonging to sanctuary; the informal oath with respect thereto. Produce about to be harvested. Demand to produce writing containing evidence of demandant's rights. Claim by the deaf-mute, the incompetent, or the minor. The informal oath with respect to claim by minor. Claims against minor; growing out of transactions beneficial to minor; growing out of torts committed by minor 207

Chapter 6. The effect of various allegations of the parties. Allegations of fact and of conclusions of law. General denial changed to plea of payment. Plea of payment in presence of witnesses denied by same. Production of witnesses to payment. Withdrawal of admission of indebtedness made in presence of witnesses 212

Chapter 7. Recognizances and admissions. Recognizance in presence of two witnesses. Reducing recognizance to writing. Recognizance before court of three sitting in regular session. Admission of indebtedness changed to plea of payment. Change of plea 217

Chapter 8. Seizin of chattels. Seizin and possession. Things designed to be lent or rented out. Plea of purchase from third party. Plea of purchase from claimant. Distinction between things designed to be lent or rented out and things fit to be lent or rented out. Things deteriorating from use 221

Chapter 9. Seizin of chattels. The craftsman. Person seen carrying utensils out of householder's possession. Person chopping off tree in other person's garden under claim of purchase. Two persons having hold of a chattel 225

Chapter 10. Seizin of chattels. Guarded and unguarded animals. Infant bondmen. Boats 230

Chapter 11. Seizin of land. Seizin and possession. Taking of profits for three year period. Protest by original owner during three year period. Original owner's absence from locality. Time of war

CONTENTS

or unsafe roads. Presumption of lost grant. Protest made in distant
land. Form of protest. Reducing protest to writing 233
Chapter 12. Seizin of land. The three year period required to
constitute seizin. Seizin of houses. Itinerant merchants. Continu-
ous possession during three year period. Adding up periods of
possession by grantor and grantee or ancestor and heir. Possession
without taking of profits. Seizin of easements. Taking profits
from part of a field 236
Chapter 13. Seizin of land. Craftsmen, tenants on shares, guardians, partners, husband and wife, father and son. The exilarchs,
robbers, and the heathen 241
Chapter 14. Seizin of land. Proof of purchase. The craftsman's or
the robber's son. An Israelite claiming through a heathen. Seizin
of property belonging to a minor. Seizin of property belonging to
a person who escaped because of danger to his life. Seizin of a
married woman's property. Seizin not coupled with a claim of
rightful ownership. Seizin coupled with a claim of rightful ownership by ancestor. Seizin coupled with claim of purchase from
third party 245
Chapter 15. Seizin of land. Precedence of proof by deed over
proof of seizin. Testimony of witnesses to the seizin. Taking of
profits by one erroneously assumed to be heir to deceased owner.
Two claimants producing proof of ownership or of seizin of the
same property. Proof of original owner's presence in the locality
immediately before commencement of taking of profits by party
having seizin. Claim of lost right of way 250
Chapter 16. Estoppel. Claim to property by one who previously
witnessed deed. Claim to property by one who was previously
consulted by purchaser. Proof of offer by party having seizin to
purchase property from claimant. Restoration of profits taken by
party not entitled thereto 255
TREATISE FIVE: INHERITANCE 259
Chapter 1. The Order of inheritance. The order of priority. Distribution per stirpes. Illegitimate heirs. Husband and wife. Vested
property and property in expectancy of the wife. The deceased
husband's heirs and the inheritance of the wife. The deceased
son's heirs and the inheritance of the mother 260
Chapter 2. Primogeniture. The double portion of the first-born
son. The first born whose birth occurred after his father's death.
The first born who was operated upon by section. Doubt as to
order of birth. The taking of the primogeniture portion by representation. The first born of the heathen turned proselyte. The

illegitimate first born. Credibility of father, mother, and midwife with respect to order of birth 264

Chapter 3. Primogeniture. Vested property and property in expectancy of deceased. Improvements of the property occurring after ancestor's death. Debts owing to deceased. Sale and relinquishment of primogeniture portion. The yaḇam and the yěḇama 267

Chapter 4. Proof of heirship. Statement made by ancestor. Heirship by reputation. Son born of a bondwoman. Heir acknowledged by some of the other heirs but not by all of them 270

Chapter 5. Proof of heirship. The heir certain and the heir doubtful. Doubtful filiation. Death of ancestor and heir in common disaster 273

Chapter 6. Disinheritance. Heirship determined by law and not by will of ancestor. Attempt to disinherit lawful heir. Unequal distribution of inheritance among lawful heirs. Language of inheritance and language of gift. Stipulations between husband and wife with respect to wife's inheritance. The rule of inheritance applicable to the heathen. Gift by ancestor to others than his lawful heirs. The renegade Israelite. Arousing jealousy among children 277

Chapter 7. Proof of death of ancestor. Clear proof of death required. Proof of drowning at sea. The captive rumored to have died in captivity. Care of property belonging to captive or to one who escaped because of danger. Property belonging to one who departed from locality voluntarily 280

Chapter 8. Care of captive's property. Property not to be delivered for caretaking to minor. Minor's property not to be delivered to relative 283

Chapter 9. The undivided inheritance. Common use of property by heirs before division. Improvements made. One of the heirs engaging in business with money taken from common fund; holding a bond made in his own name; taking money out of the common fund and departing to study the Torah or to learn a trade. Adult and minor heirs. Reciprocation of wedding gifts. Purchase of clothes by oldest brother in charge of the inheritance 285

Chapter 10. Division of inheritance and appointment of guardian. New heir appearing after division of inheritance. Legatee claiming legacy after division of inheritance. Appointment of guardian over minor heirs for purpose of division of inheritance. Appointment of guardian by ancestor or by court. Suspicion arising against guardian. Withholding inheritance from heir who has reached majority 289

Chapter 11. The guardian. Cash and other movable property be-

CONTENTS

longing to orphans. Appointment of guardian by court. Powers
of guardian and limitations thereon. Duties of guardian   291

NOTES   295
LIST OF ABBREVIATIONS   329
GLOSSARY OF TECHNICAL TERMS   330
ANALYTICAL INDEX   335

INTRODUCTION

The Book of Civil Laws as a Whole

BOOK Thirteen of the Code bears the Hebrew title of *Sefer Mišpaṭim,* literally, *The Book of Judgments,* which, for the purpose of clarity has been rendered as *The Book of Civil Laws.* This title, it must be admitted, is somewhat misleading, for the Book is one of four Books of the Code (the Eleventh, the Twelfth, the Thirteenth, and the Fourteenth), all of which deal with matters pertaining to civil law, as distinguished from ritual and ceremonial law.

The reason for the name of the Book may only be surmised. After the author had compiled the two preceding Books, *The Book of Injuries* and *The Book of Property,* with their well-defined subject matter, there still remained several subjects to be treated which did not belong under either of these headings. The author decided to group these subjects together in a separate Book containing, as it were, a miscellany of laws belonging to neither of the two legal categories treated, respectively, in the two preceding Books. The name to be chosen for the present Book therefore had to be so general in nature as to fit all of the five treatises it contains —treatises that are decidedly disparate in subject matter. In addition, there may have been another consideration which prompted the author to adopt this name. The Pentateuchal pericope (Exod. 21 ff.) that involves many of the laws dealt with in the present Book is referred to in rabbinical literature and in the Synagogue as *Mišpaṭim* in keeping with the opening words of the pericope, *Now these are the judgments* (Exod. 21:1).

The Treatises

The Book consists of five Treatises in the following order:
1) The Laws Concerning Hiring;
2) The Laws Concerning Borrowing and Depositing;

3) The Laws Concerning Creditor and Debtor;

4) The Laws Concerning Pleading;

5) The Laws Concerning Inheritance.

The Treatise on Hiring contains several subjects which, from the modern viewpoint, are diverse in nature. It includes most of the law of bailment, the law of landlord and tenant, and the law of employer and employee.

The Treatise on Borrowing and Depositing includes that part of the law of bailment which relates to the commodatary and gratuitous bailee.

The Treatise on Creditor and Debtor includes the law relating to the enforcement of obligations, written and oral; usury; pledges; the creditor's lien on the debtor's immovable property; suretyship and guarantee; the validity and effect of the writing obligatory; and the confirmation and construction thereof.

The Treatise on Pleading treats of the effect of certain types of pleading, the burden of proof, oaths, presumptions, and seizin.

The Treatise on Inheritance deals with the order of inheritance, primogeniture, wills and gifts *mortis causa,* and guardianship.

The Book of Civil Laws and The Mishnah

Book Thirteen is based for the most part on certain tractates of the mishnaic "Order" called *Nĕziḳin,* "Injuries," namely, the tractates *Baḇa Ḳamma, Baḇa Mĕṣi'a, Baḇa Baṯra,* and *Šĕḇu'oṯ,* although some propositions are derived from other "Orders." But the sequence of topics follows a plan which is independent of that of the Mishnah. None of the treatises of this Book corresponds in subject matter to a tractate of the Mishnah, nor is there a single chapter in the entire Book which corresponds to a chapter of the Mishnah. Even where the subject matter of several successive chapters of this Book corresponds to that of one chapter in the Mishnah, as is the case with chapters 4–10 of treatise III, on the one hand, and chapter 5 of *Baḇa Mĕṣi'a,* on the other, the arrangement of the material within these chapters differs widely from that of the Mishnah.

The legal propositions contained in this Book are derived for the most part from Talmudic sources, that is from the Mishnah, the Tosefta, the Halakhic Midrashim, and the Gemara, Babylonian and Palestinian. There are in this Book, however, several important rules of law which either lack Talmudic sanction or are in outright derogation of the rule of the Talmud, being based solely upon Geonic authority. An example of the former type is the rule requiring a debtor claiming insolvency to take the "oath of insolvency" (iii, ii, 2); an example of the latter type is the rule making chattels belonging to the estate of a deceased debtor and in the possession of his orphans subject to seizure by the creditors of the deceased (iii, xi, 11).

Points of Special Interest

a. In iii, xx, 3, the author refers to an old copy of the Babylonian Talmud "written [apparently on papyrus] as they were wont to write approximately five hundred years ago," which he consulted for the purpose of ascertaining the correct reading of a certain Talmudic passage. He seems to have proceeded on the quite modern principle of textual criticism that the older the copy, that is, the nearer it is to the original, the less likely it is to have undergone corruptions at the hands of copyists. The reference may also have some bearing on the question of the state of Talmudic studies in Egypt in the seventh century.

b. In the final form in which the Code has come down to us the name of the third treatise of our Book is *Malweh wĕ-Loweh,* "Creditor and Debtor." However, in IV, 1, xx, 6–7, the author refers twice to this treatise as *Halwa'ah* "Lending." This would seem to give us some insight into the author's method of work. He seems to have had from the very beginning a comprehensive plan of the entire Code, with the names of the various treatises tentatively fixed, and to have made revisions of the plan as his work progressed.

c. In v, vi, 12, the author states that although under the rule of the Law an Israelite who has become an apostate is nonetheless entitled to inherit from his Israelite ancestors, the court may, if it so chooses, deprive him of the inheritance, and that such was the custom in the West. This custom, which was apparently widespread among the Jews of medieval Europe, seems to have been incorporated in a charter granted to the Jews of Speyer by Henry IV in 1090.[1] Paragraph 7 of this charter provides that no one shall presume to baptize the children of the Jews by force. It further provides that if any Jews should, of their own free will, choose to be baptized, a waiting period of three days should be allowed to elapse in order to ascertain whether they have renounced their law for the sake of the Christian religion or because of some grievance suffered by them, and that "just as they shall relinquish the law of their ancestors, so shall they relinquish their possession" (et sicut patrum legem reliquerunt, ita etiam et possessionem eorum).

d. In three of the five treatises of our Book (i, iv, v) the last section represents a sort of peroration, with an appropriate passage from Scripture skilfully woven into the text. These perorations, which are also found in many of the other treatises of the Code, reveal a depth of feeling and a beauty of style rarely matched in Halakhaic literature.

The Translation

Throughout this translation our main objective has been to render the meaning of the text into precise and understandable legal English. Very often literalism had to yield to this objective.

In the explanatory notes we have confined ourselves to the explanation of technical terms and locutions and of difficulties due to the extreme conciseness of the Jewish legal style. Notes of a comparative and historico-legal nature were deemed outside the scope of this work, although the translator was very often under strong temptation to call attention to similarities with other systems of law. A volume dealing with the subject of the relationship

1. Aronius, J., *Regesten zur Geschichte der Juden im fränkischen und deutschen Reiche* (Berlin, 1902), p. 73.

between Jewish law and various other systems of law is under preparation by the translator.

The use of untranslated Hebrew terms has been avoided, wherever possible. However, in a few instances of technical legal terms it was deemed advisable to leave the Hebrew terms untranslated. In the case of one very important technical term— *ḥăzaḳah* (literally, "holding, seizing, taking hold")—which is used in legal Hebrew in several different senses, the untranslated Hebrew term is given in parentheses next to its appropriate equivalent in English at its first occurrence in the text. This term is used extensively in Jewish legal literature in the following senses: 1) a legal presumption; 2) reputation; 3) the formal taking of possession of real property or bondmen; [2] 4) possession under circumstances giving rise to a presumption of rightful ownership. When used in the last sense, ḥăzaḳah is translated by the term "seizin" of English law.

To be sure, ḥăzaḳah and "seizin" are highly technical terms each of which was developed in a system of law widely different from that in which the other was developed. However, the points

---

2. The *hif'il* of the verb *ḥāzaḳ*—to hold, seize, take hold of—is used in the same sense in Jer. 31:32. V. 31–32 of chap. 31 read: *Behold, the days come, saith the Lord, that I will make a new covenant with the house of Israel, and with the house of Judah; not according to the covenant that I made with their fathers in the day that I took them by the hand to bring them out of the land of Egypt; forasmuch as they broke My covenant, although I had acquired ownership in them, saith the Lord.* The phrase "I took them by the hand" is used here in the sense of taking formal possession, such as one would take when acquiring ownership of a slave, and the phrase "although I had acquired ownership in them" (*ba'alti bam*) refers to this formal act; see also Zech. 14:13. This is to be compared with *mancipium*—the act of taking formal possession under Roman law—which, leading Romanists believe, originally applied only to slaves. See H. F. Jolowicz, *Historical Introduction to The Study of Roman Law* (Cambridge, 1932), pp. 140, 141 n. 4, 145. More striking perhaps is the parallel to the Roman *mancipium* in Isa. 41:9: *Thou whom I have taken hold of from the ends of the earth, and called thee from the uttermost parts thereof, and said unto thee: "Thou art My servant," I have chosen thee and not cast thee away.* The phrase "and said unto thee: 'Thou art My servant'" is strongly suggestive of the formula "Hunc ego hominem ex jure Quiritium meum esse aio" (I say that this man is mine by Quiritarian law) which, under the Roman procedure, the transferee was required to pronounce at the time of taking formal possession of the slave.

of similarity between the doctrine of seizin in English law and the doctrine of ḥăzaḳah in Jewish law are so fundamental that the translator felt warranted in translating the one term by the other. Without expressing any opinion as to the possible historical connection between these doctrines, we may call attention to two striking similarities between them. Pollock and Maitland, in their discussion of seizin—which they start off by saying, "In the history of our law there is no idea more cardinal than that of seisin" [3] —state: "The idea of seisin seems to be closely connected in our ancestors' minds with the idea of enjoyment. A man is in seisin of land when he is enjoying it or in a position to enjoy it." [4] Precisely the same idea prevailed in Jewish law with respect to ḥăzaḳah. Possession not coupled with enjoyment or the taking of profits did not constitute ḥăzaḳah (see iv, xii, 9–20). Another point of similarity between the two doctrines is found in the rule with regard to formal protest. Under Jewish law, formal protest by the original owner within the three-year period of possession (coupled with the taking of profits, as required to constitute ḥăzaḳah) was sufficient to overcome the presumption of rightful ownership arising from such possession (see iv, xi, 2–8). To be effective, protest had to be renewed every three years. A similar rule of continual protest preventing the party in possession from acquiring seizin also prevailed, under certain circumstances, in medieval England (see Littleton, Sec. 414, *et seq.*).

Finally, a word should be said about the text of the Code used for this translation. In the absence of a critical text edition of the Code, one of the editions commonly in use, that of Vilna (1900), was used by the translator. However, in some instances (iii, xx, 4; iii, xxi, 1; iv, xiv, 8; v, i, 1; v, v, 5), where the text of this edition presents obvious difficulties, the translator examined several early editions, including the two independent first editions of Rome (?), before 1480, and Constantinople (1509), as well as several manuscripts stemming from Yemen, for the purpose of ascertaining the

---

3. History of English Law (2nd ed., Boston, 1899), II, 29.
4. *Ibid.*, p. 34.

correct reading. In most of these cases the examination of the Yemenite manuscripts yielded the best results, and the readings contained therein were adopted in the translation. In the case of one passage (III, xiii, 3) an emendation was made on the basis of one of Maimonides' *Responsa*. All the deviations from the text of edition Vilna (1900), have been noted and explained in the Notes.

The manuscript of this translation was already in the hands of the printer when a photostatic copy of the Oxford Codex of Maimonides' *Mišneh Torah* reached the Yale University Library, and, through the kindness of Professor Julian J. Obermann and the staff of the Yale Library, a copy of the text of *Mišpaṭim* was made available to me. I have examined in this copy the passages in which the translation follows the Yemenite MSS in the Library of the Jewish Theoloical Seminary, rather than the Vilna edition of 1900, and other printed editions, and found that in three of these passages (iv, 14: 8; v, 1: 1; v, 5: 5), the Oxford Codex is in accord with the Yemenite MSS, while in one passage (iii, 2: 4), it is in accord with the printed editions. The gloss to iii, 21: 1, which does not occur either in the Yemenite MSS or in the two independent first editions, of Rome (?), before 1480, and of Constantinople, of 1509, is incorporated in the text of the Oxford manuscript.

As the translation is about to be published my thoughts turn to those who have made the fulfillment of this task possible. To my father and teacher, Rabbi Moshe Zevi b. Rabbi Shalom Joseph, of blessed memory, a truly pious man and a great scholar with whom in my younger days I spent many a long winter evening poring over the folios of the Talmud and other books of Jewish lore, I owe a debt which words are inadequate to express. To Professor Louis Ginzberg of the Jewish Theological Seminary of America, the acknowledged master of Halakhah and Aggadah, I am indebted for his help, so readily and generously extended, in solving some of the most intricate problems of textual interpretation. To Professor Julian J. Obermann of Yale University, whose fine discernment, keen sense of style, and incisive logic have made themselves felt throughout my work, I owe a debt of gratitude for numerous valuable suggestions. In a true sense, he has nursed the project along with tender care from its very inception to its completion. To Professor Harry A. Wolfson of Harvard University I am indebted for several penetrating criticisms and constructive suggestions. Professors Alexander Marx and Boaz Cohen and Mr. M. Luzki of the Library of The Jewish Theological Seminary of America have eagerly extended to me every form of assistance in the use of the excellent facilities of that library.

THE BOOK OF
CIVIL LAWS

COMPRISING FIVE TREATISES IN THE
FOLLOWING ORDER

I. LAWS CONCERNING HIRING

II. LAWS CONCERNING BORROWING AND
DEPOSITING

III. LAWS CONCERNING CREDITOR AND
DEBTOR

IV. LAWS CONCERNING PLEADING

V. LAWS CONCERNING INHERITANCE

I will give thanks unto Thee with uprightness of heart,
When I learn Thy righteous laws (Ps. 119: 7).

TREATISE I

LAWS CONCERNING HIRING

Involving Seven Commandments
Three Affirmative and Four Negative
To Wit

1. To administer the Law with respect to the bailee for hire;
2. To pay the hire of the hired man on the day when due;
3. That payment of the hired man's hire, when due, shall not be delayed;
4. That the hired man may eat of that at which he works, if it is attached to the soil;
5. That, even of what is attached to the soil, the hired man shall not eat during working time;
6. That the hired man shall not carry away with him aught in addition to what he has eaten;
7. That the ox shall not be muzzled when he treads the corn.

An exposition of these commandments
is contained in the following chapters.

CHAPTER I

1. Four different types of bailees are mentioned in the Law, but only three different rules are applicable to them. The four types of bailees are: a. the gratuitous bailee; b. the commodatary; c. the bailee for hire; d. the hirer.

2. The three different rules applicable to them are:

a. A gratuitous bailee from whose possession the object bailed was stolen or *lost*—and needless to say if it was lost through *force majeure*, as in the case of an animal that died or was captured—must swear that he kept the object bailed after the manner of bailees, and he is quit. For it is said *If a man deliver unto his neighbour money or stuff to keep, and it be stolen out of the man's house . . . the master of the house shall come near unto God* (Exod. 22:6–7).

b. The commodatary is liable in all cases, whether the object bailed was lost or stolen, or even if the loss occurred through a force greater than these, as in the case of an animal that died, or was crippled, or captured. For with regard to the commodatary it is written *And if a man borrow aught of his neighbour, and it be hurt, or die, the owner thereof not being with it, he shall surely make restitution* (Exod. 22:13).

c. The bailee for hire and the hirer both are subject to one rule. If the object which one hired or for the keeping of which one received hire was stolen or lost, the said bailee must pay therefor. But if the loss occurred through a force greater than these, as in the case of an animal that died, or was crippled, captured, or torn, the bailee for hire or the hirer must swear to the force, and then is quit. For it is said *If a man deliver unto his neighbour an ass, or an ox, or a sheep, or any beast, to keep, and it die, or be hurt, or driven away, no man seeing it; the oath of the Lord shall be between them both* (Exod. 22:9–10). And it is also written *But if it be stolen from him, he shall make restitution unto the owner thereof* (Exod. 22:11).

It follows therefore that the gratuitous bailee is subject to an oath in every case; that the commodatary is subject to payment in every case—except in the case of an animal that died while working, as hereinafter stated; that the bailee for hire and the hirer are subject to payment in the case of *loss* or theft, and to an oath in the case of force majeure, as where an animal died a natural death, was crippled, captured, or torn; or where the object bailed was lost in shipwreck, or taken by armed robbers and the like.

3. If a man deposited something with another, whether it was to be kept gratuitously or for hire, or if he lent or let something to another and the bailee borrowed or hired the services of the owner together with the object bailed, the bailee is quit in every case of loss of the object, even if he was negligent with regard thereto and the loss occurred through his negligence. For it is written *If the owner thereof be with it, he shall not make it good; if it be a hireling, he loseth his hire* (Exod. 22: 14).

All this applies only if the bailee borrowed or hired the services of the owner at the time of the bailment, even though the owner was not present when the theft, loss, or force occurred. But if he first took the object, becoming a bailee with regard thereto, and later hired or borrowed the services of the owner, he must pay for the loss of the object even if the owner was present at the time when the loss through force occurred. For it is written *The owner thereof not being with it* (Exod. 22: 13). From the "oral tradition" it has been learned that this verse is to be understood thus: if he (the lender) was with him (the borrower) at the time of the borrowing, though he was not present at the time of the theft or death of the animal, the borrower is quit. But if the lender was not with him at the time of the borrowing, though he was present at the time of the death or capture, the borrower is liable. And this applies to all other bailees as well; they are quit in case of a bailment *with the owner* even if they were negligent.

4. Every bailee who was negligent at the beginning, though in the end a loss occurred through force, is liable, as hereinafter stated.

The commodatary is not permitted to lend to others the object lent to him. Even if he borrowed a scroll of the Law, the reading of which is a pious deed, he must not lend it to another. Similarly, the hirer is not permitted to let to another even if the object hired be a scroll of the Law, for the bailor may say to him, "I do not wish to have my property entrusted to another."

However, if the bailee in transgression of this precept delivered the object bailed to a second bailee, and witnesses testify that the second bailee kept the object after the manner of bailees but that it was lost through force, the first bailee is quit, since there is testimony that the loss occurred through force. But if there are no witnesses, the first bailee is liable to compensate the owner because it was he who delivered it over to the second bailee. He may, however, sue the second bailee.

Even if the first bailee kept the object gratuitously but delivered it over to a bailee for hire, he is liable, since the owner may say to him, "It is your oath that I relied on and not the oath of the other man." But if the owner was wont to entrust the said object to the keeping of the second bailee, the first bailee is quit since he may justly say to the owner, "This object, which you deposited with me, or lent to me, is one that you have recently been wont to deposit with the man with whom I deposited it"; provided, however, that the standard of care required by law was not lowered by the change of bailees.

What is meant by lowering the standard of care? Where the object had been bailed to him for hire and he bailed it to the second bailee gratuitously, or where it had been lent to him and he bailed it to the second bailee for hire. Since the standard of care was lowered, it is negligence per se, and he must pay.

5. Even if the first bailee either borrowed the object or hired it *along with its owner,* he is liable, since he delivered it from his possession to the possession of another bailee. But if the second bailee produces proof which is sufficient to absolve the first bailee from liability in accordance with the standard of care required of him, the first bailee is quit. How is this to be understood? Where, e.g., a bailee for hire delivered an animal bailed to him over to a

gratuitous bailee, and the second bailee produces witnesses to the effect that the animal died a natural death, the first bailee is quit. And so it is in all similar cases.

6. If a bailee delivered the bailed object over to another bailee, raising the standard of care, the resulting benefit accrues to the owner. How is this to be understood? If, for example, a man hired a cow from another and then lent her to a third party, and she died a natural death while in the possession of the third party—who, being a commodatary, is liable in all cases of loss—it is the owner, and not the first bailee, to whom the value of the cow is to be restored, since a bailee is not permitted to traffic with his bailor's property for his own profit. And so it is in all similar cases.

If a bailee turned the object deposited with him over to another bailee for the purpose of delivering it to the owner, the first bailee may reclaim it from the second bailee since it is he who bears the risk of its loss until it reaches the owner's possession. But if the first bailee is one whose dishonesty has been established he may not reclaim the object from the second bailee, though he continues to bear the risk of its loss.

CHAPTER II

1. The three rules that are mentioned in the Law with regard to the four types of bailees apply only to profane movables belonging to an Israelite. For it is said *Silver or vessels* (Exod. 22:6) *Or any beast* (Exod. 22:9). Landed property is thus excluded; slaves are likewise excluded because they are likened to landed property; bonds are excluded because, unlike the things enumerated in the Law, they have no value inherent in themselves. Property belonging to the sanctuary is also excluded. For it is said *If a man deliver unto his fellow* (Exod. 22:6). This also excludes property belonging to a heathen.

Making their deduction from the above passages of Scripture the Sages said: the gratuitous bailee of slaves, bonds, landed property, and property belonging to the sanctuary is not subject to an oath, and the bailee for hire or hirer of these is not subject to payment. But if he undertook by *kinyan* to be liable he is liable.

2. In order to discourage disregard for property belonging to the sanctuary the Sages have established the rule that a bailee of such property must swear a quasi-Pentateuchal bailee's oath.

3. It seems to me that if the bailee was negligent with regard to slaves and the like, he is liable since the exemption from liability in the case of slaves, landed property, and bonds applies only to theft, loss, natural death, and the like.

The rule, then, is that a gratuitous bailee, who must swear in the case of movables that were stolen or lost, is quit of an oath in the case of slaves, landed property, or bonds. Similarly, a bailee for hire, who is liable to pay in the case of movables that were stolen or lost, is quit of payment if one of the aforementioned classes of property was bailed to him. But if he was negligent, he is liable, for a negligent bailee is a wrongdoer, and there is no difference between a wrongdoer who does injury to land and one who does injury to movables.

This rule is in accord with the truth, as the discerning will recognize, and in accordance therewith decisions should be rendered in practice.

With regard to a similar case my teachers have taught: if one delivered his vineyard to another, either under a crop-sharing agreement or as a gratuitous keeper, with the party who received the vineyard agreeing to dig, prune, or sweep at his own expense, and if, the said party, neglecting his duty, fail to do as agreed, he is just as liable as though he had caused damage with his hands. And so it is in all similar cases, for he who causes damage with his hands is always liable.

4. If a man delivered to his fellow for safekeeping something which is attached to the soil, even if it be grapes ready to be cut, it is deemed like landed property with respect to the Law of bailment.

5. If a man deposited with a bailee property dedicated to the sanctuary and, while the property was in the bailee's possession, the bailor redeemed it, so that it again became profane property; or if one lent to another profane property and, while it was in the borrower's possession, the lender dedicated it to the sanctuary; or if a heathen made a deposit of property and then became a proselyte—in all of these cases the rules mentioned in the Law with regard to bailees do not apply. For in order that these rules may be applicable, it is necessary that the property bailed be profane and that it belong to an Israelite from the beginning to the end of the bailment.

6. A woman as well as a man, whether as bailor or as bailee, comes within the scope of the aforementioned rules of the Law of Bailment.

7. If a minor bailed or lent something to an adult, the adult, under the aforementioned circumstances, must swear the bailee's oath to the minor. My teachers have taught that this does not come within the rule exempting a defendant from an oath with regard to a claim made by a minor, since the bailee's oath is merely designed to remove a doubt and not to overcome a positive assertion by the defendant's adversary.

8. Just as in the case of a purchaser of movable property the Sages have established the rule that he does not acquire title to the property except by the act of *drawing it to himself,* so in the case of a bailee they have established the rule that he does not become such except by a drawing to himself of the property bailed.

If a man said to another, "Keep this for me," and the other said, "Leave it with me," he became a gratuitous bailee. But if he said to the would-be bailor, "Leave it where you please," or just "Leave it," or if he said to him, "Why, the house is at your disposal," he did not become either a gratuitous bailee or a bailee for hire and is not liable to swear the bailee's oath. However, the would-be bailor may have the anathema proclaimed generally against him who took the object and would not return it to its owner. And so it is in all similar cases.

With regard to the bailee's liability to swear the bailee's oath, it matters not whether the deposit, loan, or letting was made in the presence of witnesses. If the bailee admits the bailment he is liable to the oath, for the inference of credibility is not resorted to in order to acquit one of an oath but only in order to acquit him of payment.

Even if the object lent, deposited, or let was worth only one *pĕruṭah* the bailee must swear; nor is the requirement of a partial admission applicable to any of the bailees.

9. A gratuitous bailee may stipulate that he be quit of an oath, and the commodatary may stipulate that he be quit of payment. Similarly, the bailor may stipulate with a gratuitous bailee, with a bailee for hire, or with a hirer, that he be liable in every case of loss as a commodatary is liable; for every stipulation with regard to matters pecuniary or with regard to oaths concerning matters pecuniary is valid and does not require either ḳinyan or the presence of witnesses.

10. If the bailor claims that there was a stipulation attached to the bailment, and the bailee says that there was no such stipulation, the bailee swears the bailee's oath and, by accumulation, he also swears that there was no stipulation.

11. If a man claims to have made a deposit with another, and the other says, "I only said to him, 'Leave it where you please,' and I did not become bailee for him," the defendant swears the informal oath to the effect that he did not accept the deposit except in the manner stated by him, and he also includes in his oath an asseveration that he did not misappropriate the property in question, or destroy it, or cause it to be destroyed so as to render himself liable to compensation to the owner.

12. If a man says to another, "I lent, let, or bailed certain property to you," and the other denies the allegation, or admits

it but pleads that he has returned the property to the plaintiff and terminated the bailment without leaving any demand outstanding against him with regard thereto, the defendant swears the informal oath and is quit.

The above rule applies only where there is no writing. But where a deposit, letting, or loan is made by writing and the bailee pleads return, he must swear while holding a sacred object. Seeing that the gratuitous bailee could absolve himself from liability by pleading that the object bailed was stolen or lost—and the commodatary by pleading that the animal died while working—he is believed if he pleads return. Nevertheless, just as when he pleads loss through force he must swear the Pentateuchal oath while holding a sacred object, so in this case when he pleads return he must swear the quasi-Pentateuchal oath since the plaintiff holds a writing.

The above rule with regard to a bailment by a writing applies only to the case wherein the bailee could have pleaded loss through force without being required to produce proof of the force. But if the case is such that he would have been required to produce proof in support of a plea of loss through force, as hereinafter stated, the bailor who holds the writing is to swear to his denial of the return, and the bailee must pay.

The case of a bailee by a writing, who is required to swear while holding a sacred object, is an exception to the general rule, the general rule being that he who is awarded the proof by oath because of the inference of credibility swears the informal oath only.

CHAPTER III

1. A bailee who claims that the object bailed was lost through force majeure, such as the breaking of a limb or natural death of an animal, in a place where witnesses are ordinarily to be found, is required to produce witnesses to the force and is quit of the bailee's oath. If he fails to produce witnesses, he must pay. For it is said in Scripture *If a man deliver unto his neighbour an ass, or an ox, or a sheep, or any beast, to keep, and it die, or be hurt, or driven*

away, no man seeing it; the oath of the Lord shall be between them both (Exod. 22:9–10). The implication is that where it is possible to produce witnesses there is to be no oath; the bailee must either produce witnesses or pay.

But if the bailee claims that the force occurred in a place where, it is known, witnesses are ordinarily not to be found, he is not required to produce witnesses; he only swears to the force and is quit; and if he produces witnesses testifying that he was not negligent he is quit even of an oath.

It once happened that a barrel of wine, which was being transported by a hired man, was broken in the market place of *Mahoza*. The case came before the Sages who said to the hired man, "This market place, where you claim the barrel was broken, is a place frequented by many people. You must either produce witnesses who will testify that you were not negligent but that you stumbled and fell, or you must pay the value of the barrel of wine." And so it is in all similar cases.

2. Where one transports a barrel from place to place for hire and it breaks, the rule of the Law is that he must pay because it is not force majeure, the breaking of the barrel being like theft and loss, for which he is liable. But the Sages have established the rule that he is only liable to an oath that he was not negligent, for if we were to say that he must pay there would hardly be a man who would be willing to undertake to transport anything for his fellow. Therefore they made the breaking of a barrel tantamount to the natural death or the breaking of a limb of an animal.

Another rule that has been established in this matter is that if two persons carried a barrel on a pole and it was broken, they are to pay only half of its value. Since the burden was too heavy to be carried by one person and too light to require two persons to carry it together, the situation is like that of force, though it is not a case of force. Therefore they pay only half the value if there are witnesses testifying that they were not negligent.

If the object was broken in a place where witnesses are not likely to be found, they swear that it was not broken through their negligence and pay half its value since neither of them ought to have carried a greater burden than he alone could carry. From this it may be deduced that where one carries a large barrel, such as is not customary for other carriers to carry, he is negligent, and if it is broken he pays its full value.

3. If a porter broke a barrel of wine belonging to a shopkeeper, thus becoming liable to pay therefor, and the wine was worth four *zuz* on the market day but only three on other days, then, if the porter was to deliver the wine to the shopkeeper on the market day, he must either deliver another barrel of wine or pay four zuz—provided, however, that the shopkeeper had no other wine for his trade; but if he had other wine, the porter is to pay him only three zuz—and if the porter was to deliver the wine on any day other than a market day he is to pay only three zuz.

In any event, the shopkeeper is to deduct from the value of the wine the value of the labor he would have had to expend in selling it, as well as the expenses he would have had to incur in boring an aperture in the barrel. And so it is in all similar cases.

4. If wolves came and tore an animal in the custody of a herdsman, if it was one wolf that came upon the herdsman, even at a time of a visitation of wolves, it is not a case of force; but two wolves do constitute force.

Two hounds do not constitute force even if they came from two different directions; but more than two do constitute force.

An armed robber constitutes force even if the herdsman be armed, for the herdsman is not under a duty to risk his life contending with an armed robber.

The lion, the bear, the leopard, the hyena, and the snake constitute force.

The herdsman is free from liability in the cases just enumerated only when the wild beasts or the armed robbers hit upon the place where he happened to be. If, however, the herdsman led the herd to a place where wild beasts or armed robbers were known to abide, it is not a case of force and he is liable.

5. If a herdsman saw an armed robber and began to challenge him and to show him that he did not fear him, saying, "There are so many of us and we have so many weapons"; and the robber came and subdued them and carried off the herd, the herdsman is liable. For there is no difference between a herdsman who brings the animal to the place of the robber and one who brings the robber, by challenging him, to the place of the animal.

6. If the herdsman with the aid of other herdsmen and clubs could have saved the animal from being torn or captured but did not call the other herdsmen or bring clubs for the rescue, he is liable, whether he was a gratuitous keeper or one for hire.

There is, however, a difference in this respect between a gratuitous keeper and one for hire. The former is only under a duty to call other herdsmen and to bring clubs if he can do so without making any expenditures—and if he cannot find any he is quit— while the latter is under a duty to hire other herdsmen and clubs and to pay therefor up to the value of the animal—to be later reimbursed by the owner—and if, having had an opportunity to hire men and clubs, he failed to do so, he is liable.

7. A herdsman who claims to have saved an animal with the aid of other herdsmen, hired by him for that purpose, swears and takes what he claims, for he can only claim up to the value of the animal and, as to that, he could claim that the animal had been torn. He is to swear while holding a sacred object, as is the rule with regard to all those who swear and take.

8. If a herdsman left his herd and went to the near-by town, whether or not during the time when herdsmen usually go to the town, and wolves came and rent the herd, or a bear came and attacked it, we do not say, "Had he been there he would have saved the herd," but we make an appraisal of the situation to determine whether with the aid of other herdsmen and sticks he could actually have saved the herd. If he could, he is liable; if he could not, he is quit; and if it cannot be ascertained whether he could or could not, he is equally liable.

9. If the animal died a natural death, it is a case of force and the herdsman is quit. If he starved the animal and it died, it is not a case of force. If the animal tore itself from him and ascended to the peak of a precipice and then again tore itself from him and fell down, it is a case of force. If, however, he brought the animal up to the peak of the precipice, or if it ascended there by itself when he could have prevented it from doing so, he is liable, even though the animal tore itself from him before it fell down and died or broke its limbs. For he who is negligent in the beginning, though in the end the loss occurs through force, is liable.

Similarly, if a herdsman was leading his herd over a bridge and one animal pushed another, causing it to fall into the current of the river, he is liable because he ought to have led the animals over the bridge one by one, since a bailee receives hire for keeping the object entrusted to him under good care. Having been negligent in the beginning, by leading all the animals together over the bridge, although in the end when the animal fell down it was a case of force, he is liable.

10. If a bailee was negligent, allowing an animal entrusted to him to leave his care and proceed to the meadow, and the animal died there a natural death, he is not liable because it was not the animal's leaving the bailee's care that caused its death. Since the animal died a natural death, what does it matter whether it died in the bailee's house or in the meadow?

If, however, the animal was stolen from the meadow and died a natural death in the thief's house, the bailee is liable even if he kept the animal gratuitously. For even if the animal had not died it would have been lost to the owner through the theft which was caused by the animal's leaving the bailee's care. And so it is in all similar cases.

CHAPTER IV

1. If a man hired an ass to lead it through mountain country but led it through a valley instead, and the ass suffered injury

through slipping, he is quit, although he deviated from what the owner had consented to. But if the animal suffered injury through excessive heat, he is liable. If he hired the animal to lead it through a valley but led it through mountain country instead, he is liable if the injury occurred through slipping, because slipping is more likely to occur on a mountain; but he is quit if it occurred through excessive heat, because the heat is greater in the valley than on the mountain, where the breezes blow on the mountain tops. If, however, the animal's heat was caused by the ascent he is liable. And so it is in all similar cases.

Similarly, if a man hired a cow for ploughing on the mountain but ploughed in the valley instead, and the *kankan,* that is the instrument by means of which the ploughing is done, was broken, he is quit, and the owner of the cow has an action against the ploughmen. If he did not deviate from the owner's intention, the owner's action is likewise against the ploughmen. But if he hired the cow for ploughing in the valley and ploughed on the mountain instead and the kankan was broken, he is liable to the owner and has an action over against the ploughmen.

2. What is the rule with regard to two ploughmen who, while ploughing, break the implement and become liable to pay? Who pays? He who holds the implement at the ploughing. But if the field was uneven, both the one who guides the cow with the goad and the one who holds the implement are liable.

3. If a man hired an animal for threshing pulse but made it thresh grain instead, and the animal suffered injury through slipping, he is quit. If, however, he hired it for threshing grain but made it thresh pulse instead, he is liable because pulse is likely to cause slipping.

It once happened that a man let an ass to another, saying to him, "Do not go by way of *Nehar Pekod,* because there is usually water on that road, but go by way of *Naras,* where there is no water." He went by way of Nehar Pekod and the ass died. There were no witnesses who could testify which road he took. He admitted, however, that he went by way of Nehar Pekod, but said that there was no water there and that the animal died from internal causes. The Sages said: since there are witnesses testifying that there is water in Nehar Peḵod, and since he deviated from the owner's permission, he is liable—the inference of credibility not being resorted to in the face of witnesses contradicting the defendant's assertion.

4. If a man hired from another an animal for carrying 200 pounds of wheat but made it carry 200 pounds of barley instead, and the animal died, he is liable because bulkiness makes carrying more difficult, and barley is bulkier. If he hired the animal for carrying barley and made it carry an equal weight of straw, he is likewise liable. But if he hired it for carrying barley and carried wheat instead, he is quit. And so it is in all similar cases.

5. He who hires an animal for the purpose of having a man ride it may not have a woman ride it. But if he hired the animal for the purpose of having a woman ride it, he may have a man ride it and may also have any woman, whether large or small—even if she be pregnant and nursing—ride it.

6. If a man hired an animal for the purpose of having it carry a load of a certain weight but made it carry a greater load, and it died, he is liable if the additional quantity amounted to one thirtieth of the stipulated weight; if it amounted to less than that, he is quit, but he must pay for the extra weight.

If he hired the animal without a specific stipulation as to weight, he may not cause it to carry a greater load than is customary in that locality for that type of animal to carry; and if he augmented this load by one thirtieth thereof—e.g., where it was customary for the animal to carry 30 units and he made it carry 31—and the animal died or broke a limb, he is liable. Similarly, in the case of a ship that sank after its agreed cargo had been augmented by one thirtieth, the hirer is liable for the value of the ship.

7. If a man augmented a porter's load by one *ḵaḇ* and the porter was injured, he is liable for the injury. For although the porter is a rational being who feels the heaviness of a load, it may have oc-

curred to him that the sense of heaviness was perhaps due to his being ill.

8. He who hires an ass for riding may put thereon his garments, flask, and food required for the journey, since it is not customary for the hirer to stop at every inn and buy food; to more than that the owner of the ass may object.

Similarly, the owner of the ass may put thereon barley and straw sufficient to feed the ass for the day; to more than that the hirer may object since he can buy forage at every inn. If, therefore, there is no place on the road where food may be bought, he may put on the animal his own food and that of the animal as required for the entire journey.

All these rules apply where the hiring is made without specific stipulation and where there is no known custom. However, where there is a custom everything is governed by it.

CHAPTER V

1. If a man hired an animal and it became sick or mad, or was taken into the king's service, even if taken permanently, while he was proceeding on a journey, the owner may say to the hirer, "What you have bargained for I have delivered to you," and the hirer must pay to the owner the full amount of the hire. This applies only where he hired the animal for carrying a load of such a nature that one does not mind if it is thrown down. But where he hired it for riding or for carrying thereon glassware and the like, the owner must furnish another ass to the hirer, if it was an ass that he hired, and if he does not do so he must return to the hirer the amount of the hire, deducting therefrom the hire for that part of the journey which the hirer had already traversed when the mishap occurred.

2. If the animal, whether hired for carrying a load or for riding, died or broke a limb and the owner had said to the hirer, "I am letting *an ass* to you," the said owner must furnish another ass to the hirer; if he fails to do so, the hirer may sell the carcass or the

animal with the broken limb and buy another animal with the
money realized from the sale, or, if the money so realized is not
sufficient to buy another animal, he may hire one to bring him to
the place agreed upon. If the owner had said, "I am letting *this ass*
to you," and the hirer had hired the animal for riding or for
carrying glassware, and it died while on the road, the hirer
may buy another animal for the price of the carcass, or, if this does
not suffice to buy an animal, he may hire another animal at a price
up to the full value of the carcass to bring him to the place agreed
upon. If, however, the value of the carcass does not suffice either
to buy or to hire another animal the hirer must pay to the owner the
hire for half of the journey, and he has but a grievance against the
owner.

If he hired the animal for carrying an ordinary load and the
animal died while on the road, the owner is not bound to
furnish another animal to him, since the owner had said, "I am
letting *this ass* to you." The hirer in such case must pay the owner
the hire for half of the journey and also let him have the carcass.

3. If a man hired a freighter and it sank in the middle of the
voyage, then, if the owner had said, "I am letting *this freighter*
to you," and the hirer had hired it for carrying a cargo of unspecified wine, the owner must return the freightage even if prepaid, since the hirer may say, "Produce the very same ship which
I hired, and for which I had a great preference, and I will produce *any* wine to transport thereon." If he had said, "I am letting
a ship to you," and the hirer hired it to transport thereon a cargo
of *specified wine,* the hirer is bound for the full freightage even if
not prepaid, for the owner may say, "Produce the very same wine
and I will bring *any* ship to transport the wine thereon." But the
owner must deduct from the freightage the value of the labor
he would have expended during the incompleted half of the
voyage, since one who sits idle is not to be likened to one who
busies himself with conducting a ship on a voyage.

If he had said, "I am letting *this ship* to you," and the hirer
hired it to transport *specified wine,* then, if the hirer paid the full

freightage in advance, the owner cannot claim it, since the owner cannot produce the very same ship nor can the hirer bring the very same wine.

If he had hired an *unspecified ship* for carrying *unspecified wine,* the freightage is apportioned between the owner and the hirer.

4. If a man, who had hired a freighter, unloaded the cargo in the middle of the voyage, he must pay the full freightage to the owner. But if the hirer finds another hirer for the rest of the voyage agreed upon between him and the owner of the ship, he may let the ship to the second hirer, and the owner has but a grievance against him.

Similarly, if in the middle of the voyage he sells the merchandise to another, disembarks, and has the purchaser embark, the owner of the ship receives half of the freightage from the seller and the other half from the purchaser of the merchandise, and he has but a grievance against the seller for causing him to endure the inclinations of another man to whom he is not accustomed. And so it is in all similar cases.

5. On the basis of the rule immediately preceding I hold that if a man let a house to his fellow and the lessee wishes to let the house to another, he may do so, provided the size of the second lessee's family is the same as that of the first lessee's. If, for example, there were four members in the lessee's family, he may not let the house to one having five members.

When the Sages said, "The hirer may not let," they had in mind movables only, where the owner may say, "I do not wish to have my property entrusted to another." But with regard to landed property, or with regard to a ship whose owner is present thereon, the owner will not be permitted to say so.

I also hold that if the owner of the house said to the lessee, "Why should you trouble yourself to let my house to another? If you do not wish to stay therein, you may vacate it and be quit of the payment of rent," the lessee may not let it to another, for this comes within the Scriptural injunction of *Withhold not good from him to whom it is due* (Prov. 3: 27). Rather than let the house to another leave the house to its owner.

There is one authority holding that the lessee may never let the house to another. But this does not appear to me to be the correct rule.

6. If a man said to another, "I am letting *this house* to you," and after the letting the house collapsed, he is not bound to rebuild it. The lessor is to make deduction from the rental paid by the lessee for the use of the house during the period it was occupied by the lessee and return the balance. If, however, the lessor demolished the house, he is bound either to rebuild it or to let to the lessee another house that is similar to the one demolished.

Similarly, if the lessor, after having let the house to the first lessee, re-let or sold it to a heathen or to a lawless person who dispossessed the first lessee, he is bound to let to the first lessee another house similar to the one from which he was dispossessed.

7. If a man let to another an *unspecified house* and after he delivered possession to the lessee the house collapsed, he is bound to rebuild it or to supply the lessee with another house. If the second house is smaller than the one that collapsed the lessee cannot object, provided it may be classified as a house, for it was but an *unspecified house* that the lessor let to the lessee.

If, however, the lessor said, "I am letting to you a house like this one," he must supply the lessee with a house of the length and width of the one he indicated to him. He cannot say, "What I meant was only that the house be near the river or the market or the bathhouse like the one I indicated," but must supply the lessee with a house of the dimensions and appearance of the one indicated. If, therefore, the house he indicated was small he shall not deliver to the lessee a large one; and if it was large he shall not deliver a house which has more or fewer windows than there were in the house he indicated, except with the consent of both parties.

CHAPTER VI

1. If a man let to another a house in a large court, the lessee may use the projections of the court and its walls up to four ells, as well as the hall and the open space behind the houses. Where custom allows it, the lessee may also have the use of the cavities of the walls. In all these matters the custom of the locality is to be followed, in accordance with the nomenclature prevailing there, as we have stated with regard to the Law of Purchase and Sale.

2. If a man let his court, without further specification, the cattle shed is not included therein.

3. He who lets a house to another is bound to supply doors, keep the windows in repair, reinforce the ceiling, and provide props for the broken beam, as well as to make a bolt and a lock and similar things which are produced by the craftsman and are essential to the habitability of houses and courts.

The lessee is bound to make a railing and to provide a *mĕzuzah* scroll as well as to keep the place of the mĕzuzah in repair at his own expense.

Similarly, if he wishes to make a ladder or a spout, or to plaster the roof, he is to do it at his own expense.

4. If a man let an upper story to another, he is bound to repair the ceiling and the concrete pavement thereon, since the pavement reinforces the ceiling.

5. The manure in the courtyard belongs to the lessee, and it is he who has to attend to the removal thereof. But if there is a custom with regard thereto, the custom is to be followed.

All this applies where the animals producing the manure belong to the lessee. If, however, they belong to others the manure becomes the property of the lessor. For a man's courtyard acquires title to property for him even without his knowledge and even if the courtyard is under lease to another.

6. He who lets a house, courtyard, bathhouse, shop, or other premises to another for a definite period may compel the lessee to

vacate the premises at the end of such period without even a single hour's delay.

If the letting is made for a night rest, it is to be for not less than a full day; if for a Sabbath rest, for not less than two full days; and if for a wedding, for not less than 30 days.

7. He who lets a house to another for an unspecified term may not dispossess the lessee from the house unless he notifies him 30 days in advance, so as to enable him to find a place and prevent his being thrown into the street. At the end of the 30 days the lessee must vacate the premises.

The 30-day period is applicable only during the warm season. In the rainy season, from the Feast of Succoth to the Feast of Passover, the lessor may not dispossess the lessee.

If notice to vacate is given by the lessor to the lessee before the Feast of Succoth, and the 30-day period of notice ends even one day after the feast, the lessor may not dispossess the lessee until after the Feast of Passover next following and until he has given him another notice of at least 30 days in advance.

8. Just as the lessor is bound to give notice to the lessee, so is the lessee bound to give notice to the lessor—30 days in small towns and 12 months in cities—so as to enable the lessor to find another tenant to fill the vacancy. If the lessee fails to give notice, he may not quit the premises but must pay the rent.

9. Although the lessor may not dispossess the lessee and the lessee may not vacate the premises without advance notice, yet if rents have increased, the lessor may demand a higher rent saying to the lessee, "Either pay the prevailing rent or vacate the premises," and if rents have decreased the lessee may insist upon paying a lower rent, saying to the lessor, "Either accept the prevailing rent or retake possession of the house."

If the lessor's dwelling collapsed, he may remove the lessee from the leased premises. For he may say to him, "It is not right that you should remain in my house until you find another dwelling place, while I am lying on the street; your right in this house is not greater than mine."

10. If the owner gave the house to his son for the purpose of establishing a home for him upon his marriage, and, though he knew in advance that the son was to be married on a certain date, so that notice could have been given to the lessee, did not give him such notice, he may not dispossess him. If, however, the opportunity of marrying the woman presented itself to the son without previous knowledge and he decided to marry her at once, the lessor may dispossess the lessee without notice. For it is not right that the lessee should remain in the house while the lessor's son is compelled to rent a house for a postnuptial home.

11. If the lessor transferred the house, by way of sale or of gift, or if he died leaving it to his heirs, neither the transferee nor the heirs may remove the lessee without 30 days'—or 12 months'—notice in advance. For the lessee may say to them, "Your power is not greater than that of the lessor from whom your right is derived."

CHAPTER VII

1. One may make any stipulation he wishes with regard to hiring just as one may do with regard to purchase and sale, since hiring is but a sale for a specified time.

He who may sell may also let, and he who may not sell may not let either, unless he be a usufructuary of land, who may let but may not sell.

2. If a man let a house for a year, and an additional month was intercalated, the benefit of the intercalation accrues to the lessee. If the letting was made by the month, the benefit of the intercalation accrues to the lessor.

If the lessor mentioned both months and a year, whether he said, "One *denar* a month; 12 denar a year," or "Twelve denar a year; one denar a month," the benefit of the intercalation accrues to the lessor because the land is in the owner's possession (*ḥăzaḳah*), and one cannot recover anything from the party in possession without clear proof.

Similarly, where the lessor says, "I let the house to you for such a term," and the lessee says, "I rented the house for an indefinite term" or "for a longer term," it is the lessee who has the burden of proof, and, if he fails to produce proof, the lessor swears the informal oath and removes the lessee from the premises.

3. If the lessee says, "I have paid the rent I owed," while the lessor says, "I have not received it," whether the letting was by a writing or without witnesses, then, if the lessor made demand within 30 days, the lessee must either produce proof or pay. He may, however, have the anathema proclaimed generally against him who took the rent from him once before. He may also present a separate claim against the lessor for the amount of the payment he claims to have made to him previously, subjecting him to the informal oath. If, however, the lessor made demand after 30 days, or even on the thirtieth day, he must produce proof, or the lessee swears and is quit.

Similarly, if at the time of the letting the lessee agreed to make payment annually, and the lessor made demand within the year, the lessee is to produce proof. If, however, the lessor made demand after the year was over, and even on the twenty-ninth day of *Elul,* the lessor is to produce proof.

4. If a man let a house for 10 years by a writing which did not contain a date and the lessee says that only one year has elapsed from the time of the letting, while the lessor says that the entire term has expired, the lessee is to produce proof. If he fails to do so, the lessor swears the informal oath and dispossesses him.

5. If a man let or mortgaged an orchard for 10 years, and it dried up during the term of the lease or of the mortgage, the dead trees are to be sold and for the money realized from the sale land is to be bought, the fruit of which is to be enjoyed by the lessee or the mortgagee until the end of the lease or the mortgage. Because of the prohibition of usury neither the creditor nor the debtor may take the trees that dried up or were cut.

6. If a writing of lease or of mortgage contains the word *years*, without specification of the number of years, and the lessee or the mortgagee says, "The writing was made for three years," while the owner says, "It was made for two years only," then, if the lessee or the mortgagee has already enjoyed the fruit of the land for three years, the fruit is presumed (ḥăzaḳah) to have belonged to the lessee or the mortgagee unless the owner produces proof to the contrary; and if the lessee or the mortgagee has enjoyed the fruit of the land for three years and, without producing the document, claims that he is entitled to the fruit for five years, while the owner claims that the letting or mortgage was for three years only, and when told to produce the document the lessee claims to have lost it, he is believed; for, relying upon his enjoyment of the fruit for three years, the lessee could plead that the property was his by purchase.

7. If a man brought his produce to the house of his fellow without his consent or through deceit, the owner of the house may sell so much thereof as is necessary to pay workers to have it removed and thrown into the street. However, the moral rule (ḥăsiḏuṭ) requires that the court be notified so as to enable them to hire a place for part of the value of the property, thereby fulfilling the commandment relating to the return of lost property to its owner, although the owner did not act properly.

8. If a man let a mill to another on condition that the lessee grind for him 20 sĕ'ah of wheat per month in lieu of rent, and thereafter the owner of the mill became rich and no longer needed to have flour ground for himself in the mill, then, if the lessee has other wheat to grind either for himself or for others he is compelled to pay to the owner in cash the value of grinding 20 sĕ'ah of wheat, since not to do so would be to follow the ways of the Sodomites; but if the lessee cannot find other wheat he may say, "I have no money to pay you. I am ready to grind for you wheat as stipulated. If you do not need the flour for yourself, sell it to others." And so it is in all similar cases.

CHAPTER VIII

1. There is but one rule applicable to both a lease of a field or vineyard for a stipulated amount of money and a lease for a stipulated amount of the produce, as where one rents a field for 20 *ḳor* a year or a vineyard for 20 jars of wine a year. He who rents for produce is called the *ḥoḳer*.

2. He who takes a field or an orchard on condition that he is to cultivate it, incur the necessary expenditures of cultivation, and deliver to the owner of the land one third, one fourth, or any other stipulated portion of the produce is called the *měḳabbel*.

Whatever is essential to the protection of the land is chargeable to the owner and whatever constitutes added precaution is chargeable to the farmer or tenant on shares.

The spade with which one digs the ground, the vessels in which the dirt is carried, the pole and the bucket with which water is drawn are chargeable to the owner; the digging of ditches where water is gathered for irrigation is chargeable to the farmer or tenant on shares.

3. He who leases a field or takes it on shares for a few years is not allowed to sow it to flax. If he rented or took the field for seven years he may sow it to flax the first year. Also, if he rented or took a field for seven years the Sabbatical year is not included.

4. If a man leased a field from his fellow or took one on shares, and it was an irrigated field or a tree plantation, and the spring feeding the irrigated field dried up—but the main river did not cease flowing and it was still possible to fetch water therefrom by pail—or the trees of the tree plantation were cut down, the lessee may make no deduction from the rental. But if it was a misfortune widespread in that region, such as the river drying up, he may make a deduction from the rental.

If, at the time of the letting, the lessor was standing in the field and said to the lessee, "I am letting *this* irrigated field or *this* tree plantation to you," and thereafter the spring dried up or the trees were cut down, the lessee may make a deduction from the rental. Since the lessor stood in the field at the time of the letting and said *"this* field," it is as though he had said, "I am letting it to you as it is now." But if he was not standing in the field at the time of the letting and said, "I am letting *an* irrigated field or *a* tree plantation to you," and thereafter the spring dried up or the trees were cut down, the lessee may make no deduction from the rental.

5. If a man leased a field or took one on shares from his fellow and the locusts devoured the crop or the tempest blasted it, then, if the mishap occurred to most of the fields in that town, the lessee may make a deduction from the rental in accordance with the loss he sustained; but if the misfortune did not spread to most of the fields, he may make no deduction from his rental even though the crops in all of the lessor's fields were blasted by the tempest.

If the crops in all of the lessee's fields were blasted by the tempest, even though the misfortune spread to most of the fields of the neighborhood, he may not make any deduction from the rental, the loss being attributable to him, since the crops in all of his fields were blasted.

If the lessor stipulated with the lessee that he sow wheat and he sowed barley instead, or did not sow at all, or sowed and it did not grow, even though a locust plague or a tempest came and most of the fields in the region were afflicted, the lessee may make no deduction from his rental.

To what point of time is the lessee bound to busy himself sowing again if no crop grew? All the time which is appropriate for sowing in that locality.

6. If a man leased a field or took one on shares from his fellow, and the custom of the place was to cut the crops, he must cut them and may not uproot them; if the custom was to uproot them, he must uproot and may not cut them, and either one may object to a contemplated deviation from custom by the other; if the custom was to plough after reaping, he must plough.

If the custom of the place was to let the trees along with the land leased, the trees are included, even though the lease was made with-

out specification and at a rental which was less than the prevailing
one; and if the custom of the place was not to include the trees, the
trees are not included, even though the lease was made at a rental
which was higher than the prevailing one. It is all according to
local custom.

7. If a man leased a field from his fellow for 10 kor of wheat a
year and it yielded bad wheat, he may pay him out of the crop of
the field; and if the yield was of exceptionally good wheat, he may
not say, "I will buy wheat for you from the market," but must
pay him out of the crop of the field.

If a man leased from his fellow a vineyard for 10 baskets of
grapes and the grapes became sourish after they had been cut, or,
in the case of a field leased for sheaves of grain, the grain was
spoiled after it had been cut, he may pay the lessor out of the yield.
If he leased the vineyard for 10 jars of wine and the wine turned
sour, he is bound to give the lessor good wine.

If he leased the field for 100 sheaves of clover and sowed it to
another crop and then ploughed up the field and sowed it to clover,
and it yielded poor clover, he may not give him out of the yield,
but must pay him good clover since he deviated from the terms
of the lease. And so it is in similar cases.

8. If a man leased a field from his fellow and, not wishing to
weed it, said to the lessor, "What loss will you sustain, since I will
pay you your rental in any event?" No heed is to be paid to him,
since the lessor may reply, "At a later time, when you will have
vacated the field, it will yield to me naught save weeds"; even if the
lessee said, "I will plough it up at the end of my term," no heed is to
be paid to him.

9. If a man leased a field from his fellow upon condition that he
sow it to barley, he may not sow it to wheat because wheat impairs the fertility of the soil more than does barley; if he leased it
upon condition that he sow it to wheat, he may sow it to barley; if
upon condition that he sow it to pulse, he may not sow it to grain,
and if upon condition that he sow it to grain, he may sow it to

pulse. But in regions like Babylonia he may not sow it to pulse because there pulse impairs the fertility of the soil.

10. If a man took a field from his fellow on shares for but a few years, he has no share in the beams cut from the sycamore tree and the like or in the profits resulting from trees which sprouted forth in the field of themselves during that time. However, credit is to be given to him for the space occupied by the trees, as though it had been sown with the same seed with which the rest of the field was sown, provided the trees sprouted forth in a place which was fit for sowing. But if they sprouted forth in a place which was unfit for sowing, no credit is to be given to him.

If he took the field for seven years or more, he has a share in the beams cut from sycamore trees and the like.

If, when the time came for him to vacate the field there were crops which had not yet ripened to be sold, or, if ripe, the market day had not yet come when they could be sold, an appraisal thereof is made, and he takes his share in money from the owner of the land.

Just as the tenant on shares and the owner of the land divide the grain between themselves so they divide the chopped straw and the stubble; just as they divide the wine so they divide the dead branches. But the reed props which are placed under the vines are divided between them only if they were purchased by both of them, and if they were purchased with the money of one of them, they belong to him who purchased them. And so it is in all similar cases.

11. If a man took a field from his fellow on shares for planting, the owner of the field takes upon himself 10 empties to the sĕ'ah, but if there were more than that the tenant is charged with everything.

12. If a man took a field from his fellow on shares and it failed to bear fruit, he is nevertheless bound to cultivate it if there is a prospect of a yield of two sĕ'ah over and above the expenditures. For he writes to the owner of the field thus: "I will arise and plough and sow and cut and bind up and thresh and winnow and

place the heap before you, and you will take thereof one half [or whatever they may agree upon] and I will take the balance as a reward for my labor and for what I shall have expended."

13. If a man took a field from his fellow on shares and, after having taken possession thereof, he let it lie fallow, an appraisal is made of how much the field was likely to yield, and the tenant must pay the owner the share which would have come to him. For he writes to the owner of the land thus: "If I let the land lie fallow and do not till it I will pay you out of the fairest of my property." The same rule applies if he allows part of the property to lie fallow. And why is he bound to pay? Because he did not stipulate to pay a specified sum—in which case we would say that it was like 'asmaḵta—but he agreed to pay out of his fairest property and therefore he determined to obligate himself.

But if he said, "If I let the field lie fallow and I do not till it, I will give you 100 denar," it is 'asmaḵta and he is not bound by his promise. He must give to the owner of the land only that which the field was likely to yield.

14. If a man took a field from his fellow on shares on condition that he sow it to sesame, and then sowed it to wheat instead, and it yielded a crop of wheat which was worth as much as the probable crop of sesame would have been worth, the owner of the land has but a grievance against the tenant.

If the land yielded in wheat less than the value of the probable crop of sesame, the tenant must pay to the owner of the land in accordance with the value of the probable crop of sesame. If the land yielded in wheat more than the value of the probable crop of the sesame, they divide the wheat between themselves in accordance with their agreement, even though a gain accrues to the owner of the land.

CHAPTER IX

1. If a man hired laborers and bade them to work early or to work late, he has no right to compel them to do so where the custom is not to work early or not to work late. Where the custom is to

give them their food, he must give it to them and where the custom is to provide them with dry figs, dates, or the like, he must do so. It is all according to local custom.

2. If a man hired a laborer and said to him, "I will pay you like one or another of the inhabitants of the town," we take the lowest and the highest wage and strike an average between them.

3. If a man said to his messenger, "Go out and hire laborers for me at three zuz," and he went and hired them at four, then, if the messenger said to them, "I am responsible for your wages," he must give them four, although he takes only three from the employer, losing one out of his own pocket; and if he said to them, "The employer is responsible for your wages," the employer pays them in accordance with local custom. If there were in the locality some who hired themselves out at three and some who hired themselves out at four, the employer pays them only three and they have but a grievance against the messenger. This applies only where the product of their work is not measurable, but if it is measurable and it is worth four, the employer must give them four, for if his messenger had not told them that they would receive four, they would not have exerted themselves to produce what is worth four.

If the employer said to the messenger, "Go and hire laborers at four," and the messenger went and hired them at three they are entitled but to three, even though the product of their labor is worth four, since they voluntarily undertook to work for three, and they have but a grievance against the messenger.

If the employer told the messenger to hire laborers at three and the messenger went and, without disclosing the employer's instructions, offered them four, and they said, "We accept that which the employer offered," we may assume that they had in mind only the possibility that the employer told the messenger to hire them at *more than four*. Therefore an appraisal of what they produced is made and if it is worth four, they receive four from the employer; and if the value is unknown or if it is not more than three they receive only three. If the employer told the messenger to hire them at four, and the messenger went and offered them three, and they said, "We accept what the employer offered," they receive only three, even though the product of their labor be worth four, since they heard him say three and they accepted.

4. If a man hired laborers and they disappointed him, or if he disappointed them, the disappointed party has but a grievance against the other. This applies only where the employer reneged before the laborers came to work, but if the ass drivers came and found no grain to haul, or the laborers came and found the field wet, or if the employer hired them to irrigate the field and the field was filled with water, then, if the employer inspected his work the previous evening and found that it required laborers, the laborers have no claim against him. What could he do? But if he did not inspect the field he pays them a wage like the one which he would pay to a laborer who is staying idle, for he who proceeds on a journey while laden is unlike him who proceeds while empty, and he who is working is unlike him who is staying idle.

This applies only if the laborers had not begun to work when they reneged, but if a laborer began to work and then withdrew in the middle of the day, while he may not be compelled to return to work—for it is said *For unto me the children of Israel are servants* (Lev. 25:55) and not servants to servants—there is more than just a grievance involved.

What is the rule with respect to a laborer who withdrew after he had begun to work? An appraisal is made of the value of the work he has done, and he is paid therefor. But if he was an entrepreneur an appraisal is made of the work left undone by him. Whether or not labor was cheap at the time when the entrepreneur entered into his contract with the employer, and whether or not the price of labor dropped thereafter, an appraisal of that which he left undone is made. How is this to be understood? If he undertook to harvest a crop for two *sela'* and he harvested one half thereof and left the other half unharvested, or if he undertook to weave a garment for two sela' and he wove one half thereof and left the other half unwoven, an appraisal is made of the value of the work left undone; if it is worth six denar he must either finish the work or take one *shekel,* or if what was left undone is worth two denar the employer pays him only one sela', since he only performed one half of the work.

This applies only where no irretrievable loss is involved, but if there is an irretrievable loss, as where the employer hired him to remove his flax from the vat in which it was steeped, or if he was to bring flutes for a funeral or for a bridal procession and the like, neither a laborer nor an entrepreneur may withdraw unless overtaken by force majeure, as when he took sick or received tidings that a near relative of his had died. But if he was not overtaken by force majeure and he withdrew, the employer may hire other laborers at his expense or may, through false promises, induce him to return to his work.

What is meant by inducement through false promises? The employer may say, "I have stipulated with you for one sela', come to work and you will receive two instead," holding out this promise to him until he has completed his work and, upon the completion of the work, he may pay him only what he originally stipulated; and even if he paid the additional sum he may recover it from him.

What is meant by hiring other laborers at his expense? He may hire other laborers who will finish the work, thus preventing an irretrievable loss, and whatever additional sum he may have to pay to the other laborers in excess of the sum agreed upon by the first laborer he takes from the first laborer. Up to what? Up to the wages owed by him to the first laborer; if the laborer has money in the employer's hands, the latter may hire another laborer at a wage up to 40 and 50 zuz per day, even though he hired the first laborer for three or four zuz per day.

This applies only if there are no laborers available to be hired at the wages of the original laborer, but if there are such laborers available and the retracting laborer says to the employer, "Go forth and hire these and complete your work, and no irretrievable loss will result"—whether the employee is a day laborer or an entrepreneur—the employer has but a grievance against him. In the case of a day laborer an appraisal is made of the work he has done, while in the case of an entrepreneur the appraisal is made of the work he has left undone.

5. If a man hired a laborer and thereafter the laborer was seized for royal service, the employer may not say to him, "I am ready and willing to have you complete the work"; he must pay the laborer for the work he has performed.

6. If a man hired a laborer to water a field from *this* river, and in the middle of the day the river ceased flowing, the worker is entitled to be paid only for the work he has performed, provided it was not the way of the river to cease flowing. Similarly, if it was customary for the inhabitants of the town to stop the course of the river, and they stopped it in the middle of the day, the workers are entitled to be paid only for the work they have performed, since they knew that it was customary to stop the course of the river. But if it was the way of the river to cease flowing of itself, the employer must pay the workers the full day's wages, since he should have given them notice.

If a man hired a worker to water his field, and rain came and watered it, the worker is entitled to receive wages only for the work he has performed. But if the river overflowed and watered the field, the employer must pay the worker his wages in full, for it was heaven that helped him.

All this applies to a worker; but if a man stipulated with his tenant on shares that, if he should water the field four times a day, he would take one half of the produce, while other tenants on shares, who watered their fields only twice a day, took only one quarter of the produce, and rain came and the field was watered, so that the tenant was not required to draw water with a pail, he takes one half of the produce, in accordance with the stipulation, because a tenant on shares is like a partner and not like a worker.

7. If a man hired a worker to do a certain task for a full day, and the task was finished in the middle of the day, then, if the employer has another task like the previous one, or a lighter one, the laborer works on it the balance of the day; but if he has no work for him

he pays him a wage such as one would pay a worker who is staying idle. However, if the worker was of the diggers or of the tillers of the soil and the like, who are accustomed to great exertion and who would be weakened by lack of work, he must pay him his full wage.

8. If a man hired a worker to go on a mission for him and bring a certain thing from another place, and he went and did not find that which he was to bring, the employer must pay him his full wage.

If he hired him to bring reed props for a vineyard, and he went and did not find any, the employer must pay him his full wage.

If he hired him to bring cabbage and damascene plums for a sick person, and he went and found that the sick person had died or had recovered, the employer may not say to him, "Take what you brought for your wage," but must pay him his full wage. And so it is in all similar cases.

9. If a man hired a worker to work on what belongs to himself but directed him to what belongs to his fellow, the employer must pay to the worker his wage and he in turn takes from his fellow the value of the benefit the latter received from the work.

10. If a man hired a worker to work for him on chopped straw or stubble and the like and he said to the worker, "Take from what you produce for your wage," no heed is to be paid to him; but if after the worker had accepted such an offer from the employer the latter said, "Here is your wage in money and I will take what is mine," no heed is to be paid to him.

11. What a worker finds belongs to himself, even though the employer said to him, "Work for me today," and needless to say if he said, "Hoe for me today." But if the employer hired the worker to collect things, as may be the case, for example, after an overflowing river had subsided and he hired him to collect fish in the marshland, what he finds belongs to the employer, even if it be a purse full of denars.

CHAPTER X

1. If a man made a loan to his fellow on a pawn, whether he loaned him money or produce, whether he took the pawn at the time he made the loan or afterward, the lender is deemed a bailee for hire with respect to the pawn. If, therefore, the pawn was lost or stolen the lender is liable for its value; but if the pawn was lost through force majeure, as where it was taken by an armed robber or through similar force, the lender must swear that it was lost through force majeure and the owner of the pawn must pay his debt to the last pĕruṭah.

2. Whenever one says to his fellow, "Keep (certain property) for me and I will keep (certain property) for you," it is a keeping with the owner. But if he said to him, "Keep for me today and I will keep for you tomorrow," "Lend to me today and I will lend to you tomorrow," "Keep for me today and I will lend to you tomorrow," "Lend to me today and I will keep for you tomorrow"—in all of these cases each becomes a bailee for hire for the other.

3. All craftsmen are deemed bailees for hire. But if a craftsman said, "Take what is yours and bring money," or "I have completed my work," and the owner did not take the object, the craftsman becomes a gratuitous bailee. If, however, the craftsman said, "Bring money and take what is yours," he continues to be a bailee for hire as before.

4. If a man gave something to a craftsman for repair and he spoiled it, the craftsman is liable to pay for it. How is this to be understood? If he gave a carpenter a box, chest, or cupboard to have a nail driven into it and he broke it, or if he gave him wood to make therefrom a box, chest, or cupboard and after it was made it was broken, the craftsman must pay the value of the box, chest, or cupboard. For a craftsman does not acquire title to the improvement wrought by him in the object on which he works.

If a man gave wool to a dyer and it was burnt in the caldron the dyer must pay him the value of his wool. If he dyed it in unseemly fashion, or if the owner gave it to him to dye red and he dyed it black, to dye black and he dyed it red; or if the owner gave wood to a carpenter to make therefrom a seemly chair and he made an unseemly chair, or a stool, then, if the value of the improvement was greater than the expenditure, the owner of the object pays the expenditure, and if the expenditure was greater than the value of the improvement, he pays the value of the improvement only.

If the owner of the object said, "I do not wish to avail myself of this enactment, but let him give me the value of the wool or of the wood," no heed is to be paid to him. Similarly, if the craftsman said, "Here is the value of your wool or the value of your wood, take it and go," no heed is to be paid to him, because the craftsman does not acquire title to the improvement he wrought in the object.

5. If a man brought wheat to a mill for grinding, and the miller did not moisten it, or ground it into bran flour or into coarse bran; or if a man gave flour to a baker and the baker baked Neapolis bread therefrom; or if a man gave an animal to a butcher and he made it a *nĕbelah,* they are each liable because they are receivers of hire. But if the butcher was skilled and slaughtered the animal gratuitously, he is quit of payment, and if he was not skilled, even though he slaughtered the animal gratuitously, he is liable to pay.

Similarly, if a man showed a denar to a banker, and the banker told him that it was a good coin, and it proved to be bad, then, if the banker received hire for the inspection, he is liable to pay, even though he is experienced and does not need to learn; but if he made the inspection gratuitously he is quit, provided he is experienced and does not need to learn. If he is not experienced, however, he is liable to pay, even though he made the inspection gratuitously, provided the owner of the coin said to the banker, "I am relying upon you," or it was evident that he was relying upon the banker's inspection and that he was not going to show it to others.

A butcher who slaughtered an animal gratuitously and made it a něbelah, or a banker who said, "The coin is good," and it proved to be bad, or the like, must produce proof that he is skilled and if he fails to produce such proof, he must pay.

6. If the local custom was that the tree planter should take one half of the improvement made by him on the land and the owner of the land should take the other half, and the planter planted, causing improvement in some places and loss in others, one half of the improvement is reckoned in his favor, a deduction is made therefrom of the loss caused by him, and he takes the balance. Even if he stipulated that if he caused loss he should not take anything, it is 'asmakta, and only the loss caused by him is deducted from his share.

If the local custom was that the planter should take one half and the owner of the land should take the other half, and also that a tenant on shares should take one third, and the planter planted, causing improvement, and then decided to withdraw, so that it was necessary for the owner of the land to put a tenant on shares on the property, he may put such tenant thereon and the owner of the land takes one half, losing nothing, the tenant on shares takes one third, and the planter takes only the remaining one sixth, since the latter withdrew of his own accord.

7. A planter of trees for the inhabitants of a locality who caused damage, or a butcher for the inhabitants of a town who made *něbelot* of the animals, or a bloodletter who caused injury, or a scribe who made errors in deeds, or a teacher who, being negligent of the children, failed to teach or taught error, and all similar skilled persons, who cannot repair the damage caused by them, may be removed without warning because, having been appointed by the public, they have a standing warning to exert themselves in their work.

CHAPTER XI

1. It is an affirmative commandment to give to the hired man his hire in time, for it is said *In the same day thou shalt give him his hire* (Deut. 24:15). And he who delays payment until after the

time when the hire is due transgresses a negative commandment. For it is said *Neither shall the sun go down upon it (ibid.).* But no lashes are to be administered for the transgression of this commandment since the transgressor is liable to pay. A man's hire, the hire for an animal, and the hire for utensils, all alike, must be paid in time, and if one delays payment until after the time when it is due he transgresses a negative commandment. In the case of a resident alien the affirmative commandment of *In the same day thou shalt give him his hire* applies, but no negative commandment is violated by a delay.

2. Whoever withholds the hire of a hired man is deemed as though he took away his livelihood from him. For it is said *And he setteth his soul upon it* (Deut. 24:15). And he transgresses four negative and one affirmative commandments, to wit: *Thou shalt not oppress* (Lev. 19:13), *Thou shalt not rob (ibid.), Thou shalt not cause the wages of a hired man to abide with thee all night until the morning (ibid.), The sun shall not go down upon it,* and *In the same day thou shalt give him his hire* (Deut. 24:15).

What is the time when wages are due? A hireling for the day collects his hire all night, and with respect to him it is said *Thou shalt not cause the wages of a hired man to abide with thee all night until the morning;* a hireling for the night collects all day, and with respect to him it is said *In the same day thou shalt give him his hire;* a hireling by the hour during the day collects all day; a hireling by the hour during the night collects all night; a hireling by the week, by the month, by the year, by the septennium if his term ends in the daytime, collects all day, and if in the nighttime, all night.

3. If a man gave his garment to a craftsman and the craftsman finished the work that was to be done on it, giving the owner notice thereof, the latter does not violate the Law concerning timely payment, even if he delayed payment for ten days, as long as the object remains in the hands of the craftsman.

If the craftsman returned the garment in the middle of the day, the employer transgresses the commandment of *Thou shalt not cause the wages of a hired man to abide with thee, etc.* as soon as the sun goes down; for an undertaking to do a specific task is like a hiring for a specified time, and the employer is bound to pay the employee in time.

4. If a man said to his messenger, "Go and hire workers for me," and the messenger went and said to the workers, "The employer will be responsible for your hire," neither of them transgresses the commandment of *Thou shalt not cause the wages of a hired man to abide with thee, etc.*—the employer because he did not hire them, and the messenger because they did not work for him. But if the messenger did not say to them, "The employer is responsible for your hire," he commits a transgression.

The employer does not commit a transgression unless the hired man made demand upon him and he failed to pay. But if the hired man did not make demand, or if he made demand and the employer did not have the money to pay him, or if the employer gave the hired man a draft upon another, and the hired man accepted it, the employer is quit.

5. He who has withheld the hire of a hired man until after it was due is still bound to pay him immediately, even though he has transgressed an affirmative and a negative commandment; during the whole time in which he continues to withhold the hire from the hired man he transgresses an extra-Pentateuchal negative commandment. For it is said *Say not unto thy neighbour, Go, and come again* (Prov. 3: 28).

6. If a hired man, who had been hired in the presence of witnesses, made timely demand and the employer said, "I have paid you your hire," while the hired man said, "I have not received anything," the hired man, by virtue of an enactment of the Sages, swears while holding a sacred object and takes what he claims—in accordance with the rule applicable to every other claimant who is to swear and take—because the employer is preoccupied with his workers, while the hired man looks eagerly to his hire upon which he depends. Even if the employer is a minor the hired man swears and takes.

If the man was hired in the absence of witnesses the employer is believed when he says, "I have hired you and paid you your hire," since he could say, "No such thing ever occurred." The employer therefore swears the informal oath that he has paid—or the Pentateuchal oath if he made a partial admission—as in the case of all other claims.

If the hired man had one witness testifying that the employer had hired him, such testimony is of no avail to him.

Similarly, if the hired man made demand subsequent to the time when the hire was due, even though he had been hired in the presence of witnesses, the rule that he who claims anything from his fellow must produce proof applies, and if he does not produce proof, the employer swears the informal oath.

If the hired man produces proof that he made demand continually during the time when the hire was due, he swears and takes, if he sues on the day when he made the demand. How is this to be understood? If the hired man was working for the employer on a Monday until evening, the time of payment thus being the whole night of Monday, and he sues on Tuesday he does not swear and take. But if he produces witnesses that he was continually making demand the whole night of Monday he swears and takes, if he sues at any time during the day of Tuesday, and from Tuesday night onward the rule that he who claims anything from his fellow must produce proof applies.

Similarly, if he produces witnesses that he was continually making demand until Thursday he swears and takes, if he sues at any time during the day of Thursday.

7. If the employer says, "I have stipulated with you for two zuz," while the hired man says, "You have stipulated for three zuz," there is no enactment of the Sages that the hired man should swear and take, and the rule that he who claims anything from his fellow must produce proof applies.

If the hired man does not produce proof, the employer swears while holding a sacred object, even though he has already paid him two zuz or made tender thereof.

The rule requiring that the employer swear while holding a

sacred object is an enactment of the Sages instituted in order that the hired man should not walk away discouraged. This applies only where the hiring was done in the presence of witnesses, who did not know how much was stipulated, and the hired man made timely demand; but if the hiring was done in the absence of witnesses, or if the hired man made demand subsequent to the time when the hire was due, the employer is to swear the informal oath that he did not stipulate for more than he has already paid him, or that he does not owe him more than what he has tendered, as is the rule with respect to all other claims.

8. If a man gave his garment to a craftsman for repair and thereafter the craftsman said, "You have stipulated with me for two zuz," while the owner of the garment said, "I have stipulated with you for one zuz only," the rule is that as long as the garment is in the hands of the craftsman and the circumstances are such that he could claim that it had come to him by way of purchase, he swears while holding a sacred object and takes what he claims.

Under this rule he may claim as stipulated hire up to the value of the garment. But if the garment is out of his possession or if he has no seizin (ḥăzaḳah) therein and could not claim that it had come to him by way of purchase the rule that he who claims anything from his fellow must produce proof applies.

If the craftsman does not produce proof, the owner of the garment is to swear the informal oath—or the Pentateuchal oath if he made a partial admission—as is the rule with respect to all other claims, the rule of the hired man not being applicable to such a case.

9. A hired man who comes to swear an oath is not to be treated with strictness, and no oath by accumulation is to be imposed upon him at all; he is to swear only that he has not received his hire and is to be paid.

All others who come to take an oath are not treated with leniency except the hireling who is treated with leniency and in whose case the court must open the proceedings by saying to him, "Do not grieve, swear and take."

Even if his hire was one pĕruṭah and the employer says, "I have paid him," he does not take what he claims except by oath.

The same rule applies to all other claimants who swear and take. Even if the claimant does not claim more than one pĕruṭah, he does not take except by a quasi-Pentateuchal oath.

CHAPTER XII

1. Whenever workers are working at anything which grows from the soil and has not been completely processed, whether severed from the soil or still attached to it, and their work constitutes a final processing the employer is enjoined to allow them to eat of that at which they are working. For it is said *When thou comest into thy neighbour's vineyard, then thou mayest eat grapes until thou have enough at thine own pleasure . . . When thou comest into thy neighbour's standing corn, then thou mayest pluck ears with thy hand* (Deut. 23: 25–26). From the oral tradition it has been learned that these passages of Scripture refer only to a man who was hired by the owner. For if he was not hired, who permitted him to come into his neighbor's vineyard or standing crops without his neighbor's consent? These passages can therefore be understood only thus: when you come into the domain of the owner to work you may eat of that at which you are working.

2. What is the difference between him who is working at that which is severed from the soil and him who is working at that which is attached to the soil? He who is working at that which is severed from the soil may eat thereof until it has been completely processed and is forbidden to eat thereof once it has been completely processed; while he who is working at that which is attached to the soil, such as a harvester of grain or a plucker of grapes, may not eat thereof until a stage of his work has been completed. If, for example, a hired man is plucking grapes, putting them in a basket until it is filled, shaking the contents of the

basket out into some other place, returning, plucking grapes, and filling the basket again, he may not eat of the grapes until he has filled the basket. But by reason of the commandment relating to the restoration of lost property to its owner the Sages have said: workers may eat while walking from one row of vines to another and while returning from the wine press, in order that they should not neglect their work by sitting down to eat, but should rather eat in the midst of their work, while walking from one place to another, without neglecting their work.

3. He who neglects his work and eats, or eats not at the time when a stage of the work has been completed, transgresses a negative commandment. For it is said *But thou shalt not move a sickle unto thy neighbour's standing corn* (Deut. 23:26). From the oral tradition it has been learned that this passage is to be interpreted thus: so long as you are occupied with reaping you must not move a sickle for your own eating. And so it is in all similar cases.

Similarly, a worker who carries off in his hands of that at which he is working, or takes more than is required for his eating, giving it to others, transgresses a negative commandment. For it is said *But thou shalt not put any in thy vessel* (Deut. 23:25). However, no lashes are to be administered for the transgression of these two negative commandments because the transgressor is liable to pay.

4. He who milks an animal or makes curds or cheese may not eat thereof, because it is not a product of the soil.

He who weeds among the onions and garlic, even though he uproots the small ones from among the large ones—and in all similar cases—may not eat thereof, because his labor does not constitute a final stage of the work, and, needless to say, they who guard gardens and orchards and every other thing that is attached to the soil, such as cucumbers and gourds, may not eat thereof at all.

5. He who separates dates or dry figs may not eat thereof, because they have been completely processed for tithes.

He who is working at wheat and the like after tithes have been set apart—as when the owner hired him to pick pebbles from the wheat, or to cause it to swell, or to grind it—may eat thereof, because it has not been completely processed for *ḥallah*. But he who kneads dough, or forms it, or bakes it, may not eat thereof, because it has been completely processed for ḥallah and tithes.

6. A worker may eat only of that which has not been completely processed for ḥallah and tithes. If one's fig cakes broke up, or his jars burst open, and he hired workers to work at them, they must not eat thereof since they have been completely processed, thus becoming subject to tithes, and are therefore *ṭeḅel*. If the employer did not give the workers notice that the figs or the wine had become subject to tithes, he must first set apart tithes and then suffer them to eat.

Workers who are working at anything which belongs to the sanctuary may not eat thereof while working. For it is said *When thou comest into thy neighbour's vineyard, etc.* (Deut. 23:25).

7. If a man hired workers to work at his fourth-year plantings, they may not eat thereof, and if the owner did not give the workers notice that these were fourth-year plantings, he must first redeem the fruit and then suffer them to eat.

8. He who is reaping, threshing, winnowing or sifting grain, harvesting olives, cutting or pressing grapes, or doing similar work, is allowed to eat thereof by virtue of Pentateuchal Law.

9. Those who are guarding grapes in the wine press, or stacks of grain, or any other thing which is severed from the soil and has not been completely processed for tithes, may eat thereof by virtue of the customs of the country, because he who guards is unlike him whose task requires action. But he who is working at anything with the members of his body, whether with his arms, or legs, or even with the shoulders, may eat thereof by virtue of Pentateuchal Law.

10. If a worker is working at figs he may not eat grapes. For it is said *When thou comest into thy neighbour's vineyard, then*

thou mayest eat grapes until thou have enough at thine own pleasure (Deut. 23:25). And he who is working at one vine may not eat of another vine; nor may a worker eat grapes together with another thing—not even with bread or with salt. But if the measure of that which the worker should be allowed to eat was fixed by agreement between employer and worker, the latter may eat either with salt, or with bread, or with anything else at his pleasure.

A worker is forbidden to press the juice out of the grapes and consume it. For it is said *Thou mayest eat grapes* (*ibid.*). Nor may his children or his wife parch ears of corn for him over the fire. For it is said *Thou mayest eat grapes until thou have enough at thine own pleasure* (*ibid.*)—grapes as they are. And so it is in all similar cases.

11. A worker is forbidden to overeat of that of which he is allowed to eat. For it is said *Until thou have enough at thine own pleasure* (Deut. 23:25). But he may refrain from eating until he reaches the best fruits and then eat. He may eat cucumbers, even to a denar's worth, and dates, even to a denar's worth, even if he was hired for only one *ma'ah* of silver. For it is said *Until thou have enough at thine own pleasure* (*ibid.*). But a man is to be taught not to be so gluttonous as to shut the door against himself.

If he was guarding four or five stacks, he must not eat his fill from one of them but must eat from each one proportionately.

12. Workers who have not yet trodden on the grapes in the wine press once, lengthwise and crosswise, may eat of the grapes but may not drink of the wine, because they are as yet working at the grapes only; but as soon as they have begun to press the grapes, having trodden once on the grapes, lengthwise and crosswise, they may eat of the grapes and drink of the must, since they now are working at the grapes and the wine.

13. If a worker said, "Give to my wife and children that which I am allowed to eat," or if he said "I am going to give to my wife and children a little of that which I have taken for myself to eat," his words may remain unheeded, because the Law conferred the

right only upon the worker himself. Even if the worker was a Nazarite working at grapes and he said, "Give to my wife and children," his words may remain unheeded.

14. If a worker, who was working together with his wife, children, and bondmen, had stipulated with the employer that neither he nor they should eat of that at which they were going to work, they may not eat thereof. This applies only to adults, because, possessing understanding, they may renounce their rights. But with respect to minors, one may not stipulate that they should not eat, because what they eat is neither their father's nor their employer's but belongs to heaven.

CHAPTER XIII

1. An animal is to be allowed to eat of that at which it is working whenever it is working at anything which grows from the soil, whether attached to the soil or severed from it. It is also to be allowed to eat of the burden on its back, provided one does not take with his hand and feed to it.

2. Whoever prevents an animal from eating while it is working is subject to lashes. For it is said *Thou shalt not muzzle the ox when he treadeth out the corn* (Deut. 25: 4). This applies to all other animals, whether clean or unclean, as well as to an ox; it also applies to all other types of work at that which grows from the soil as well as to threshing, *The ox when he treadeth out the corn* having been specified in Scripture only because that is the usual thing. But he who prevents a worker from eating is quit of lashes.

If one muzzled the animal while it was working, or before it had begun to work, and worked with it while it was muzzled—and even if he prevented it from eating by shouting at it—he is subject to lashes.

If one hired an animal and muzzled it and then threshed with it, he is subject to lashes and must pay to the owner four ḳab for a cow and three ḳab for an ass, because, while he became liable to pay for the animal's food from the moment he drew it to himself, he did not become subject to lashes until he threshed with it while it was muzzled.

3. An Israelite who threshes with a cow belonging to a heathen transgresses the commandment of *Thou shalt not muzzle, etc.*

If a man said to a heathen, "Muzzle my cow and thresh with it," or if a thorn happened to be stuck in the animal's mouth, and he threshed with it while it was unable to eat, or if he caused a lion to lie down nearby, or if he caused the animal's offspring to lie down nearby, or if the animal was thirsty and he failed to give it to drink, or if he spread a skin over the threshing floor in order to prevent the animal from eating—all this is forbidden but does not make the transgressor subject to lashes.

If the thing at which the animal was working was bad for its stomach or injurious, or if the animal was sick and, if it ate of that thing, its stomach would become loose, it is permissible to prevent it from eating because the Law is only concerned with that which is beneficial to the animal, and here the animal would derive no benefit.

4. If a priest is threshing grain, which is known for certain to be *tĕrumah* or tĕrumah of tithes, with a cow belonging to an Israelite, or if cows are threshing grain which has been set apart as second tithes, or if cows happen to be passing over grain because the roadway is blocked, the negative commandment of *Thou shalt not muzzle, etc.* does not apply. However, in the case of cows threshing tĕrumah or second tithes it is incumbent upon the person working with the animal, for the sake of appearances, to bring some of the kind of grain the animal is threshing and put it in the basket which is around its neck.

5. If a man is threshing second tithes of *dĕmai,* or tĕrumah of tithes of dĕmai, or that which grew from seeds of tĕrumah, the negative commandment of *Thou shalt not muzzle, etc.* applies.

6. The owner of the cow is permitted to withhold food from her in order that she should eat more of the grain which she is going to thresh, and the hirer of the cow is permitted to feed to her

from the bundles of sheaves in order that she should not eat much from the grain she is threshing.

Similarly, an employer may give his workers wine to drink in order that they should not eat much of the grapes, and the workers may dip their bread in brine in order that they may eat much of the grapes.

But a worker may not do his own work at night and hire himself out for the day, or thresh with his cow in the evening and hire her out for the day; nor may he starve himself, giving away his own food to his children, because by doing so he weakens himself physically and mentally and renders himself incapable of exertion in his work, thus depriving the employer of what is due to him.

7. Just as the employer is enjoined not to deprive the poor worker of his hire or withhold it from him when it is due, so is the worker enjoined not to deprive the employer of the benefit of his work by idling away his time, a little here and a little there, thus wasting the whole day deceitfully. Indeed, the worker must be very punctual in the matter of time, seeing that the Sages were so solicitous in this matter that they exempted the worker from saying the fourth benediction of grace.

The worker must work with all his power, seeing that the just Jacob said *And ye know that with all my power I have served your father* (Gen. 31:6), and that he received his reward therefor in this world, too, as it is said *And the man increased exceedingly* (Gen. 30:43).

TREATISE II

LAWS CONCERNING BORROWING AND DEPOSITING

Involving Two Affirmative Commandments

To Wit

1. To administer the Law of the commodatary;
2. To administer the Law of the gratuitous bailee.

An exposition of these commandments
is contained in the following chapters.

CHAPTER I

1. If a man borrowed from his fellow utensils, an animal, or any other movable, and the object borrowed was lost or stolen—or even if the damage occurred through force majeure, as where the animal broke its limb, was captured, or died—he is liable to pay in full. For it is written *And if a man borrow aught of his neighbour, and it be hurt, or die, the owner thereof not being with it, he shall surely make restitution* (Exod. 22:13).

This applies only if the force occurred while the animal was not working, but if a man borrowed an animal to plough with it, and it died while ploughing, he is quit. If, however, the animal died before or after he ploughed with it; or if, instead of ploughing with it, he rode on it or threshed grain with it, and the animal died during the riding or the threshing, he is liable to pay. And so it is in all similar cases.

Similarly, if a man borrowed an animal to ride on it to a certain place, and it died while he was riding in the direction of that place, or if he borrowed a pail to draw water therewith from a well, and it fell into the well while it was being filled, or if he borrowed an axe to chop wood therewith, and it was broken during the chopping and because of it—and in all similar cases—he is quit, since he borrowed the thing but for the purpose of doing with it the work which he actually did without deviating from that purpose.

2. If a man borrowed an animal, and it died, and he claims that it died while working, then, if the place to which he was to take the animal under the terms of the borrowing was one which was frequented by people, he must produce proof that the animal died a natural death or through force while working, and that he did not deviate from the terms of the borrowing, and he is quit; if he fails to produce such proof, he must pay.

If he borrowed the animal for the purpose of carrying dirt to fill therewith the ruins of his house, where witnesses are not likely to be present, or if he borrowed a pail to draw water therewith from his private well, and the pail fell into the well, then, if he produces proof to that effect, he is quit even of an oath, and if he fails to produce such proof, he must swear the bailee's oath that the animal died while working, and is quit. And so it is in all similar cases.

3. If a man borrowed a utensil, and it was broken, the assessment of damages is made in the same manner as in torts. An estimate is made of how much the utensil was worth when whole and of how much it was worth after it was broken. The borrower returns the broken utensil, or the animal with the broken limb, to the lender and pays the amount of the depreciation. Similarly, if the animal died, the borrower returns the carcass to the lender and pays the depreciation.

4. He who borrows an animal is bound to feed it from the moment he draws it to himself until the end of the term for which he borrowed it. If the animal becomes lean of flesh he is liable to pay the amount of its depreciation. If, however, the animal became lean of flesh because of its work, he is to swear the bailee's oath to that effect and is quit.

5. If a man borrowed a utensil or an animal without specifying the time for which he borrowed it, the lender may demand its return at any time at his will. If he borrowed the object for a specified time, then, once he drew it to himself acquiring a right therein, the lender may not demand its return until the end of the term of the borrowing. Even if the borrower died, his heirs may use the object borrowed until the end of the term.

This rule is based upon the following analogy: a vendee acquires the corpus of the property in perpetuity with the money he gives to the vendor, while a donee acquires the corpus in perpetuity without giving anything in return; a hirer acquires the usufruct of the property for a specified time with the money he gives to the lessor, while a borrower acquires the usufruct of the property for a specified time without giving anything in return. Just as the donor is likened to the vendor in that he may at no time retract from the gift, so the lender is likened to the lessor in that he may not retract from the lending during the term thereof.

If a father left to his heirs a cow he had borrowed, and she died, the heirs are not liable. If the heirs, thinking that the cow belonged to their father, slaughtered her and consumed the meat, they are to pay only the value of the meat at the lowest price. If, however, the father had left property to the heirs, they must pay out of their father's property the full value of the animal that died or was slaughtered.

6. If a man borrowed a tool to perform with it a certain task, the lender may not demand its return until the task has been performed. Similarly, if one borrowed an animal to carry him to a certain place, the lender may not demand its return until the borrower has gone to that place and returned therefrom.

7. If a man said to another, "Lend me a hoe with which to hoe *this orchard,*" he may hoe only that orchard and no other; if he said *an orchard* he may hoe any orchard; if he borrowed the hoe to hoe *his orchards* he may hoe all the orchards he has, and even if all the metal disintegrates in the process of hoeing, the borrower may return the wooden handle. And so it is in all similar cases.

8. If a man borrowed a tool for use, saying to the lender, "Lend this thing to me out of your kindness," that is, "You are not to lend this thing to me in the manner of all other lenders but in accordance with the kindness of your heart and your liberality, which make you unconcerned about the period of time during which the thing may be kept by me, even if it be long," then, if kinyan was performed at the time of the borrowing, the borrower may use the tool until it is rendered unusable, returning only its broken parts or what remains of it. But the borrower may not repair the tool or make another one out of its broken parts.

9. If a man said to another, "Lend me *this water tank,*" and the tank was destroyed, he may not rebuild it; if he said, *"Lend me a water tank,"* and the tank was destroyed he may rebuild it; and if he said, "Lend me a place for a *water tank,*" then, if kinyan was

performed, he may continue building on the lender's land until a water tank is produced sufficient to keep his animals watered, or his land irrigated, in accordance with his agreement with the lender.

10. If a man borrow a lodging place for a night's rest, the borrowing is for not less than a day; if for a Sabbath rest, it is for not less than two days; and if for a wedding, it is for not less than 30 days.

If a man borrowed a garment in which to pay a visit to a mourner's house, he may keep it for as long as it takes to go there and return; if he borrowed the garment to wear at a wedding feast, he may keep it the whole day; and if for his own wedding, he may keep it up to seven days.

CHAPTER II

1. He who borrows anything with the owner is quit of payment in case of loss, even if the object borrowed be stolen or lost through his negligence. For it is written *If the owner thereof be with it, he shall not make it good* (Exod. 22:13), provided, however, that he borrowed the services of the owner together with the object as hereinabove stated.

Whether the commodatary borrowed the services of the owner or hired them, whether he borrowed the services for the same work, or for other work, or for anything in the world, even if he said to the owner, "Give me water to drink," and asked him at the same time to lend his animal to him, and the owner gave him water and lent him the animal, it is a case of borrowing with the owner and the commodatary is quit. If, however, he borrowed the animal first, and then the owner gave him water to drink, it is not a case of borrowing with the owner. And so it is in all similar cases.

2. If a man lent or let to his fellow an animal to carry a load and went forth to assist the borrower or hirer in loading the animal, it is a case of keeping with the owner. If, however, he came to examine the load and to see to it that it was not greater than is proper, it is not a keeping with the owner.

3. If a man, who exercises the calling of a town's schoolmaster, planter, bloodletter, scribe, and the like, lent or let anything to one of those in whose work he was engaged, on the day he was so engaged, it is a case of keeping with the owner, and even if the bailee was negligent with regard thereto, he is quit. But if the person exercising such calling borrowed or hired anything from one of those in whose work he was engaged, he is liable since they are not lent to him.

4. A teacher who is free to lecture to his students at any time and on any treatise, the students attending regularly, though he may skip from one treatise to another, is not deemed to be lent to his students; but the students are deemed to be lent to him. However, on the day of the prefestival assembly, when all come to be instructed in the subjects pertaining to the festival, he is deemed to be lent to the students, while the students are not deemed to be lent to him.

5. If a man said to his messenger, "Go forth and lend yourself together with my cow," it is not a borrowing with the owner. For it is written *If the owner thereof be with it, he shall not make good* (Exod. 22: 14). This has reference to the owner himself and not to his messenger.

If a master said to his Canaanite bondman, "Go forth, lend yourself together with my cow," it is a borrowing with the owner, the hand of the bondman being like the hand of the master. If, however, the bondman lent himself together with the cow, without the master's knowledge, it is not a borrowing with the owner.

6. If a man borrowed something from a married woman, and, at the same time, her husband lent himself to the borrower, it is not a borrowing with the owner—ownership of the usufruct being unlike ownership of the corpus, and the husband having only the usufruct of his wife's property.

7. If a man borrowed something from his wife, or if partners borrowed from one another, it is a borrowing with the owner. But

if a man said to another, "Make a loan to me today and I will make one to you tomorrow," it is not a borrowing with the owner.

8. If a man borrowed something from partners, and one of the partners lent himself to the borrower, or if partners borrowed something, and the lender lent himself to one of the partners, it is doubtful whether or not it is a borrowing with the owner. If, therefore, the animal died the borrower does not pay. But if the lender seized property belonging to the borrower, up to the value of the animal, it may not be reclaimed from him. If the borrower was negligent he must pay.

9. If a man borrowed an animal with the owner for the purpose of committing buggery, or for ostentatious display, or for doing therewith work worth less than one pĕruṭah, or if one borrowed two cows for doing with both of them work worth one pĕruṭah—in all of these cases it is doubtful whether or not it is a borrowing with the owner.

10. If a man borrowed an animal with the owner and then hired it without the owner, he is quit, since the liability of the hirer is comprised within that of the borrower. But if one hired an animal with the owner and then borrowed it without the owner; or if he borrowed it with the owner, then hired it without the owner, and then again borrowed it without the owner; or if he hired it with the owner, then borrowed it without the owner, and then again hired it without the owner—in all of these cases it is doubtful whether or not it is a keeping with the owner.

11. If a woman borrowed something and then married, the husband is deemed a purchaser; he is neither a bailee for hire nor a borrower. If, therefore, it was an animal that she borrowed and it died, the husband is quit, even if he used the animal during the term of the borrowing and even if he was negligent with regard thereto, since he is deemed a purchaser. The woman, however, is liable to pay when she comes into money.

If the woman gave the husband notice that the animal had been borrowed, he takes her place with regard to liability therefor.

Wherever we said that a case constitutes a borrowing with the owner, the same case would constitute a hiring with the owner, and the bailee would be quit, if he was a hirer or a bailee for hire. Whatever is not a borrowing with the owner would not be a hiring with the owner, and wherever there is doubt in this respect with regard to borrowing, there would also be doubt with regard to hiring.

CHAPTER III

1. If a man borrowed a cow from his fellow, and the lender sent it to him by the hand of his (the lender's) son, messenger, or bondman, or even if he sent it by the hand of the borrower's son, messenger, or bondman, and it died before entering the borrower's possession, the borrower is quit.

But if the borrower said, "Send it to me by the hand of my son, bondman, or messenger, or by the hand of your Hebrew bondman or messenger"; or if the lender said, "I am sending it to you by the hand of your son, bondman, or messenger, or by the hand of my son, Hebrew bondman, or messenger," and the borrower said, "Send it so," and he sent it, and it died on the way, the borrower is liable. If, however, the lender sent the cow by the hand of his Canaanite bondman, even after having been told by the borrower to do so, and it died, the borrower is quit, because the possession of the bondman is the possession of the master, and hence the cow had not left the lender's possession when she died.

2. If the borrower said to the lender, "Strike the animal with a stick and it will come by itself," and the lender did so, the borrower is not liable until the animal enters his possession, and if it died on the way, he is quit.

A similar rule applies when the borrower returns the animal to the lender. If the borrower sent it by the hand of another person, and it died before reaching the lender's possession, the borrower is liable, because the risk was still his at the time of the animal's death. But if he sent it by the hand of another person with the lender's knowledge, and it died, he is quit.

If, however, he sent it by the hand of his Canaanite bondman, even after having been told by the lender to do so, and it died on the way, he is liable, because the possession of the bondman is the possession of the master, and hence the animal had not left the borrower's possession when it died.

The above rules apply only where the borrower returned the animal within the term of the borrowing. But if he returned it after the term of the borrowing expired, and it died on the way, he is quit, because after the expiration of the term the case no longer comes within the rule of borrowing, the borrower having become like a bailee for hire; hence the borrower is quit, if the animal was captured or died after the expiration of the term of the borrowing. And so it is in all similar cases.

3. If a man borrowed an animal for half a day and hired it for the other half, or borrowed it for one day and hired it for the next day, or if he borrowed one animal and hired another, and one of the animals died, and the lender says, "The one that died was the one that was borrowed, the day when it died was the day for which it was borrowed, the time at which it died was the time for which it was borrowed," while the bailee says, "I do not know"; or if the borrower says, "The one that died was the one that was hired, the day when it died was the day for which it was hired," while the lender says, "I do not know"; or if each one of the two says, "I do not know," the rule that he who claims anything from his fellow must produce proof applies. If no proof is available, the bailee must swear either that it was the hired animal that died or that he does not know, and he is quit.

If the owner says, "It was the borrowed animal that died," while the bailee says, "It was the hired one that died," the bailee must swear that it died a natural death, as he claims, and, by accumulation, that it was the hired one that died.

4. If a man lent two animals for half a day and let them for the other half, and the lender says, "The time when the animals died was the time for which they were borrowed," while the bailee says, "One of them died at the time for which it was borrowed, and

as to the other, I do not know," the bailee, being unable to swear, must pay for the two animals.

Similarly, if the bailor delivered to the bailee three animals, two on loan and one for hire, and the bailor says, "The two that died were the ones that were on loan," while the bailee says, "One of those that died was surely on loan, and as to the other one I do not know," the bailee, being unable to swear by reason of his assertion of lack of knowledge, must pay for the two animals.

The rule with regard to litigants who are unable to swear—how and for what reason they must pay—will be stated in the Law Concerning Pleading.

CHAPTER IV

1. If a man deposited something with his fellow gratuitously, and it was stolen or lost, the bailee swears to that effect, and is quit. For it is written *If a man deliver unto his neighbour money or stuff to keep, and it be stolen out of the man's house . . . the master of the house shall come near unto God to see whether he have not put his hand unto his neighbour's goods* (Exod. 22:6). He also swears, by accumulation, that he was not negligent with regard to the deposit but kept it after the manner of bailees and that he did not misappropriate it before it was stolen. For if a bailee misappropriates the deposit before it is stolen, he is responsible for its loss.

2. Seeing that Scripture acquits the gratuitous bailee in the case of theft, he is *a fortiori* quit in the case of loss through force, as where an animal broke its limb, was captured, or died a natural death, provided he did not misappropriate the thing bailed before the mishap occurred. If, however, he misappropriated it, he is liable, even if it was subsequently lost through force.

What is meant by *the manner of bailees?* It is all according to the deposit. There are deposits, such as beams or stones, for which the proper manner of keeping is to place them in an open yard; there are others, such as large bundles of flax and the like, for which the proper manner of keeping is to place them in the courtyard; there are still others, such as a garment or a cloak, which it is proper to place in one's house; and there are still others, such as silk garments and silver or gold utensils, which it is proper to place under lock in a box or closet.

3. If a bailee placed the deposit in an unsuitable place, and it was stolen or lost—even if it was lost through force, as where a fire broke out and consumed the whole house—he is chargeable with negligence and liable to pay.

Even if the bailee placed the deposit together with his own goods, the rule is that if the place is one that is suitable, he is quit and if it is unsuitable, he is liable. With what belongs to himself he may do as he pleases, but he may not do so with what belongs to others.

4. There is no suitable place in which to keep silver coins and denars except in the ground with a handbreadth of dirt above them, or in the wall within a handbreadth of the beam, but not in the middle of the wall lest thieves dig there and steal them. Even if the bailee placed them in a well-locked box, or hid them in a place which no one knew or was aware of, he is chargeable with negligence and liable to pay.

Some authorities hold that the same rule, requiring the keeping of the deposit in the ground, applies to everything that is of light weight and is not perishable when hidden away in the ground, as silver bars and, needless to say, gold bars and precious stones. And to this my own opinion inclines.

5. If a man deposited money with his fellow on the eve of the Sabbath at twilight, the bailee is not bound to take the trouble of burying it in the ground until the night following the Sabbath. If on the night following the Sabbath an interval of time within which the money could have been buried elapsed, and, the bailee having failed to bury it, the money was stolen or taken by force, the bailee is liable. But if he is a scholar he is not liable, unless a like interval elapsed after his recital of the *habdalah* and before the money was stolen.

6. If a man entrusted money to his fellow that it be brought to his (the bailee's) house, or sent it through him from one place to another, the bailee is required to put the money in a purse and tie it around the front part of his belly until he reaches his house, whereupon he is to bury it in a suitable place. If he did not tie up the money in this manner, he is liable, even if it was taken by force, since he was negligent at the beginning.

It once happened that a man deposited money with his fellow who put it in a fence made of reeds. The money lay well hidden in a pocket within the fence, whence it was stolen. The Sages said, "Although this is a proper safeguard against thieves, it is not a proper safeguard against fire. Since he did not hide the money in the ground or in the wall of a building, he was negligent, and whenever a bailee is negligent at the beginning, though in the end the loss occurs through force, he is liable. And so it is in all similar cases.

7. If a bailor, who deposited either utensils or money with his fellow, says to the bailee, "Give me my deposit," and the bailee says to him, "I do not know where I placed this deposit or where I buried the money; wait until I find it and I will return it to you," the bailee is chargeable with negligence and must pay at once.

8. He who deposits either utensils or money with the head of a household does so with the knowledge that the keeping of the deposit may be entrusted by the bailee to his wife, adult sons, or other adult members of his household. If, however, the bailee delivered the deposit to his minor sons, or other members of his household who were minors, or to his bondman, whether adult or minor, or to one of his relatives who did not live with him in his house or depend upon him for board—and, needless to say, if he delivered it to a stranger—he is deemed to have been a negligent bailee and is liable to pay, unless the second bailee produces proof that there was no negligence on his part as hereinabove stated.

It once happened that a man deposited money with his fellow, and the bailee gave it to his mother, who concealed it from view but did not hide it well, and it was stolen. The Sages said the bailee is not liable to pay, because he gave the money to his mother, and he who deposits anything with his fellow does so with the knowledge that it may be entrusted to the bailee's sons or other members of his family. Although the bailee did not tell his mother that the money had been deposited with him, he may claim that he thought she would exercise greater care if she believed that the money was his. Nor is the mother liable to pay, since the bailee did not tell her that it was deposit money. The Sages further said the bailee shall swear that it was the deposit money that he gave to his mother, and the mother shall swear that she concealed it from view and it was stolen, and both of them shall be quit. And so it is in all similar cases.

9. From the above case it may be deduced that if the bailee delivered the deposit to his wife or to one of the other members of his family, informing them that it was a deposit, and they did not keep it after the manner of bailees, they are liable to the bailor, and the head of the household is quit. For he who deposits anything with his fellow does so with the knowledge that it may be entrusted to the bailee's wife and sons.

It once happened that a man deposited hops with another who happened to have hops of his own. The bailee said to his servant, "Put some of these hops into the beer," pointing to his own hops, and the servant went and put some of the deposited hops into the beer. The Sages said: the servant is quit, because his master did not say to him, "Put some of these, and not some of those hops into the beer," and he thought that the master, by pointing to the hops, intended only to facilitate his task by showing him where he could find hops, but that it did not matter to him which hops were to be used. The master is likewise quit of liability for negligence, because he said to his servant, "Put some of these hops into the beer." What he must pay to the bailor is only the value of the benefit he derived from the hops. Hence, he is altogether quit of payment if the beer turned sour. In any event, the bailee must swear to the truth of his allegations. And so it is in all similar cases.

CHAPTER V

1. If a man accepted a deposit of money dedicated to the poor or to the redemption of captives, and the money was stolen through his negligence he is not liable. For it is written *If a man deliver unto his neighbour money or stuff to keep* (Exod. 22:6)—*to keep* but not *to distribute among the poor*. The money comes within the class of property for which there are no claimants. Even if thieves came upon him and he hastened to save himself with the money dedicated to the captives, he is quit, since there is no greater redemption of captives than this.

All of the above applies only if the money deposited was not dedicated to the poor of a definite locality or to the redemption of specified captives. If, however, the money was intended for specified poor or captives and was so designated, it is property for which there are claimants, and the bailee must pay if he was negligent or swear like all other bailees that he was not negligent.

2. If a man deposited with his fellow money or valuable utensils, and thieves came upon the bailee and he hastened to give them the deposit in order to save himself, then, if the bailee was reputed to be a wealthy person, he is liable, because the presumption (ḥazaḳah) is that the thieves came on his account and that, consequently, he saved himself with his fellow's money. But if he was not reputed to be wealthy, the presumption is that they came but for the deposit, and he is quit. And so it is in all similar cases.

3. If a man deposited with his fellow utensils or produce, and thieves came and stole the deposit in the bailee's presence under such circumstances that, if he had raised a hue and cry, people would have come and saved it, his failure to do so is deemed negligence, and he is liable to pay. And so it is in all similar cases.

4. If two persons made deposits with another, one of them depositing 100 zuz and the other 200, and each one of the two says, "I am the one who has deposited the 200," while the bailee says, "I do not know," each of the depositors swears that he is the one who

has deposited the 200, and takes 200 in accordance with the rules concerning those who swear and take. The bailee must pay 200 to each, losing 100 out of his purse, because he was negligent in not writing down the names of the depositors and the amount each one deposited.

It follows therefore that if both depositors together brought the 300 zuz in one bundle, and later each demands 200, the bailee is to give 100 to each and keep the third 100 indefinitely or until one of the depositors makes an admission to the other. For the bailee may say to them, "Since I saw that you did not distrust each other, I did not take the trouble of learning and always remembering who was the owner of the 200 and who of the 100 zuz.

Similarly, if they deposited two utensils, one large and one small, and each one claims to be the owner of the large one, while the bailee says, "I do not know," each of the two depositors swears to the truth of his allegation, and the bailee gives the large utensil to one of them and the value of such utensil to the other, keeping the small one for himself. But if they brought both utensils in one bundle, he gives the small one to one of them and its value to the other, keeping the remainder until one of them makes an admission to the other, or indefinitely.

Similarly, where two persons lay claim to the same deposit and the bailee says, "I know that one of you is the depositor, but I do not know which one," he must pay to both of them.

Similarly, if two persons entrusted two animals to a herdsman, and one of the animals died, and the herdsman does not know whose animal it was that died, he must pay to both of them. But if they placed the animals in his herd without his knowledge, he may leave the living animal between them, abandoning control over it, and the animal is to remain there until one of the depositors makes an admission to the other or until they agree to divide it between themselves.

5. If a man deposited produce with his fellow, the bailee must not commingle it with his own produce. If the bailee, transgressing the precept of the law, commingled the deposited produce with his

own, he must compute what part the deposited produce is of the total mass, see how much the total mass shrank, compute the shrinkage of the deposited produce, and, after taking an oath, return the remainder of the deposited produce, as computed, to the bailor.

If the bailee was taking from the total mass for his own needs and did not know how much he took, he may deduct for shrinkage as follows: for wheat and peeled rice, four and a half ḳaḇ to the kor; for barley and durra, nine ḳaḇ to the kor; for spelt, linseed on the stalk, and unpeeled rice, three sĕ'ah to the kor. These deductions, in the measures stated, may be made by the bailee for every year.

This applies only where the bailor deposited the produce by measure during the harvest season, and the bailee returned it during the harvest season; but if the bailor deposited the produce during the harvest season, and the bailee returned it during the rainy season, the latter may not deduct anything for shrinkage, because the produce swells.

The bailee may similarly deduct one sixth for wine and three *log* for each 100 log of oil—one and a half log for sediment, and one and a half log for absorption. However, if the oil was refined, the bailee may not deduct for sediment, and if the jars were old, he may not deduct for absorption.

6. If a man deposited with his fellow an unmeasured mass of produce, and the bailee commingled it with his own produce, without measuring it, the bailee is deemed negligent. If the bailor says, "There was so much," and the bailee says, "I do not know," the bailee must pay without an oath on the bailor's part. Since by the bailee's own admission he is liable to pay, but he does not know for how much he is liable, he is in the position of one who is liable to an oath but is unable to swear. So have ruled my teachers, Rabbi Joseph Hallevi and his teacher, of blessed memory.

Similarly, in the case of every other bailee who has become liable to pay and who says, "I do not know for how much I am liable," while the bailor says, "I do know that the thing bailed was worth so much," the bailor takes what he claims without being subjected to an oath, provided his claim was in accord with what he was reputed to possess. But the bailee may have the anathema proclaimed generally against him who took from him more than his due.

Whence do we know that such is the rule? Suppose a purse full of gold coins was deposited with a bailee and was lost through his negligence. Suppose further that the bailor said, "There were 200 denar in the purse," while the bailee said, "There surely were denar there, but I do not know how many." The bailee would be in the position of a defendant who, in answer to a claim for 200 denar, admitted part and pleaded ignorance with regard to the remainder. Like such a defendant, he would be liable to an oath but unable to swear, and, consequently, he would be required to pay, as hereinafter stated.

7. If a tied-up pouch was left to one by his deceased father, and he deposited it with his fellow, and it was lost through the bailee's negligence, and the bailor says "I do not know that the pouch did not contain gems," while the bailee says, "Perhaps it was full of glass," the rule under such pleading is that the bailee, in accordance with the enactment of the Sages, must swear that the deposit is not in his possession. He must also include in his oath an asseveration that he does not know with certainty that the pouch contained more than so much in value, whereupon he must pay what he admits as owing from him. And so it is in all similar cases.

It once happened that a man deposited with his fellow a pouch that was tied up, and it was lost through the bailee's negligence. The bailor said "The pouch contained gold and gems and the like," while the bailee said, "I do not know what it contained, perhaps dross or sand." The Sages said: let the bailor swear and let him take what he claims.

But this rule applies only where the bailor claims something which, in view of his reputation for wealth, he is likely to have possessed, or which, in view of his reputation for honesty, people are likely to have deposited with him.

The rule being what it is, that he who is liable to an oath but is unable to swear must pay, why does the bailor have to swear in this case? Because the bailee is *not* liable to an oath. For even if the bailee had said "I am certain that the pouch was full of dross," against the bailor's assertion that it contained gems, the bailee would have been subjected only to the informal oath and would have been quit, just as in the case where the plaintiff claimed wheat and the defendant admitted that he owed him barley. And so it is in all similar cases.

CHAPTER VI

1. If a gratuitous bailee says, "I am ready to pay, and prefer to do so rather than swear," then if the thing bailed belonged to a class that is uniform—and there are others like it available for sale in the market—such as produce, or sheets of woolen or linen cloth that are identical in every respect, or undecorated beams and the like, the bailee pays and does not swear. But if the thing bailed was an animal, or a decorated garment, or a specially wrought utensil; or if no others like it are available in the market, a suspicion may be entertained that the bailee took a liking to the thing bailed. By virtue of an enactment of the Sages he is therefore subjected to an oath while holding a sacred object that the thing bailed is not in his possession, whereupon he pays.

The same rule applies to the other bailees, such as a commodatory who pleads that the animal died or was stolen, or a bailee for hire, or a hirer, who pleads that the animal was stolen or lost. Although they are liable to pay, they are subjected to an oath that the thing bailed is not in their possession, whereupon they pay the value of the animal or thing, the oath being required because of the suspicion that the bailee took a liking to the thing bailed.

If the bailor claims that the thing bailed was worth more than what the bailee alleges, the bailee must also include in his oath an asseveration as to the value of the thing.

It follows therefore that every bailee who is required to swear the bailee's oath must include therein three matters: 1. that he kept the thing bailed after the manner of bailees; 2. that thus and so happened to it; 3. that he did not misappropriate it before the event absolving him from liability occurred. And if he wishes to pay, he swears that the thing bailed is not in his possession, including in his oath an asseveration as to the value of the thing.

2. A bailee may stipulate that he shall not be bound to keep the thing bailed after the manner of bailees. He may say, "I shall put the money you are depositing with me in a corner of my house," and the like.

If the bailee pleads that there was a stipulation, and the bailor says that there was no stipulation, the bailee's plea is believed, even though the deposit was made in the presence of witnesses, since he could plead that he kept the deposit after the manner of bailees and that it was lost through force. The bailee is therefore allowed to swear that he did not misappropriate the deposit, that it is not in his possession, and that there was a stipulation.

3. If a gratuitous bailee produces proof to the effect that he was not negligent, he is quit of an oath, the possibility of his having misappropriated the deposit being disregarded.

If the bailor produces proof by witnesses to the effect that the bailee was negligent, the bailee must pay. If the bailee pleads that there was a stipulation between them, he is not believed, since there is no inference of credibility in his favor when witnesses testify that he was negligent.

4. If a man deposited anything with his fellow in the presence of witnesses and the witnesses come and testify that it was so deposited, the bailee may not enter a plea saying, "I purchased it from him," or "He gave it to me as a gift afterward." If, therefore, the bailee died, the deposit may be reclaimed from his heirs without an oath. Moreover, even if one comes and says to another, "I deposited with your father such and such a thing," giving distinguishing marks, and the deposit is found to correspond to the description given, and the judge knows that the deceased was not esteemed to be the owner of this deposit, the judge is to award the deposit to him who has given its distinguishing marks, pro-

vided the claimant was not accustomed to visit with the deceased during his lifetime. If, however, he was so accustomed, we say, "Perhaps it belongs to another, but the claimant came to know its distinguishing marks."

If witnesses come and testify before the judge that the deceased was not esteemed to be the owner of the thing in dispute, the testimony is not sufficient to take the thing away from the heirs. For this is not clear proof, and the witnesses' estimate is not the judge's estimate. The judge is to be guided only by that on which he, in his own mind, is inclined to rely, as will be stated in the Laws Concerning The Sanhedrin.

It once happened that a man deposited a quantity of sesame with his fellow in the presence of witnesses. When the depositor came to demand the sesame the bailee said to him, "I have returned it to you." To this the depositor replied, "Was not the quantity of the sesame thus and so, and is it not kept in your barrel?" Again the bailee said, "Your sesame I have returned, and this is other sesame." The Sages said: the sesame is not to be taken away from the bailee, there being a possibility that it is his. But the bailee must swear while holding a sacred object that he has returned the deposit, as hereinabove stated.

5. If the bailor demands the deposit and the bailee gives it to him, but the bailor says, "This is not my deposit but something else," or "It was unbroken, and you broke it," or "It was new, and you used it," or "I deposited with you 100 sĕ'ah, and here you have only 50," while the bailee says, "This is what you deposited, and what you gave me you are now receiving," the bailee is to swear the informal oath, and not the bailee's oath, like any other defendant who is subjected to an oath under similar circumstances. For not every bailee swears the bailee's oath which is mentioned in the Law; only a bailee who admits that the deposit was made with him, as claimed by the bailor, but pleads that it was stolen, or, if it was an animal, that it died or was captured, is subjected to such an oath.

The general rule is: a bailee who pleads a plea which, if true, would acquit him of payment, swears the bailee's oath. But if he says, "This is what you lent or hired to me, or for which I received hire," while the owner says, "This is not it but something else," or "It is different now from what it was," the bailee swears the informal oath or, if he makes a partial admission, the Pentateuchal oath.

How is this to be understood? If the bailor says, "I deposited with you 100 sĕ'ah," while the bailee says, "You deposited but 50," he swears the Pentateuchal oath because he has made a partial admission, and not because he is subject to the bailee's oath; but if the bailor says, "I deposited with you 100 kor of wheat," while the bailee says, "You deposited with me 100 kor of barley," he swears the informal oath like all others who are subjected to an oath upon a similar plea.

CHAPTER VII

1. If a man deposited produce with his fellow, the bailee may not touch it, even if it keeps shrinking in volume, provided the shrinkage is not greater than the normal yearly shrinkage. If, however, the shrinkage is greater than normal the bailee is to sell it under the court's supervision, such sale being in the nature of retrieving lost property for the benefit of its owner. When selling such produce, the bailee must sell it to priests at the prevailing price for tĕrumah, since the owner may have set it apart as tĕrumah or tĕrumah of tithes with respect to other produce.

2. If a man deposited with his fellow produce, honey, or wine, and it became rotten, spoiled, or sour, the bailee may sell it for the owner's benefit under the court's supervision. He may do so even if the deterioration of the produce, honey, or wine has come to an end, progressing no further, since the deterioration of the casks or baskets continues.

3. If a man deposited leavened matter with his fellow, and the Feast of Passover is approaching, the bailee may not touch the deposit until the fifth hour of the fourteenth day of the month of

Nisan. From then on, during the remaining hour, he is to sell it at the market, thereby retrieving lost property to its owner. The same rule applies to other deposits as well. The bailee may not touch them, even though he knows that if nothing is done, they are going to depreciate in value, or will be forcibly taken by the king, since it is possible that in the meantime the owner will come and take the property.

4. If a man deposited a scroll of the Law with his fellow, the bailee is to unroll it once in 12 months. If, while unrolling it, he happens to read it, he does not act unlawfully; but he may not open it for his own sake and read it.

The same rule applies to other books as well. If the bailee opens the book for his own sake and reads it, it is a misappropriation, and he becomes subject to liability for its loss through force.

If a man deposited with his fellow a woolen garment, the bailee is to dust it once in 30 days. What the Sages have said with regard to the care of a lost object applies equally to a deposit. It is the bailee's duty to prevent deterioration of the deposit on the principle that one is bound to retrieve lost property for the benefit of its owner. This applies only with regard to a deposit whose owner has gone abroad. But if the owner remains in the country, the bailee must leave the deposit untouched, even if it is perishing.

5. He who sells a deposit by court order must sell it to others, and not to himself, because of suspicion. The money realized from the sale is to remain with him and he is permitted to use it. He is therefore deemed a bailee for hire with respect to such money, even before he had occasion to use it.

6. If a man deposited money with a shopkeeper or a money-changer, the bailee is not permitted to use the money if it is contained in a purse which is sealed or tied with a peculiar knot. If, therefore, the money was lost or stolen the bailee is not answerable for its loss. If the money was neither sealed nor tied with a peculiar knot, although it was contained in a purse, the bailee may use it, and, therefore, he becomes a bailee for hire with respect

thereto. If the money was lost or stolen the bailee is answerable; if it was stolen through force, such as that of armed robbers, he is quit.

7. All of the above applies only before the bailee has made use of the money; after he has made use of it he bears the risk of its loss until it is returned to its owner, just as in the case of an obligation arising out of a loan of money.

8. If a man deposited money with a householder, whether it was contained in a purse or not, the bailee may not use it. If, therefore, the money was lost or stolen, the bailee is not answerable, provided he hid it in the ground, as we have stated above.

9. If a man deposited a barrel with his fellow, whether a specific place was designated for it or not, and the bailee moved it for his own sake, and it was broken, either while he was handling it or after it was returned to the place designated for it, the bailee is liable to pay. If, however, he moved the barrel for its own sake, he is quit, whether it was broken while he was handling it or after it was put in place.

10. Deposits are not to be accepted from women, bondmen, or minors. If a man accepted a deposit from a woman he is to return it to her or, if she died, to her husband; if he accepted a deposit from a bondman, he is to return it to him or, if he died, to his master; if from a minor, he is to purchase for the minor a scroll of the Law or a date tree, so that the minor may enjoy its fruit.

If one of those enumerated above made a deathbed declaration that the deposit belonged to a certain person, then, if the bailee believes him, he may act in accordance with such declaration, and if he does not believe him, he is to return the deposit to the depositor's heirs.

11. No demand may be made for the return of a deposit or of a lost object except in its place. How is this to be understood? If a man deposited something in Jerusalem, he may not demand it in Nebo. If, however, the bailee offered to return it in Nebo, the

bailor must accept it from him. But if the deposit was made in an inhabited place, and the bailee brought it to the bailor in the desert, the latter may refuse to accept it and may say to the bailee, "The risk is yours until you return it to me in an inhabited place, just as I deposited it with you in an inhabited place."

12. If a man who had deposited something with his fellow went abroad, and the bailee wished to undertake a sea voyage or to join a caravan, the bailee may, according to one authority, bring the deposit into court and is thereby relieved of all responsibility for its safekeeping. There is good reason for this rule. The bailee is not to be kept confined in the country on account of the deposit belonging to the man who left the country; nor is it feasible for him to take the deposit with him lest a mishap occur to it and he be held responsible. The court is to deposit it with a person whom they consider trustworthy, thereby retrieving lost property for its owner.

CHAPTER VIII

1. If a man deposited an animal or utensils with his fellow, and they were stolen or lost, and the bailee said, "I will rather pay than swear," and then the thief was found, the thief pays twofold or, if he slaughtered or sold the animal, fourfold or fivefold to him who held the deposit and had previously agreed to pay therefor. If the animal itself was recovered, it, together with its shorn wool and offspring, belongs to the owner; for the bailee does not acquire a right to the appreciation which comes out of the animal's body, but only to that which comes of itself.

We have already stated that the thief does not return the shorn wool and the offspring, unless he was apprehended before abandonment.

If the bailee swore, refusing to pay, and then the thief was apprehended the latter pays twofold or, if he slaughtered or sold the animal, fourfold or fivefold to the owner of the deposit.

Similarly, if a man hired an animal from his fellow, and it was stolen and the bailee said, "I will rather pay than swear," and then the thief was apprehended, he pays twofold, fourfold, or fivefold, to the bailee, since the latter, who would have been quit if he had sworn that the animal had been stolen by force, voluntarily offered to pay therefor.

2. A gratuitous bailee who said, "I was negligent," thereby acquired the right to the double payment, since he voluntarily subjected himself to liability to pay, when he could have said "The animal was stolen or lost," and would have been quit.

Similarly, the bailee for hire or the hirer who said, "The animal was stolen," is entitled to the double payment, since he voluntarily subjected himself to liability to pay, when he could have said, "The animal died," and would have been quit. But the commodatary does not acquire the right to the double payment until he voluntarily pays for the loss. If he paid voluntarily before the thief was apprehended, the fourfold or fivefold payment is to be made to him.

3. He who acquires the right to the double payment acquires also the right to the appreciation which comes of itself. How is this to be understood? If a man deposited with his fellow four sĕ'ah, which were worth at the time one sela', and they were stolen or lost, and the bailee said, "I will rather pay than swear," and then they were found, and when found were worth four sela', they belong to the bailee, and he pays only one sela' to the owner.

This applies only where the bailee did not cause to the owner the trouble of having resort to a court to compel payment. If, however, he admitted that he had been negligent, and the court adjudged him liable to pay, but he did not pay voluntarily until he was compelled by the court, and payment was exacted from him against his will, and then the thief was apprehended, or the deposit found, it is to be returned to the bailor as it is, and the money recovered by the bailor from the bailee is to be returned to him; and if the bailee's utensils or landed property were levied upon by the court and taken by the bailor by appraisal, such utensils or landed property are to be returned to the bailee.

4. If the bailor made demand upon the bailee and the latter swore but thereafter paid, and then the thief was apprehended, the bailee is entitled to the double payment, although he subjected the bailor to the trouble of having resort to a court and took an oath, since he paid voluntarily. If the bailee first said, "I will not pay," and then said, "I will pay," he is entitled to the double payment.

5. If the bailee first said, "I will pay," and then said, "I will not pay," or if he said, "I will pay," and then died and his children said, "We will not pay"; or if before the bailor was able to make demand upon him the bailee died, and the bailor thereupon made demand upon his children, and they paid; or if the bailee's children paid to the bailor's children; or if the bailee paid half; or if he borrowed two cows and paid for one of them; or if he borrowed from partners and paid to one of them; or if partners borrowed something and one of them paid therefor; or if the bailee borrowed from a woman and paid to her husband; or if a woman borrowed, and her husband paid—in all of these cases there is doubt as to what the rule should be. The ownership of the double payment being thus subject to doubt, and the money not being under the hand of either the bailor or the bailee, it, or the appreciation of the deposit, is divided between them. But if one of them hastened and seized the whole, it is not to be taken away from him, even outside of the Land.

6. If the deposit was stolen by force, and thereafter the thief was apprehended, the bailee, whether he kept the deposit gratuitously or for hire, sues the thief and does not swear. If he swore and thereafter the thief was apprehended, then, if he was a gratuitous bailee, he may either stand on his oath or sue the thief, and if he was a bailee for hire he must sue the thief.

If the deposit was stolen by force, and the thief returned it to the bailee, or, if it was an animal, it died through the bailee's negligence, it is doubtful whether or not the bailment had come to an end when the animal died and, consequently, the bailee is quit of payment. But if the bailor seized property belonging to the bailee in satisfaction of his claim, it is not taken away from him.

TREATISE III

LAWS CONCERNING CREDITOR AND DEBTOR

Involving Twelve Commandments

Four Affirmative and Eight Negative

To Wit

1. To lend money to him who is poor and indigent;
2. Not to exact payment from him;
3. To exact payment from the heathen;
4. Not to distrain upon the debtor by force;
5. To return the pledge to its owner when he is in need thereof;
6. Not to delay the return of the pledge to an owner who is poor when he is in need thereof;
7. Not to make distraint upon the widow;
8. Not to take in distraint utensils necessary for the preparation of food;
9. That the lender shall not lend on usury;
10. That the borrower shall not borrow on usury;
11. That one shall not lend his aid either to the lender or the borrower in a usurious loan by being a witness thereto, writing the bond therefor, or guaranteeing payment thereof;
12. To borrow from the heathen and to lend to him on usury.

An exposition of these commandments
is contained in the following chapters.

CHAPTER I

1. It is an affirmative commandment to lend to the poor of Israel. For it is written *If thou lend money to any of my people, to the poor with thee* (Exod. 22:24). From this passage one might infer that lending money to the poor is optional, but when we read in another passage *Thou shalt surely lend him* (Deut. 15:8), we know that it is obligatory.

Lending money to the poor man is a more meritorious deed than giving charity to him who begs for it, for the one has already been driven to begging, while the other has not yet reached that stage.

Severe, indeed, is the censure of the Law against him who withholds a loan from the poor. For it is written *Beware that there be not a base thought in thy heart . . . and thine eye be evil against thy needy brother, and thou give him naught* (Deut. 15:9).

2. He who exacts payment when he knows that the debtor has not the wherewithal to pay transgresses a negative commandment. For it is written *Thou shalt not be to him as a creditor* (Exod. 22:24). But it is an affirmative commandment to exact payment from a heathen debtor. For it is written *Of the heathen thou shalt exact payment* (Deut. 15:3). From the oral tradition it has been learned that this is an affirmative commandment.

3. One is forbidden to appear before his debtor, nay even to pass before him, even though he does not make demand upon him—and, needless to say, if he does make demand upon him—lest he frighten or shame him.

Just as the creditor is forbidden to demand payment, so is the debtor forbidden to withhold from the creditor the money that is in his hands and to say to him "Go forth and come back again," provided he has the means of paying. For it is written *Say not unto thy neighbour, Go, and come again* (Prov. 3:28).

The debtor is also forbidden to borrow money and spend it unnecessarily or dissipate it, so that the creditor will not find anything from which to collect, even if the creditor be very rich. He who does this is classified as a wicked man. For it is written *The wicked borroweth, but payeth not* (Ps. 37:21). And the Sages have enjoined us: *your fellow's property shall be as dear to you as your own* (Ab. 2:12).

4. When the creditor demands payment of the debt, even if he is rich, and the debtor is in straits and exerting himself to earn his subsistence, there is to be no compassion in the administration of the Law; the entire debt, to the last pĕruṭah, must be levied from all the movables belonging to the debtor, wherever found, and if the movables do not suffice, the debt is to be levied from the landed property, after the anathema has been proclaimed against him who has movables belonging to the debtor, or knows of such movables, and would not bring them to court.

Levy is to be made upon any landed property which the debtor may possess, even though it is bound for the payment of his wife's kĕṭubbah or of a prior debt, and if the prior debtor should later come to *seize* the property let him seize it.

If the debtor pleads, "These movables which I have in my possession are not mine; they have been deposited with me, or hired, or lent to me," no heed is to be paid to his plea; he must either produce proof of his allegation or, if he fails to produce such proof, allow the creditor to collect from these movables.

5. The creditor may not levy upon the garments of the debtor's wife and children, nor upon the dyed garments which were dyed for them, although they have not yet worn them, nor upon the new shoes which were purchased for them. This has reference to everyday apparel only; but the Sabbath and festival apparel is subject to levy by the creditor, and, needless to say, if it includes rings and gold or silver articles, they are at the creditor's disposal.

6. If the debtor has movables or landed property, but there are bonds outstanding against him in the hands of heathen creditors, and he says, "All my property is obligated to the heathen creditor and if the Israelites will levy upon it for their debts, the heathen

creditors will imprison me for theirs, and I will be a captive," no heed is to be paid to his plea; let the Israelite creditors levy upon the property, and if the heathen creditors should come and imprison the debtor, it would then be incumbent upon all Israel to redeem him. So my teachers have ruled.

7. An exemption from levy of a portion of his property is made for the debtor, just as such an exemption is made for the person who has taken a vow of valuation. How is this to be understood? The debtor is told to bring all the movables he possesses, without leaving even a single needle, and he is given food for 30 days and such clothing as is suitable for him for 12 months; but he may not don silk clothes or a gilded headgear, and if he does, it is to be removed from him, and he is to be given instead suitable clothes for 12 months. The debtor is also to be allowed a couch on which to sit and bed and bedding suitable for him on which to sleep, or, if he is a poor man, a bed and a straw mattress on which to sleep. But such articles are not to be allowed for his wife or children, although he is obligated to support them.

He is also to be allowed his shoes and phylacteries. If he is a craftsman, he is to be allowed two tools of each kind, such as, if he is a carpenter, two adzes and two saws.

If he has an abundance of one kind of tools and a deficiency of another kind, he is to be allowed only two of the kind which he has in abundance and whatever he has of the other kind. The deficiency may not be made up by purchasing the tools of which he is short with money which may be realized from the sale of some of the tools which he has in abundance.

If he is an agricultural worker or an ass-driver, he is not to be allowed his team of oxen or his ass; and if he is a ship captain he is not to be allowed his ship, although he has no other means of earning a livelihood. For these are not tools but property, which is to be sold together with all of his other movables at a judicial sale, and the proceeds turned over to the creditor.

8. If the creditor came to collect his debt in the debtor's absence, as when the debtor was away in a distant land, and the debtor's

wife had taken some of the debtor's property in order to maintain herself out of it, the property is to be taken away from her and given to the creditor. For even if the debtor had been there he would not have been allowed to support his wife and children out of the property before paying the debt in full.

CHAPTER II

1. The rule of the Law is that when the creditor demands the debt an exemption is to be set apart for the debtor, if he has property, and the remainder is given to the creditor as we have stated. If no property belonging to the debtor is found, or if only such property as is exempt is found, the debtor may go free. He is to be neither imprisoned nor told, "Produce proof that you are poor," nor subjected to an oath, as the heathen are wont to judge. For it is written *Thou shalt not be to him as a creditor* (Exod. 22:24). The creditor is only told by the court "If you know of any property belonging to the debtor, go and levy upon it."

2. If the creditor claims that the debtor has property which he is concealing, and that it is in his house, it is not lawful either for the creditor or for the court's representative to enter the debtor's house, the Law being strict in this respect. For it is written *Thou shalt stand without* (Deut. 24:11). But the creditor may have the anathema proclaimed generally against him who has property and withholds it from the creditor.

When the first *Geonim* that arose after the compilation of the *Gemara* saw that deceivers had multiplied and that, consequently, all doors had become closed to would-be borrowers, they enacted the regulation that the debtor be subjected to a strict oath, akin to the Pentateuchal oath, while holding a sacred object that he has nothing over and above his exemption, that he has not concealed anything in the hands of others, and that he has made no gift upon condition that it be returned to him. He is also to include in this oath a promise that whatever he may earn or whatever may come into his hands or possession as his own he will not spend on food, clothing, and the maintenance of his wife and children, or give it away to any person whatsoever, but will only take therefrom 30 days' food and 12 months' clothing, that is, food which is appropriate and clothing which is appropriate, not the food of gluttons and drunkards or that which is served before kings, and not the clothing of grandees and high officers, but that to which he is accustomed. And he must continually hand over to the creditor all surplus over and above his needs until the entire debt has been paid. And at the very beginning the anathema is to be proclaimed against him who knows of property, open or concealed, belonging to the debtor and would not notify the court.

Even now, after the above regulation has been enacted, neither the creditor nor the court's representative may enter the debtor's house for the purpose of making distraint, since the enactment was not intended to abolish an essential rule of the Law; the debtor himself must bring out his movables or say, "This or that is what I have." He is then allowed to keep what is properly to be kept by him and must turn the remainder over to the creditor and take the oath provided for by the above enactment. And so the courts of Israel rule everywhere.

If the debtor is seen to be in possession of property after he has taken the above oath, and he pleads, "The property belongs to others," or, "It was entrusted to me for the purpose of engaging in an enterprise on shares," no heed is to be paid to his plea unless he produces proof. So my teachers have ruled.

3. He who is required to take an oath that he has no property and that whatever he may earn he will turn over to his creditor, is not to be subjected to such an oath by each one of his creditors. For this oath is inclusive of all creditors and, moreover, it is an enactment of the later Sages, which is not to be applied with strictness but with leniency.

4. If a man is generally reputed to be poor, honest, and walking in integrity, the matter being manifest and known to the judge and to the majority of the people, and his creditor comes to subject him to an oath by virtue of the above-mentioned enactment, the

creditor not being satisfied with the poverty of the debtor, but being desirous of tormenting him with this oath, of causing chagrin to him, and disgracing him in public, so as to take revenge of him or to force him to go to a heathen and borrow money or to take his wife's property and turn it over to him in order to be saved from this oath—it seems to me that a God-fearing judge is forbidden to subject the debtor to the oath, and that if he does cause him to swear, he renders null the negative commandment of the Law of *Thou shalt not be to him as a creditor* (Exod. 22:24). Moreover, it is fitting for the judge to reprimand the creditor and to discomfit him because he is bearing ill will and walking in the hardness of his heart. For the Geonim made this enactment only because of the deceivers, and it is written *Until thou inquire about thy brother* (Deut. 22:2)—*make inquiry about him, whether he is a deceiver or not a deceiver* (BM. 2:7). And since the man is generally reputed to be poor and not to be a deceiver, it is forbidden to subject him to the oath.

I also say that if the debtor is generally reputed to be a deceiver, and his ways in dealing with others are corrupt, and is also reputed to be a moneyed person but claims that he has nothing and is quick to swear, it is not proper for the judge to cause him to swear, but, if he has the power to do so, he should rather use compulsion against him, or declare him excommunicated, until he satisfies the creditor, since he is reputed to be a wealthy individual and since the satisfaction of a creditor is enjoined by the Law.

To put it generally: everything the judge does in these matters with the intention of pursuing justice only, as we have been enjoined to pursue it, and not of tampering with the Law to the detriment of one of the litigants, he is permitted to do and will receive heavenly reward therefor, provided always that his deeds are for the sake of heaven.

5. If a debtor, who had become liable to and had taken the above-mentioned oath at the behest of a creditor holding a writing of indebtedness against him, confessed other debts to other debtors, and thereafter acquired a surplus over and above the exemption

allowed to him by law, such surplus is to be turned over to the holder of the writing only, because it is possible that the confession was but the result of a conspiracy against the interests of the holder of the writing.

6. If Reuben is liable to Simeon for 100 denar and Levi, in turn, is liable to Reuben for 100 denar, we take from Levi and give to Simeon. If, therefore, Reuben has no other property except a writing of indebtedness against Levi, who says that he gave the writing to Reuben on faith or that he has discharged the obligation evidenced by it, and Reuben admits that it is so, his admission is to be disregarded, because it is possible that they have entered into a conspiracy to deprive Simeon of his right. Simeon is to take an oath and collect from Levi, in accordance with the rule applicable to every creditor who comes to seize his debtor's property, which rule is to the effect that the creditor is not to be satisfied unless he takes an oath.

Similarly, if a man had a writing of indebtedness outstanding against him and, of his own accord, he confessed a debt to another debtor, the holder of the writing alone collects if the debtor has not sufficient property to satisfy both creditors. This rule is designed to prevent a conspiracy directed against the rights of the debtor under the writing of indebtedness.

7. A man is forbidden to lend his money without witnesses, even to a scholar, unless he lends it on a pledge. And he who lends on a writing is still more praiseworthy.

He who lends without witnesses transgresses the commandment of *Thou shalt not put a stumbling-block before the blind* (Lev. 19:14), and brings a curse upon himself.

8. If a master borrowed money from his bondman and subsequently set him free, or if a man borrowed from his wife and subsequently divorced her, they have no claim against him. For what the bondman acquires belongs to the master, and all money in the hands of a married woman is presumptively her husband's, unless she produces proof that it is of her dowry.

CHAPTER III

1. One must not take a pledge, either at the time the loan is made or afterwards, from a widow, whether she be poor or rich; nor must one take a pledge from her by order of the court. For it is written *Thou shalt not take the widow's raiment to pledge* (Deut. 24: 17). And if one takes a pledge from a widow, he is compelled to return it against his will.

If she confesses the debt, she must pay, and if she denies it, she must take an oath. If the pledge is lost or consumed by fire before the creditor returns it, he is subject to lashes.

2. Similarly, he who lends money to his fellow, whether he makes the loan on a pledge or takes the pledge by his own hand or by order of the court, after the loan is made, must not take utensils which are used in the preparation of food, such as a mill, a wooden kneading trough, a kettle used for cooking, a slaughterer's knife, and the like. For it is written *No man shall take the mill or the upper millstone to pledge; for he taketh a man's life to pledge* (Deut. 24: 6). And if he takes one of these, he is compelled to return it against his will; if it is lost or consumed by fire he is subject to lashes.

3. If a man took as a pledge many utensils used in the preparation of food, such as a kneading trough, a kettle, and a knife, he is liable for each utensil separately. Even if he took two utensils used in the performance of a single operation, his liability is the same as for any other two utensils: he is subject to lashes for each of the two. For it is written *The mill or the upper millstone (ibid.)* which implies separate liability for each, the mill and the upper millstone; and just as in the case of the upper millstone and the mill, which are distinct as two utensils performing one operation, he is liable for each one separately, so in every case of two utensils, even though they perform only one operation, he is liable for each separately. Similarly, if he took as a pledge a team of plough oxen, he is subject to lashes twice.

4. He who has lent money to his fellow, whether the borrower be poor or rich, must not make distraint upon him except through court. Even the court's representative, who comes to make distraint upon a debtor, must not enter the debtor's house for that purpose, but must stand outside while the debtor enters the house and brings the pledge out to him. For it is written *Thou shalt stand without* (Deut. 24: 11). This being so, what is the difference in this respect between the creditor and the court's representative? The court's representative may take a pledge from the hand of the debtor by the might of his arm and give it to the creditor, while the creditor may not take a pledge unless the debtor gives it to him of his own will.

If the creditor, in transgression of the precept of the Law, entered the debtor's house and took a pledge, or if he seized the pledge from the debtor's hand by the might of his arm, he is not subject to lashes because, the negative commandment is coupled with an affirmative one. For it is written *Thou shalt surely restore to him the pledge when the sun goeth down* (Deut. 24: 13). But if he did not fulfill the affirmative commandment relative to the pledge, as when the pledge was lost or consumed by fire, he is subject to lashes, must deduct the value of the pledge from the amount of the debt, and may demand the remainder by law.

5. He who makes distraint upon his fellow, whether through court or by the might of his arm or with the debtor's consent, is enjoined to return the pledge to the debtor at the time when he needs it, if the debtor is an indigent man in need of the things taken as a pledge.

The creditor must return to the debtor the pillow at night that he may sleep on it, and the plough during the day that he may do his work with it. For it is written *Thou shalt surely restore the pledge to him* (Deut. 24: 13). If he fails to return the articles that are used in the daytime during the day, or the articles that are used at night during the night, he transgresses a negative commandment. For it is written *Thou shalt not sleep with his pledge* (Deut. 24: 12) which means thou shalt not sleep while his pledge is in thy possession. This has reference to a night garment. As to articles which the debtor uses in the course of his work, or wears during the day, Scripture says *Thou shalt surely restore to him the pledge when the sun goeth down* (Deut. 24:13), which means that the creditor is to return the pledge for the whole day.

If it is so, that the creditor is to return the pledge when the debtor needs it and to take it from him when he does not need it, what avails the pledge to the creditor? That the debt will not be canceled by the advent of the Sabbatical year, and that the property taken as a pledge will not become movables in the hands of the debtor's children but will be available to the creditor to collect his debt therefrom after the debtor's death.

From the above it follows that he who makes distraint upon an indigent debtor, taking articles of which the debtor is in need, and fails to return the articles taken in distraint at the time when they are needed by the debtor, is a transgressor under three counts: 1. *Thou shalt not go into his house to fetch his pledge* (Deut. 24:10); 2. *Thou shalt surely restore to him the pledge when the sun goeth down* (Deut. 24:13); 3. *Thou shalt not sleep with his pledge* (Deut. 24:12). This applies only where the creditor did not take the pledge at the time the loan was made; but if he took it at the time the loan was made, he is not bound to return it and is not a transgressor under any of the above counts.

6. A court's representative who comes to make distraint upon a debtor must not take things that a man could not give as a pledge, such as the garment he is wearing, the utensils with which he eats, and the like. He must leave a bed and a mattress for the rich and a bed and a mat of reeds for the indigent, and everything else that is found in the hands of the debtor he may take in distraint.

The creditor must return to the debtor in the daytime articles that are used during the day, and at night articles that are used during the night. If there are two utensils in his hands, he keeps one and returns the other.

For how long is the creditor bound to return the pledge? Forever. If the pledge is one of those things that are not needed by the debtor and therefore not required to be left with him, he keeps it for 30 days and from the thirtieth day on he may sell it at a judicial sale.

If the debtor died, the creditor is not bound to return the pledge to his children. If the debtor died after the pledge had been returned to him, the creditor may take it even from the backs of the debtor's children and is not required to return it to them.

7. A surety may be distrained upon by the creditor without the aid of a court's representative. It is also permissible to enter his house and take a pledge from him. For it is written *Take his garment that is surety for a stranger* (Prov. 20: 16).

Similarly, he who has hire owing to him from his fellow, whether it be hire for his work or for his animal, utensils, or house, is permitted to make distraint without a court's order; he may also enter his fellow's house and take a pledge for the hire. If, however, he converted the hire due to him into a loan all this is forbidden. For it is written *When thou dost lend thy neighbour any manner of loan, thou shalt not go into his house to fetch his pledge* (Deut. 24: 10).

8. He who has in his hands a pledge belonging to an indigent debtor may, without the owner's knowledge, hire it out to others—provided the hire that will be realized from it is greater than the depreciation that will ensue, as in the case of an axe, a saw, and the like—always deducting the hire from his debt, this being like retrieving lost property, which does not require the owner's consent.

CHAPTER IV

1. *Nešek* ("biting," usury) and *marbiṭ* ("increase," interest) are one and the same thing. For it is written *Thou shalt not give him thy money upon nešek, nor give him thy victuals for marbiṭ* (Lev. 25: 37). And Scripture further says *Thou shalt not lend upon nešek to thy brother: nešek of money, nešek of victuals, nešek of any thing that is lent upon nešek* (Deut. 23: 20).

Why is it called nešek? Because he who takes it bites his fellow, causes pain to him, and eats his flesh. Why did Scripture make a distinction between nešek and marbit? So that he who would take it should be chargeable with transgressing two negative commandments.

2. Just as it is forbidden to lend money on interest, so is it forbidden to borrow on interest. For it is written *Thou shalt not cause thy brother to bite* (Deut. 23:20). From the oral tradition it has been learned that this is an admonition to the borrower, the passage being understood as though it read *Thou shalt not cause thy brother to take interest*.

It is also forbidden to mediate between the borrower and the lender in a usurious transaction. He who acts as a surety, a scribe, or a witness between them transgresses a negative commandment. For it is written *Ye shall not lay interest upon him* (Exod. 22:24), which, in addition to being an admonition to the lender, is also an admonition to the witness, the surety, and the scribe. From the above it may be deduced that he who lends anything at usury transgresses six negative commandments, to wit: 1. *Thou shalt not be to him as a creditor* (Exod. 22:24); 2. *Thou shalt not give him thy money upon interest* (Lev. 25:37); 3. *Nor give him thy victuals for increase (ibid.)*; 4. *Take thou no interest of him or increase* (Lev. 25:36); 5. *Ye shall lay no interest upon him* (Exod. 22:24); 6. *And thou shalt not put a stumbling block before the blind* (Lev. 19:14); that the borrower transgresses two negative commandments, to wit: 1. *Thou shalt not cause thy brother to bite* (Deut. 23:20); 2. *And thou shalt not put a stumbling block before the blind* (Lev. 19:14); that the surety, witnesses, and the like transgresses only the commandment of *Ye shall lay no interest upon him* (Exod. 22:24); and that he who acts as a broker between the two, or assists or instructs one of them, transgresses the commandment of *And thou shalt not put a stumbling block before the blind* (Lev. 19:14).

3. Although the lender and the borrower transgress all these negative commandments enumerated above, they are not subject to lashes therefor, because usury is restorable. For if one lent money

on usury, if it was *directly stipulated* usury, which is forbidden by Pentateuchal Law, the amount paid as usury is recoverable through the court, which takes it from the lender and returns it to the borrower. But if, in the meantime, the lender died, the usury already paid is not recoverable from his children.

4. If a father left usury money to his children, they are not bound to return it, though they know that the money was received as usury. If, however, their father left them a cow or a garment or any other specific chattel received by him as usury, they are bound to return it for the sake of their father's honor. This applies only where the father repented but did not have the opportunity to make restitution before he died; but if he did not repent, they need not be solicitous of his honor and need not restore even a specific thing.

5. If robbers and lenders on usury make an offer of restitution, it is not to be accepted from them. This rule is designed to open for them the way to repentance. He who accepts restitution from them incurs the displeasure of the Sages.

If the thing which was obtained by robbery is still in existence, or if what was received as usury was a specific thing, and that very thing is still there, restitution may be accepted.

6. Only the principal is recoverable, and not the usury, on a writing which contains usury, whether it be directly stipulated usury or usury prohibited only by Rabbinical law. If the lender hastened to collect the entire amount, the directly stipulated usury included therein is recoverable from him. However, *dust of usury,* which is prohibited only by Rabbinical law, while it may not be collected by the lender from the borrower, is not recoverable by the borrower from the lender if already paid.

7. Whoever writes a writing containing usury is deemed as though he wrote, and called witnesses to attest, that he denied the Lord, the God of Israel.

He who borrows or lends on usury in privacy is deemed as though he denied the Lord, the God of Israel, and the exodus from Egypt. For it is written *Thou shalt not give him thy money upon interest* (Lev. 25:37), and this is followed by *I am the Lord your God, who brought you forth out of the land of Egypt* (Lev. 25:38).

8. A man is forbidden to cause his children and members of his household to lend him money on usury, although he does not mind making the excess payments to them, intending these as a gift, lest they become accustomed to taking usury.

10. If a man lent money to his fellow and the borrower, upon counting the money, found an excess over the agreed amount of the loan, or the lender, upon receiving repayment of the loan and upon counting the money, found an excess over the amount of the loan, then, if the excess is of an amount by which the mind is likely to err, he who received it must restore it to his fellow, and if it is not of such an amount, he may assume that the excess was either intended by his fellow as a gift or that an amount equal to the excess had come unlawfully into the hands of his fellow who, by absorbing it in the reckoning, intended to make restitution thereof.

By what amount is the mind likely to err? By one or two; also by five or ten, since it is possible that the count was made by five or ten units. Also, if the excess is of an amount equal to the number of fives or tens in the entire sum it must be restored, since it is possible that he counted the money by laying aside one unit for each five or ten, and then the units became mingled with the fives or tens.

11. If a man lent money to his fellow and provided for repayment in a given coin, or if he wrote to his wife in her ketubbah a given coin, specifying its weight, and thereafter the weight of the coin was augmented, then, if the price of commodities dropped as a result of the augmentation, the borrower may deduct the amount of such augmentation, even if it be but slight, and if prices did not drop as a result of the augmentation, no deduction may be made and the borrower must pay in the coin current at the time. This applies only where the augmentation was up to one fifth of the

weight, as where the weight had been four and was changed to five, but if the augmentation was more than one fifth, he may deduct the entire augmentation even though the price of commodities did not drop. The same rule applies where one lent money to be repaid in a given coin and thereafter the weight of the coin was decreased.

12. If a man lent money to his fellow providing for repayment in a given coin, and thereafter the coin was invalidated, then, if the coin may be uttered in another country and the lender has a way by which he can reach that country, the borrower may repay him in the coin provided in the agreement of the loan, saying to him, "Go forth and utter it in such a place," and if the lender has no way by which he can get there, the borrower must pay him in the coin current at the time. The same rule applies to a woman's kĕṭubbah.

13. Some of the Geonim have taught that where the borrower pardons the lender all interest he has already received from him, as well as that which he may receive from him in the future, such pardoning is of no avail, even though ḳinyan be performed with respect to such pardoning or gift. Since all payments of interest in the world, they said, are in the nature of a pardon, yet the Law does not pardon, but, on the contrary, forbids such pardoning, it is of no avail, even in the case of interest which is prohibited by Rabbinical law only. It seems to me, however, that this teaching is not correct. Seeing that the lender is told to make restitution, and the borrower knows that the lender acted unlawfully and that he may recover the interest from him, he may pardon him, if he wishes, just as he may pardon to a robber that which he has taken. Furthermore, the Sages have expressly said that if robbers and lenders on interest offered to make restitution, it is not to be accepted from them, which implies that a pardoning is effective.

14. Property belonging to orphans may be handed over to a person who is trustworthy and owns property of good quality, upon condition that the orphans share in the profit but not in the loss

which may result from the investment thereof. How is this to be understood? He is told "You are to engage in business, using this property, and if there is profit you will give to the orphans a share thereof, and if there is loss you alone will bear it." This is dust of usury which is forbidden by Rabbinical law only, and the Rabbis' enactment was not intended to apply to orphans' property.

CHAPTER V

1. It is permissible to borrow from a heathen or from an alien resident and to lend to him at interest. For it is written *Thou shalt not lend upon interest to thy brother* (Deut. 23:20)—to thy brother it is forbidden, but to the rest of the world it is permissible. Indeed, it is an affirmative commandment to lend money at interest to a heathen. For it is written *Unto the heathen thou shalt lend upon interest* (Deut. 23:21). From the oral tradition it has been learned that this is to be construed as an affirmative commandment. This is the rule of the Law.

2. However, the Sages have forbidden Israelites to lend money to a heathen at directly stipulated interest, except to the extent that this may be necessary for the Israelite in order to earn a livelihood. This was decreed out of fear lest the Israelite lender learn from the deeds of the heathen borrower by consorting with him frequently. It is therefore permissible to borrow at interest from a heathen, since the Israelite borrower is more likely to avoid the lender than to associate with him.

A scholar, who is not likely to associate with the heathen so as to learn from his deeds, may lend at interest to a heathen for the mere sake of making a profit. All quasi-usurious transactions with the heathen are permissible to everyone.

3. If an Israelite who had borrowed money at interest from a heathen wished to return the money, when he met another Israelite who said to him, "Give the money to me and I will pay you what you are paying to the heathen," it is directly stipulated interest, even if the second Israelite was substituted as the heathen's debtor,

unless the heathen took his money from the original borrower and gave it to the second Israelite.

4. If a heathen who had borrowed money from an Israelite at interest wished to return it, when he met another Israelite who said to him, "Give the money to me and I will pay to you what you are paying to the Israelite," it is permissible. If, however, the second Israelite was substituted as the debtor, even though it was the heathen who handed him the money, it is directly stipulated interest since the heathen handed the money to the Israelite borrower with the Israelite lender's consent.

5. An Israelite is forbidden to transfer money to a heathen surreptitiously for the purpose of lending it at interest to another Israelite.

If a heathen lends money at interest to an Israelite, it is forbidden for another Israelite to enter as a surety. Since under *their* laws the creditor makes demand for repayment upon the surety first, the surety would be demanding the principal and interest, for which he would incur a liability, from the Israelite debtor. If, however, the heathen undertook that he should not make demand upon the surety first, it is permissible for the Israelite to enter as a surety.

6. If an Israelite borrowed money from a heathen at interest and, after some interest accrued, the creditor converted the accrued interest into a new indebtedness and became a proselyte, then, if the conversion of the interest into a new indebtedness occurred before he became a proselyte, he collects the principal and the interest; and if the conversion occurred after he became a proselyte he collects only the principal and not the interest.

But if a heathen borrowed money from an Israelite at interest, and the creditor converted the accrued interest into a new indebtedness, even if this was done after the debtor became a proselyte, the creditor collects the principal and the interest in order that it should not be said "He became a proselyte for the sake of the money." Moreover, the Israelite creditor collects from him all the interest for which he became liable while he was a heathen.

7. It is a meritorious deed to give priority to a gratuitous loan to an Israelite over a loan at interest to a heathen.

8. A man is forbidden to give his money to another for the purpose of engaging in a joint venture on condition that he share in the profit but not in the loss, this being quasi usury. He who does this is called a wicked man. And if one gave money to another on such a condition, they share the loss, as well as the profit, in accordance with the nature of their venture. He who gives his money on condition that he share in the loss but not in the profit is called a pious man.

9. One may not set up a shopkeeper in a shop on condition that he receive half of the profit; nor may one advance money to another for the purpose of purchasing produce on condition that he receive half of the profit; nor may one give eggs, for the purpose of hatching, to another, who owns hens, on condition that he receive half of the profit; nor may one give to another, at an assessed valuation, calves and colts for fattening on condition that he receive half of the profit, unless he pays to the other a reward for his labor and the cost of the food, or unless the share of the one who is engaged in the enterprise is greater in the profit than in the loss, as we have stated in the matter of partnership.

10. He who enters into a partnership, in money or in landed property, with his fellow, or gives him aught for trading on shares, shall not add the anticipated profit to the principal, lest there be no profit and, consequently, they prove to have engaged in a usurious transaction. Nor shall one give to his fellow money for trading on shares or for a partnership and take a writing of indebtedness therefor, lest he die and the writing come into the hands of his heir, who will collect interest by means thereof.

11. Advance or delayed interest is prohibited. How is this to be understood? If a man set his mind upon obtaining a loan from another and sent him gifts in order to induce him to make the loan, it is advance interest. If a man borrowed money, repaid it, and then sent gifts to the lender on account of the money that was idle

it is delayed interest. He who transgresses the prohibition is guilty of quasi usury.

12. He who borrowed something from his fellow must not be quick to greet him first if he was not accustomed to do so before the loan was made and, needless to say, must not flatter him with words of praise or pay him visits frequently at his house. For it is written *Interest of any word* (Deut. 23:20), that is, even words are forbidden. Similarly, the borrower is forbidden, while the loan remains unpaid, to teach the lender Scripture or Gemara if he was not accustomed to do so before the loan was made. For it is written *Interest of any word* (*ibid.*).

13. He who has lent something to his fellow must not say to him, "Ascertain whether such a one has arrived hither from such a place," that is to say, "Pay him respect, dine and wine him fittingly," and the like.

14. There are things that are like interest and yet are permissible. How is this to be understood? A man may purchase bonds from his fellow for less than their face value, without fear of a transgression. Also, a man may give to his fellow a denar in order to induce him to lend 100 denar to a third party, the Law having prohibited only interest which comes from the borrower to the lender. Also, a man may say to his fellow, "Take this denar and tell such a one to lend me money," the denar being only a reward for telling the lender to make the loan.

15. There are things that are permissible in themselves, yet one is forbidden to do them because they constitute a device for the evasion of the Law of Usury. How is this to be understood? If one said to another, "Lend me a mina," and the other said, "A mina I have not; but wheat at a mina I have," and he gave him wheat at a mina and thereafter purchased it back from him for 90 zuz, it is permissible. But the Sages have forbidden this, because it is a device for the evasion of the Law of Usury, the lender giving only 90 zuz and receiving a mina. If the lender, transgressing the prohibition, does some such thing, he may recover the full 100 zuz at law, since this is not even quasi usury.

Also, he who is in possession of a field given him as a gage must not let it to the owner, because it is a device for the evasion of the Law of Usury, the owner remaining in possession of the field as before and paying the lender every month a reward for having made the loan to him.

16. It is forbidden to let denar at hire, the letting of denar being unlike the letting of a utensil, since in the former case the same utensil is returned, while in the latter the denar are spent and others are returned in their place resulting in quasi usury.

17. Where the law of the king is that he who has paid the head tax for a person in default may take into bondage the person whose tax he has paid, it is permissible to do so even if the value of the man's services is greater than the tax paid for him. And so it is in all similar cases.

CHAPTER VI

1. If a man lends to his fellow a sela' for five denar or two sĕ'ah of wheat for three, or a sela' for a sela' and a sĕ'ah of wheat, or three sĕ'ah of wheat for three sĕ'ah and a denar, or, to put it generally, where a loan is made on condition that it be repaid with an addition of any kind whatsoever, it is Pentateuchal usury, which is recoverable in a court of law. Also, if one lends money to his fellow stipulating that he is to occupy premises belonging to the borrower without any rent until the loan is repaid, or if the lender leases the premises from the borrower at a reduced rental, specifying the reduction which is to be made until the loan is repaid, or if the borrower delivers to the lender as a gage property which is producing profits at the time the loan is made, as where he delivers to him a house on condition that he live therein gratis, it is Pentateuchal usury which is recoverable in a court of law.

Also, if one sold to another a field or a court by way of 'asmaḵta, the profits taken by the purchaser while in possession of the property are deemed to be usury and must be returned by him to the seller since the purchaser did not acquire title to the property. The same rule applies to every purchaser who did not acquire full title to the property at the time of the purported sale: he must return to the seller the profits taken by him in the meantime, since failure to do so would make him guilty of Pentateuchal usury.

All transactions, other than those just enumerated, which are forbidden as a species of usury, are so forbidden by the decree of the Sages only, the prohibition having been enacted for fear that those who would engage in such transactions might eventually come to practice Pentateuchal usury. The gain resulting from such transactions is called "dust of usury" (quasi usury) and is not recoverable in a court of law.

2. He who has lent money to his fellow, must not have the borrower's bondman perform work for him, even though the bondman would otherwise stay idle; nor must he live in a house belonging to the borrower without paying rent, even though the house is not being offered by the owner for rent, and the owner does not usually let it to others; and if the lender did live in the house, he must pay rent, but if he does not pay, it is only quasi usury, since he did not stipulate with the borrower, at the time the loan was made, that he live in the house.

If, therefore, the borrower has not yet paid the debt and he wishes to deduct therefrom the amount of the rent, he may not deduct the entire amount if it is equal to the amount of the debt, but only so much as the judges, in their discretion, may decide. For if we were to dismiss the lender with nothing at all, it would be as though the amount of the rent was recovered from him in a court of law, and quasi usury is not recoverable in a court of law.

3. My teachers have taught that if a man lent money to his fellow and thereafter, when he demanded repayment, the borrower said to him, "Live in my house until I repay the loan," it is quasi usury, since there was no stipulation at the time the loan was made. For it is written *Thou shalt not give him thy money upon interest* (Lev. 25: 37).

4. If a man lent money to his fellow upon a field and said to the borrower, "If you do not repay the loan within three years the field

is mine," he does not acquire title to the field, because this is 'asmakta. He must therefore deduct all the profits he receives from the field, such profits being Pentateuchal usury. But if the borrower said to the purchaser, "Acquire title to the field from now on if I do not return the money to you within the three years," then, if he tenders the money within the three-year period, none of the profits belongs to the purchaser, and if after the three-year period, all of the profits belong to the purchaser.

5. If a man sold a house or a field to his fellow, and the seller said to the purchaser, "You are to return the property to me whenever I have money," the purchaser does not acquire title to the property. All the profits he receives are therefore in the nature of directly stipulated usury and are recoverable in a court of law. But if the purchaser, of his own accord, said to the seller, "I shall return the property to you whenever you have money," the transaction is lawful, and the purchaser takes the profits until the seller returns the money to him.

6. If a man sold a field to his fellow, and the purchaser paid only part of the purchase price, the following rules apply:
a. If the seller said to the purchaser, "Acquire title to such part of the property as corresponds to the part of the purchase price you are paying," each one of the two takes a share of the profits corresponding to his interest in the property.
b. If the seller said to the purchaser, "When you tender the balance of the purchase price you will acquire title to the whole from now on," both of them are forbidden to take the profits in the meantime. The seller is forbidden to take the profits, because it is possible that the purchaser will tender the money, and it will turn out that the property was his *ab initio* and that the seller took the profits as interest for the money he had in the purchaser's hands. The purchaser is similarly forbidden to take the profits, because it is possible that he will not tender the balance, and it will turn out that he took the profits as interest for the money he had in the seller's hands. The profits are therefore to be delivered to a

depositary and kept by him until it is ascertained whether the purchaser or the seller is entitled to them.

c. If the seller said to the purchaser, "When you tender the balance you will acquire title," the seller takes the profits until the balance is tendered by the purchaser, and if the purchaser took them, they may be recovered from him by the seller.

d. If the seller said to the purchaser, "Acquire title from now on, and the balance of the purchase price shall constitute an indebtedness against you," the purchaser takes the profits, and if the seller took them, they may be recovered from him by the purchaser.

7. My teachers have taught: where one lends money to his fellow, who delivers to him a field as a gage on condition that he is to take the profits therefrom during the term of the gage, it is only quasi usury and is not recoverable in a court of law, even though the agreement is that no deduction at all is to be made from the principal. For the gage of a field is unlike the gage of a house, since at the time the loan is made there is no produce in the field, and while it is possible that in the future there will be profits resulting in gain, it is also possible that seed and labor will go to nought resulting in loss. Therefore it is only quasi usury. Nor is a gage to be likened to a conveyance upon 'asmakta, for he who conveys upon 'asmakta does not deliberately intend to convey title, while he who delivers property as a gage deliberately intends to convey title to the corpus of the property, in so far as the taking of profits therefrom is concerned. This opinion seems to find support in the Gemara, where it appears that a gage is deemed to be quasi usury only. The text of the Gemara cannot be construed otherwise than that it applies to the gage of a field, which accords with my teachers' teaching.

It follows therefore that there are three types of gages: a. a gage which is in the nature of directly stipulated usury; b. a gage which is quasi usury; c. a gage which is permissible.

How is this to be understood? Where the borrower delivers to the lender a gage, such as a house, a bathhouse, or a shop, out of which profits are always available, and the lender takes the profits, it is directly stipulated usury. Where the borrower delivers a field and the like as a gage, and profits accrue, and the lender takes them, it is quasi usury. Also, where the borrower delivers a house and the like as a *gage with deduction,* it is quasi usury. But where he delivers a field as a gage with deduction, it is permissible.

How is deduction to be understood? Where one lends a 100 denar to another, who delivers to him his house or his field, and the lender says, "I will deduct one ma'ah annually as rent for the property in order that I may take all the profits therefrom," it is forbidden in the case of a house, but permissible in the case of a field.

8. Some of the Geonim have taught that every gage in which there is no deduction whatsoever constitutes directly stipulated usury. But they failed to penetrate the depth of the matter and to make a distinction between a field and a house, wherefore they had difficulty in understanding the words of the Sages of the Gemara.

They have also taught that every gage, even with deduction, is forbidden, whether it be a gage of a house or of a field. According to their opinion, there is no permissible gage except the following: where one lends 100 denar to another, who delivers to him a house or a field as a gage, stipulating that upon the expiration of a 10-year period the property is to revert back to the borrower free, the lender may take the profits during the 10-year period, even if the property be worth a 1,000 denar per year in rent, since this is in no way different from letting property for less than its true rental value.

Similarly, where the gagor stipulates with the gagee that whenever he tenders the money the gagee is to allow him a deduction therefrom of 10 denar per year and surrender the property, it is permissible.

Similarly, where the gagor stipulates that whenever the gagee so desires he will repay the loan, deducting therefrom a proportionate amount for the occupation of the property by the gagee, whereupon the gagee shall surrender the premises, it is permissible, since this is but like a letting, and since every stipulation with regard to letting is permissible, as we have stated.

CHAPTER VII

1. If a man lent money to his fellow, who delivered to him a field as a gage for a specified time or until he tendered the money, when the lender was to surrender the property, and the lender was taking all the profits, he may not be compelled to surrender the field without receiving anything on account of the loan, even if the profits equal the amount of the loan. For if he were compelled to surrender the property without receiving any payment on account of the loan, it would be as though the profits were recovered from him in a court of law. And it is needless to say that if the profits exceed the amount of the loan, the excess may not be recovered from the gagee. Also, no transfer of accounts may be made from one writing to another with respect to a gage.

If the property gaged belonged to orphans, and the profits taken by the gagee equal the amount of the loan, he is compelled to surrender the property without receiving anything on account of the loan. If the profits exceed the indebtedness, the excess may not be recovered from the gagee, but a transfer of accounts may be made from one writing to another.

What is meant by a transfer of accounts from one writing to another? As where one field was gaged to a man on a writing for 100 denar and another field was gaged to him on another writing for 100 denar, both fields belonging to the same person, and the gagee took 50 denar worth of profits out of one field and 150 denar worth out of the other, we may say to him, "You have already taken 200 denar worth of profits and you are entitled to no more," as though there was but one writing and one gage.

2. If the custom of the locality is that the lender may be compelled to surrender the gage whenever the borrower tenders the amount of the loan, it is as though it was so expressly stipulated, an express stipulation being unnecessary. Similarly, if the custom

of the locality is that the gagee may not be compelled to surrender the property until the end of the term of the gage, it is as though it was so expressly stipulated.

If a gage is made without any specification as to its duration, the gagor may not compel the gagee to surrender the property before the end of 12 months.

3. If the custom of the locality is that the gagor may compel the gagee to surrender the gage at any time, but the gagee stipulated that he was not to be compelled to surrender until the end of the term of the gage, the gagor may not compel him to surrender the gage before the end of the term.

If the custom of the locality is that the gagee may not be compelled to surrender the gage before the end of the term, but the gagee undertook to surrender the gage whenever the gagor tendered payment of the loan, the performance of ḳinyan is necessary in order to make the gagee's undertaking valid.

4. If the custom of the locality is that the gagee may be compelled to surrender the gage whenever the gagor tenders payment of the loan, the gagee's creditor does not collect his debt from the gage, as he does from other landed property, the first-born does not take a double portion therein, the advent of the Sabbatical year cancels the debt secured by it, and when the gagee surrenders it he does not take even the fruit which has already ripened and fallen to the ground. But if the gagee lifted up the fruit before he surrendered the gage, he acquired title thereto.

But if the custom of the locality is that the gagee may not be compelled to surrender the gage before the end of the term, the gagee's debtor may collect therefrom, the first-born takes a double portion therein, and the advent of the Sabbatical year does not cancel the debt secured thereby.

5. Although the above-mentioned gage is forbidden, being quasi usury, as we have stated, it is possible that it was made through error, or that it was taken from a heathen, or that it was made in violation of the prohibition, and since it is only quasi

usury, the custom of the locality is followed. But there was one authority who taught that the above-mentioned rules have reference to a gage with deduction.

6. If a heathen delivered a house to an Israelite as a gage and then sold it to another Israelite, the gagee is not bound to pay rent to the Israelite purchaser from the time of the purchase, but may live in the house without paying rent until the heathen repays the loan for which the house was gaged, since under *their* laws the property is in the ownership of the gagee until the loan is repaid and the property surrendered.

7. If a man delivered a house or a field to his fellow as a gage on condition that the gagor take the profits therefrom, and the gagee said to the gagor, "If you sell the property, you are to sell it to me for so much," it is forbidden; but if he said to him, "You are to sell it to me for what it is worth, and on such condition I am lending you the money," it is permissible.

8. It is permissible to stipulate for an increase with respect to rent of landed property. How is this to be understood? As where one lets a house to another and says to him, "If you will pay the entire rent in advance, I will give you the property for 10 sela' per year, but if you will pay in monthly installments, the rent will be one sela' per month," it is permissible.

9. If a man let a field to his fellow for ten kor per year, and the lessee said to the lessor, "Lend me 200 zuz for improving the cultivation of the field, and I will pay you 12 kor per year," it is permissible, since the rental value of the field will be greater when cultivation is improved.

Similarly, if a man let a shop or a ship to another and the lessee said to the lessor, "Lend me 200 zuz with which to rebuild, decorate, and panel the shop or repair the ship and its accessories," it is permissible. But if he said, "Lend me 200 zuz with which to carry on business in the shop, or to buy merchandise to transport on the ship, or to hire sailors," it is forbidden.

10. It is forbidden to stipulate for an increase with regard to a man's hire. How is this to be understood? One may not say to his fellow, "Do for me certain work which is worth one *kesep̄*, and I will do for you work worth two kesep̄."

11. One may say to his fellow, "Help me to hoe today and I will help you to hoe tomorrow." But he may not say to him, "Help me to weed and I will help you to hoe, help me to hoe and I will help you to weed." All days of the dry season are accounted alike and all days of the rainy season are accounted alike. Nor may a man say to his fellow, "Help me to plough during the dry season and I will help you to plough during the rainy season," since the labor of ploughing during the rainy reason is harder. And so it is in all similar cases.

If a man hired a worker in the summer, paying him his wage in advance at the rate of one denar per day for work to be performed in the winter, when his labor will be worth one sela' per day, it is forbidden, since it appears as though he was lending him the money in order to obtain his labor at a lower wage. But if he said to him, "Work for me from this day until such a time," it is permissible. Since the worker commences his work immediately, it does not appear as though the employer were receiving compensation for making the advance payment of the worker's wages.

CHAPTER VIII

1. It is forbidden to stipulate for an increase with regard to a sale. How is this to be understood? If a man sold landed property or movables to his fellow and said to him, "If you will make payment now the property is yours for 100 zuz, but if you will pay only at such a time it is yours for 120 zuz," it is quasi usury, for this is as though he were taking 20 zuz for allowing the purchaser to use the 100 zuz until the time of payment.

When the seller sues for the purchase price, the purchaser is bound to pay for the property only so much as it was worth at the time of the sale, or, if the property is still in his possession, he may return it to the seller. Similarly, if a man sold movables to another for 100 zuz payable at such a time, while the market price of the property for a cash purchaser was only 90 zuz, it is forbidden, and the purchaser pays only 90 zuz, or returns the property if it is still in his possession.

2. If a man purchases something from his fellow at its market value on condition that he pay therefor at the end of 12 months, the seller may say to the purchaser, "Pay me now and I will take less," and need not fear that the transaction is usurious.

3. If a jar of wine which is worth one denar is sold for two denar, payable at a later time, on condition that if any accident occur to the wine before the purchaser resells it, it shall be deemed to have been in the seller's ownership at the time of such accident, it is permissible. For if the jar is lost or broken, the purchaser does not pay anything, and if he cannot resell it at a profit, he may return it to the seller.

Similarly, where the seller sells the wine for two denar and says to the purchaser, "The excess over two denar which you may realize from the resale of the wine shall be your reward for your efforts in reselling it, and if you cannot resell it at a price satisfactory to you, you may return it to me," it is permissible, even though the wine is to be deemed in the purchaser's ownership if it is lost or stolen or if it turns sour.

4. If a man has produce for which he could receive only 10 denar at the market, but is not minded to sell it to a purchaser soliciting the sale for less than 12 denar, even if the purchase price were paid immediately, he may sell it for 12 denar, deferring payment for 12 months, because even if the purchaser brought the money with him, he could only purchase it for 12 denar. And so it is in all similar cases.

5. It is forbidden to purchase the produce of an orchard before it ripens, because when the vendor sells for less, say for 10 denar, produce which will be worth more, say 20 denar, when it is ripe, the difference is due to the advancing of the money.

But if one purchases a calf at a price which is lower than its market price, and the calf is to remain with the vendor until it grows up, the transaction is a permissible one, because if the calf died or became lean, the vendee would suffer the loss, and leanness and death are of frequent occurrence.

6. If a purchaser advances money to an owner of a vineyard for branches and vine rods to be delivered to him when cut off, when they sell at a high price, while he purchases them at a low price before they dry up and are cut off, he must tend them while they are still attached to the soil, in order that he be deemed like one who purchases a tree for its rods; but if he does not tend them, the money is deemed to be a loan, and the low price to be due to the advancing of the money, which makes the transaction a prohibited one.

7. Watchmen of fields, who receive their hire in wheat from the granary at a low price at the time when the wheat is stored away in the granary, must do some work on the wheat while it is in the granary, in order that the receipt of the wheat by them may take place at the end of the term of the hiring; and if they do not do so, the deferment of the payment of the hire is deemed to be a loan to the owner, and the low price at which the wheat is reckoned to them to be due to the deferment of the payment of their hire until such time as the wheat is stored away in the granary.

8. If it was customary for the owners of the fields to remove their tenants from the fields in the month of Nisan, receiving from the tenants four sĕ'ah for each *ḥomer* sown, and the owner let his tenants remain in the field until the month of *Iyyar,* receiving from them six sĕ'ah, it is permissible, and there is no usury there.

9. If a man purchased wheat at four sĕ'ah to the sela' this having been the market price, and paid the money to the vendor and when, after the lapse of some time, he came to take the wheat, the vendor added to the measure, giving him more than he had purchased, it is permissible, because the vendor made the addition of his own will, and had he not wished to do so, he could have

made no addition at all, since there was no stipulation to that effect.

10. A man may give to his fellow the purchase price of a barrel of wine saying to him, "If it turns sour from now until such a day, it is yours, but if its price drops or rises, it is mine," because the purchaser, having taken upon himself the risk of a drop in the price, has both the possibility of gain and of loss. And so it is in all similar cases.

It is also permissible for a man to purchase from his fellow 100 jars of wine in the month of *Tishri* for a denar without accepting delivery until the month of *Tebeth,* and when accepting delivery, he may examine the wine, rejecting that which has turned sour and taking only the good wine, because what he purchased from him was only good wine, and that which has become sour was from the very beginning bound to become so, although this was unknown at the time of the purchase.

11. In a locality where the custom is that the owner of a ship receive hire therefor at the time it is hired out, and that if the ship is damaged, the hirer, in addition to the hire, make good the damage by appraisal, a hiring in accordance with such custom is permissible.

It is also permissible to let on hire a copper kettle and the like, taking the hire therefor and, in addition, the value of that which the kettle loses of its weight.

12. It is not permissible to accept *iron sheep* from an Israelite because it is quasi usury. How is iron sheep to be understood? Suppose a man had 100 sheep, and another accepted them from him on condition that he take care of them and receive one half, one third, or one fourth of the wool, the offspring, and the milk for a year or two, as the case may be, and that if any of the sheep die the party accepting the sheep shall pay the value thereof, it is a prohibited transaction, since the owner of the sheep has only a possibility of gain and none of loss. If, therefore, the owner of the sheep undertook that if the price of the sheep rose or dropped, or if they were devoured, they were to be deemed to have been in his

ownership, it is a permissible transaction. And so it is in all similar cases.

13. If a man took a cow from his fellow at an appraised value and said, "If she dies I shall be liable to you from now on for 30 denar, and I will pay you a sela' per month as hire for her," it is a permissible transaction, because he did not undertake to be liable for the appraised value of the cow while she was alive, but only if she died.

14. A woman may let to another a hen, to be set on eggs, for two chicks, without entertaining any fear that the transaction savors of usury.

15. If a man made demand upon his fellow for four denar of usury, and his fellow gave him therefor a thing worth five denar, he must, when restitution is ordered, restore to his fellow five denar, since the thing came into his hands by way of usury. Similarly, if his fellow gave him therefor a garment or a utensil, he must restore that same garment or utensil. If his fellow let to him therefor a place, the rental of which is worth only three denar, he must, when restitution is ordered, restore four denar, since he rented the place for four denar, accepting it in lieu of the usury.

CHAPTER IX

1. No agreement may be made with respect to produce until the market price has been published; but once the market price has been published, such an agreement may be made, for even if the seller does not have the produce, another man has it. How is this to be understood? If the market price has become fixed at four sě'ah to the sela', one may make an agreement with a vendor for the purchase of 100 sě'ah, giving him 25 sela', and if the vendor delivers 100 sě'ah of wheat after the lapse of some time, when wheat sells at a sela' per sě'ah, there is no usury at all in the transaction, even though the vendor had no wheat at the time when he made the agreement.

This applies only if the vendor, at the time when the agreement is made, has none of the kind which he agrees to sell, but if he has some of that kind, although it has not been completely processed, it is permissible to make an agreement with respect thereto, even if the market price has not yet been published.

How is this to be understood? If a man is the first among the reapers, he may make an agreement with respect to the wheat even though it is still in the stack. One may also make an agreement with respect to wine as soon as he cuts the grapes and places them in the pressing vat, or with respect to oil as soon as he places the olives in the vat, or with respect to lime as soon as the limestone is sunk in the kiln.

One may likewise make an agreement with respect to pottery as soon as the potter makes the clay balls. This applies only to pottery made of white clay, but in the case of pottery made of black clay one may make an agreement with respect thereto, even though none of it has yet been made, because black clay is readily available and if the seller does not have it another man has it.

One may likewise make an agreement with respect to manure at any season of the year, even though he has none, because manure is always available.

2. If a thing still requires one or two processes, an agreement of purchase and sale may be made with respect thereto, but if it requires three processes, no such agreement may be made unless the market price has been published. For if the thing requires three processes, it is as though the vendor had none of its kind and as though it has not yet come into existence.

How is this to be understood? If grain in the stack requires being placed in the sun to dry, threshing, and winnowing, no agreement may be made with respect thereto, unless the market price has been published; but if it is dry and requires only threshing and winnowing, an agreement may be made with respect thereto.

If the potter's clay balls require moulding and drying, transportation to the kiln, burning, and removal from the kiln, no agreement may be made with respect thereto; but if they are dry and require only transportation to the kiln and burning, an agreement may be made with respect thereto, provided it is customary for the vendee to remove the pottery from the kiln. If, however, the vendor is the one who removes the pottery from the kiln, the clay balls require three processes, and no agreement may be made with respect thereto, unless the market price has been published. And so it is in all similar cases.

3. If a man was going to milk his goats, to shear his sheep, or take the honey out of his beehive and he met his fellow and said to him, "What my goats will yield in milk is sold to you, what my sheep will yield in wool is sold to you, what my beehive will yield in honey is sold to you," it is a permissible transaction; but if he said to him, "So much of what my goats will yield in milk is sold to you for so much, so much of what my sheep will yield in wool is sold to you for so much, so much of what my beehive will yield in honey is sold to you for so much," it is a prohibited transaction, unless the agreement was made at the prevailing market price. And so it is in all similar cases.

4. No agreement may be made on the basis of the market price in small towns, because the market price there is not a stable one, but only on the basis of the market price in the principal town of the region.

If new wheat is selling in the principal town at four sĕ'ah to the sela' and old wheat at three sĕ'ah to the sela', no agreement may be made until the market price has been published for new wheat and for old. If mixed wheat is selling at four sĕ'ah to the sela' and householder's wheat at three sĕ'ah to the sela', an agreement may be made with respect to mixed wheat at the market price for such wheat, but no agreement may be made with a householder until the market price for householder's wheat has been established.

5. Once the market price has been established, it is permissible to make an agreement to deliver at a higher rate, if such should prevail at the time of delivery. How is this to be understood? If wheat was selling at four sĕ'ah to the sela', and the vendor agreed

to deliver the wheat at a lower price, if such should prevail at the time of delivery, and afterwards wheat stood at 10 sě'ah to the sela', the vendor is to deliver the wheat to the vendee at the rate of 10 sě'ah to the sela', that is at the prevailing market price at the time of delivery, since he agreed to deliver at the higher rate.

If the vendee gave the money to the vendor without specification, that is without stipulating for a higher rate, and the price of wheat dropped, the vendor is to make delivery at the price which prevailed at the time when he received the money, and he who retracts subjects himself to the malediction of "He who punished." This applies only if one made an agreement on his own behalf, but if the agreement was made by an agent on behalf of another, whether on behalf of the vendor or on behalf of the vendee, a different rule applies: if the vendee acted through an agent who failed to stipulate for a higher rate in case of a drop in the price, the vendee may refuse to accept delivery except at the lower price, and if the vendor acted through an agent who stipulated for a higher rate in case of a drop in the price, he may return the money to the vendee, and neither of them is subject to malediction, if the agreement was entered into by an agent, since the principal may say to the agent, "I sent you to act for my advantage and not for my disadvantage," as we have stated.

6. If wheat was selling at four sě'ah to the sela' and the vendor took the money and later delivered to the vendee wheat at the rate of five sě'ah to the sela', it is a permissible transaction if the vendor had wheat at the time when he took the money. But if he had a debt of wheat outstanding against others, and he took the money, agreeing to deliver the wheat to the vendee when he shall have collected it from his debtor, it is a prohibited transaction. Since the wheat lacked collection, it is as though the vendor sold the wheat at a lower price because the vendee advanced the money to him before the time of delivery.

7. If wheat was selling at four sě'ah to the sela' in the principal town of the region and at six sě'ah to the sela' in the surrounding villages, it is permissible to give a sela' to a merchant to bring six

sĕʻah from the village, provided it is agreed that the wheat is to be deemed to be in the ownership of the purchaser while in transit, so that if it were lost or stolen, the loss would be his. However, a worthy man is forbidden to enter into such an arrangement; and with respect to all kinds of wares all men are forbidden to enter into such an arrangement, because wares are not as readily available as produce.

8. If assdrivers came to town when wheat was selling at four sĕʼah to the selaʻ, and they sold some of the wheat to their salesmen or middlemen at a lower price, say at five sĕʼah to the selaʻ, for money which the latter gave to them as soon as they came to town, before they could open up their sacks and sell to others, it is a permissible transaction, because it is assumed that the lowering of the price was not due to the fact that the vendees advanced the money on the wheat, which was not to be delivered until a later time, but to the fact that the vendees apprised the vendors of the market price and were otherwise of assistance to them.

9. If a man was transporting his produce from one place to another and met his fellow who said to him, "Give it to me and I will give you other produce which I have in the place to which you are taking yours," then, if he had produce in that place, it is a permissible transaction, and if he did not have any, it is a prohibited one.

If a man was transporting wares from one place to another and his fellow said to him, "Give them to me, and I will pay you therefor what they are worth in the place to which you are taking them," then, if the wares were to be deemed to be in the ownership of the vendor while in transit, it is a permissible transaction, and if they were to be deemed to be in the ownership of the vendee, the transaction is a prohibited one.

10. If a man gave to the owner of a garden the purchase price of *these 10 cucumbers* or *these 10 melons* while they were still small, stipulating with the owner that he should deliver them to him when they have grown large, it is a permissible transaction, since

they grow of themselves, and since no others would grow in their place if the owner cut them off immediately. And so it is in all similar cases where the vendor suffers neither damage nor loss.

CHAPTER X

1. Just as it is permissible for a vendor to make an agreement with respect to produce on the basis of the market price, so is it permissible to borrow produce, without fixing a time for repayment, on the basis of the market price. How is this to be understood? If a man borrowed from his fellow 10 sĕ'ah of wheat, the market price having been fixed and known to both of them, he is bound to return to the lender 10 sĕ'ah of wheat, even though the price of wheat rose in the meantime, since the market price of the wheat was known at the time when he borrowed it, and he could have purchased other wheat and repaid the lender at any time thereafter, no time for repayment having been fixed.

2. If the borrower has some of the kind of produce that he wishes to borrow, it is permissible to borrow, without fixing the time for repayment, even though the market price has not yet been published; even if he has one sĕ'ah only, he may borrow many sĕ'ah; if he has one drop of wine or of oil, he may borrow many jars of wine or oil; but if he has none of that kind, and the market price has not yet been fixed or has not become known to them, it is forbidden to borrow a sĕ'ah for a sĕ'ah.

Similarly, in the case of other produce, one should not borrow until he has converted the loan into terms of money, and if he borrowed without converting the loan into terms of money and the price of the produce dropped, the borrower may repay to the lender the quantity of produce, by measure or by weight, which he borrowed; if the price of the produce rose, the lender must accept an amount of money equal to the value of the produce at the time of the loan.

It is forbidden to borrow produce for produce, to be repaid at a fixed time, even though the borrower has some of that kind of produce, or the market price has become fixed; such a loan may only be made where no time of repayment is fixed.

3. A man may not say to his fellow, "Lend me a kor of wheat and I will repay you at threshing time," but he may say to him "Lend it to me until my son returns," or "until I find the key."

4. If a man borrowed produce to be repaid at a specified time, and the price thereof dropped, he may repay the produce at the time fixed for repayment; if the price rose, he may repay an amount of money equal to the value of the produce at the time of the loan.

5. A man may lend to his tenants on shares wheat for wheat, to be used for sowing, whether before or after the tenant has taken possession. This applies only in a locality where it is customary for the tenants on shares to supply the seed, since the owner may remove the tenant so long as he has not supplied the seed. But in a locality where it is customary for the owner to supply the seed it is permissible to lend to the tenant wheat for wheat only so long as the tenant has not taken possession, when the owner may still withdraw from the tenancy agreement since the tenant, when he takes possession, does so upon the understanding that he is to repay to the owner the wheat the latter has lent to him. But after the tenant has taken possession, seeing that the owner may no longer remove him, he is like every other man, and it is forbidden to lend to him wheat for wheat to be used for sowing. The owner may, however, lend to him wheat for wheat, without fixing the time for repayment, on the basis of the market price.

6. If a man made a demand upon his fellow for money he owed him saying to him, "Give me my money as I wish to purchase wheat," and the debtor said, "Convert the money into wheat at the prevailing market price and you will have with me wheat on loan," then, if the debtor had on hand a quantity of wheat equivalent to the debt, it is a permissible transaction and if he did not have the wheat on hand, it is a prohibited one; because when the Sages said that it is permissible to make an agreement with respect

to produce on the basis of the market price, even though the vendor has none of that kind on hand, they said so only with respect to one who advances the purchase price of produce in cash, but if one wishes to convert a loan of money into a loan of produce, it is forbidden unless he has the produce.

If the debtor had wheat on hand and converted the loan of money into a loan of wheat, and thereafter the creditor came and said to him, "Give me the wheat as I wish to sell it in order to purchase wine with the money," and the debtor said, "Convert the loan of wheat into a loan of wine against me at the prevailing market price," then, if the debtor had the wine on hand, it is a permissible transaction, and the loan of wheat becomes a loan of wine, and if he did not have the wine on hand, the transaction is a forbidden one. If the debtor did not have produce on hand and in transgression of the Law converted a loan of money into a loan of produce, he is not bound to repay produce, but only the money he borrowed, even though he thereafter acquired the produce.

CHAPTER XI

1. If a man lent money to his fellow in the presence of witnesses, whether the borrower said to the witnesses, "Ye be witnesses against me that I owe this man a mina," or "Ye be my witnesses that I owe this man a mina," it is called an *oral loan,* and the borrower is not required to pay it in the presence of witnesses. If, therefore, the borrower subsequently pleads, "I have paid," he swears the informal oath and is quit.

But if a man lent money to his fellow on a writing, the borrower is required to repay it in the presence of witnesses. If, therefore, the borrower subsequently pleads, "I have paid," he is not believed. Rather, we say to him, "Either produce witnesses or pay the debt."

Therefore, if a man said to witnesses, "Ye be witnesses against me that I owe this man a mina," the witnesses may not reduce their testimony to writing, thereby converting an oral loan into a loan on a writing, unless the borrower said to them, "Write a

writing, sign, and hand it to him." And even where the borrower says thus to the witnesses, they must consult him after they
have signed and only then they may hand the writing to the lender.

If ḳinyan was performed by the debtor to the effect that he was
obligated to the creditor for a mina, the witnesses may draw up a
writing and deliver it to the creditor, even if the debtor did not
say to them, "Write it down." For every ḳinyan, unless otherwise
specified, is designed to be reduced to writing, and it is not necessary to consult the party performing ḳinyan with respect to reducing the matter to writing.

2. If a borrower drew up a writing in his own hand, had it
attested by witnesses, and delivered it to the creditor it is a valid
writing. Similarly, if he drew up a writing and delivered it to the
creditor in the presence of witnesses, even though the witnesses'
signatures do not appear thereon, it is a loan on a writing, provided
the writing is such that it could not be forged and that the witnesses in whose presence it was delivered had read it. There is,
however, an opinion by one of the Geonim to the effect that the
borrower must say to the witnesses, in whose presence the writing
was delivered, "Sign and attest that the writing was delivered in
your presence."

3. Where one produces an unattested note of hand stating that
the writer thereof owes him a debt, it is to be treated as an oral debt
in every respect, even though the writer's handwriting has been
judicially established. If the debtor pleads that he has paid the debt,
he swears the informal oath and is quit. The debt evidenced by
such a writing is not collectible either from the debtor's heirs or
from the purchasers of his property.

4. Every debt is collectible from the debtor's heirs and from
the purchasers of his property, as hereinafter stated. An oral debt,
however, is collectible from the debtor's heirs but not from the purchasers of his property. Because an oral debt is not attended by
publicity, the creditor on such a debt may not *seize* the debtor's
property in the hands of purchasers. But a debt on a writing is at-

tended by publicity, and the purchaser who failed to make an inquiry, which would have revealed that the seller's property was bound for a debt outstanding against him, thereby caused a loss to himself, since all of the debtor's property is bound to the creditor by Pentateuchal Law.

5. If a man sold a field to another in the presence of witnesses, and the purchaser was evicted therefrom, the purchaser may seize the seller's *alienated* property, even though he has no writing, as hereinafter stated. For he who sells landed property sells openly, and the sale is attended by publicity.

6. An oral debt may not be collected from the debtor's heirs, except under one of the following three conditions: 1. Where the debtor admitted the debt and declared during his illness that he still owed it to the creditor. 2. Where the debt had a specific date of maturity and the debtor died before such date, the presumption being that a man does not pay a debt before its maturity. 3. Where the debtor had been put under ban until such time as he shall have repaid the debt and was still under ban when he died. In all of these cases, the creditor collects from the debtor's heirs without taking an oath.

But if witnesses came and testified that the deceased owed the claimant a mina, or that in their presence the deceased borrowed from the claimant a mina, the claimant does not collect anything from the heirs. For, the rule being what it is, that where one lends money to his fellow in the presence of witnesses the borrower is not required to repay in the presence of witnesses, there is a possibility that the deceased repaid the loan.

Similarly, if the claimant produced a note of hand written by the deceased and stating that he owes him a mina, the claimant does not collect anything on the note of hand.

7. If the debtor has no movables in his possession but owns landed property, and the court is informed that he is concealing his movables in the hands of others, they compel him to sell his movables and pay the debt. If they have no information with re-

gard thereto, they declare the anathema generally against him who knows of movables belonging to the debtor and would not bring them into court, and thereupon they levy upon the debtor's landed property of medium quality and cause the debt to be satisfied therefrom, as hereinafter stated.

All this applies only where the creditor seeks satisfaction of the debt from the debtor himself. But if he seeks satisfaction of the debt from the debtor's heir, whether minor or adult, the court may not cause him to be paid out of movables, even if they are under loan or deposit in the hands of others, since, by Pentateuchal Law, movables are not bound to the debtor.

8. Orphans are under a moral duty to pay their father's debts out of the movables he left to them. But if the heir does not wish to pay out of such movables, he may not be compelled to do so.

If the creditor seized some movables in the debtor's lifetime, he may collect his debt out of them. If the creditor claims that he seized the movables in the debtor's lifetime, while the debtor's heir claims that he seized them after the debtor's death, the heir must produce proof in support of his allegation, or, if he fails to produce such proof, the creditor swears that the deceased owed him so much—and he may claim that he owed him up to the value of the movables—and includes in the oath an asseveration that he seized the movables in the debtor's lifetime.

If the things that have been seized by the creditor consist of writings obligatory, and he claims that he holds them as a pawn for his debt and that he seized them in the debtor's lifetime, he must produce proof in support of his allegations, or, if he fails to produce such proof, he must return the writings to the heir, since he does not claim the writings themselves but only that he is holding them for the evidence which they contain.

9. If orphans have obtained landed property in satisfaction of a debt which was owed to their father, the father's creditor may, in his turn, collect his debt from such landed property, since the property is deemed to have belonged to the father.

10. If Reuben sold a field to Simeon with warranty, constituting the amount of the purchase price an indebtedness against Simeon, and Reuben died, and Reuben's creditor came to seize the field for a debt which Reuben owed to him, and Simeon settled with Reuben's creditor for a certain amount of money, the rule is that Reuben's heirs may demand of Simeon payment of the indebtedness which he owed to their father, since the indebtedness is not bound for the payment of Reuben's debts. If, therefore, Simeon would act wisely, he should give to the heirs, in satisfaction of the indebtedness which he owed to Reuben, the field which he purchased from Reuben. He would then be in a position to seize the same field from the heirs for the money for which he settled with their father's creditor, since he bought the field with warranty.

11. All of the later Geonim adopted the enactment that a creditor collect out of movables in the hands of the debtor's heirs, and so it is ruled in Israel, in all of its courts throughout the world. But in the West they were wont to write in their writings obligatory that the creditor collect out of the debtor's landed property and movables, whether in the debtor's lifetime or after his death. The creditor would therefore collect out of the heirs' movables by reason of the condition rather than by reason of the enactment.

This clause constitutes a greatly desirable safeguard against the possibility that the debtor will have been ignorant of the enactment and that, because an enactment of the later Sages does not possess the force of creating a new liability against orphans, the creditor will deprive the orphans of their property unlawfully.

CHAPTER XII

1. No execution may be had against property in the hands of the debtor's heirs unless they are adults. Property in the hands of the debtor's heirs who are minors is not subject to execution for their father's debts.

2. Even if the writing obligatory contains every conceivable condition in the world, the creditor may not enforce payment

thereof until the orphans have reached majority, since it is possible that they have evidence with which they could break the writing.

3. If the debt was contracted by the deceased from a heathen at usury, and the usury is consuming the orphans' property, a guardian is appointed and resort is had to their property, which may be sold to pay the debt. Similarly, where a woman demands her dower, whether she be a widow or a divorcee, a guardian is appointed over the orphans and resort is had to their property. This is done in order to make the woman more sought after as a mate, that is, in order that she have means which will enable her to marry another man. If, therefore, the woman hastened to remarry and then she came and demanded her dower, her demand remains unheeded until the orphans have reached majority, since she is not entitled to maintenance out of the orphans' property and since she has already remarried.

4. Some of the Geonim have taught that if the value of the orphans' property is only equal to or less than the woman's dower her demand must remain unheeded, since no advantage would ensue to the orphans from satisfying her demand immediately. These Geonim hold that when the Sages said that resort is had to orphans' property to satisfy a woman's dower out of it, they said so only in order to prevent a diminution of the property by reason of expenditures on the woman's maintenance; and in this case where the woman would take away all the property, what advantage would there be to the minor orphans if resort was had to their property? And as to the other reason—that of making the woman more sought after—they hold that it may be disregarded.

5. If the ancestor left instructions saying, "Give a mina to such a one," resort is had to the orphans' property after a guardian has been appointed to plead their cause. If he said, "Give *this* mina or *this* field to such a one," it is to be given, and it is not necessary to appoint a guardian.

6. If orphans are in possession of landed property which is not theirs, but is claimed by a claimant to have come into the hands

of their ancestor through robbery, an action lies against the orphans, and a guardian is appointed to plead and to litigate in their behalf. If the property is found to have been taken away from its owner by robbery, it is restored to him.

Similarly, if a minor, with the aid of his bondmen, descended upon a field belonging to his fellow and forcibly took possession thereof, we do not say, "We shall wait until he has reached majority," but the property is taken away from him, and when he reaches majority let him produce witnesses, if he has any.

7. If landed property is in the possession of orphans, and a claimant comes and claims that he purchased the property from their ancestor and took profits therefrom for the number of years required to constitute seizin, and he has witnesses to the effect that he was in possession of the property and took profits therefrom for the period required to constitute seizin during the ancestor's lifetime, the property may not be taken away from the orphans until they have reached majority. For the testimony of witnesses is not admissible in the absence of the litigant against whom it is offered, and a minor is deemed as though he were not present in court.

But if the claimant produces a writing to the effect that the property was his by purchase, he may have the writing confirmed and the property taken away from the orphans after a guardian is appointed for them.

8. When the court proceeds to sell property belonging to orphans they make an appraisal of the property, and then they cause proclamation of the impending sale to be made for 30 days in succession or on every Monday and Thursday during a period of 60 days. Proclamation is made in the morning and in the evening, when workers come to work and when they quit their work, in order that he who wishes to buy may be able to send his workers to examine the property for him.

When proclamation is made, the property is designated by its boundaries, and notice is given of how much the property produces and at how much it was appraised and for what purpose it is being sold, whether to satisfy a creditor or to pay a woman's dower, because there are those who prefer to pay the purchase price to a creditor and those who prefer to pay it to a woman for her dower.

9. When a writ of execution against property belonging to orphans, whether minor or adult, is drawn up it must contain the following recital: "We have ascertained that this property belonged to such a one, deceased." If the writ does not contain this recital, it is invalid and the purchaser under such a writ may not take the profits from the property, even after all proclamations have been completed.

10. If a court sold property without proclamation, it is as though they erred about a matter stated in the Mishnah, and they are to sell the property *de novo* with proclamation.

Where the court sells property belonging to orphans, the obligation of the warranty rests upon the orphans.

11. If the court made proclamation properly, investigated thoroughly, and made the appraisal painstakingly, their sale is valid, even though they erred and sold what is worth 100 zuz for 200 or 200 for 100. But if they did not investigate in making the appraisal and did not draw up a writ of inquest attesting the painstaking nature of the appraisal and the proclamation, and they erred, their sale is void, if they overestimated the property by one sixth or underestimated it by one sixth; by less than one sixth it is valid.

Similarly, if they sold landed property under circumstances in which proclamation is not necessary and they erred, underestimating or overestimating by one sixth, their sale is void, even though they made proclamation. If they erred by less than one sixth, their sale is valid, even though they made no proclamation, proclamation being unnecessary under the circumstances.

What are the circumstances in which proclamation is not necessary? When landed property is sold for burial expenses, for the maintenance of the decedent's wife and daughters, or for the king's portion. Proclamation is not required in these circumstances because the matter is urgent. Similarly, if the court sold things that do not require proclamation and erred by one sixth, their sale is void; by less than one sixth it is valid.

Following are the things that do not require proclamation: a. Bondmen; b. Writings obligatory; c. Movables. Bondmen—lest they hear and escape; writings obligatory and movables—lest they be stolen. These are therefore sold immediately upon being appraised by the court. But if there is a market near the locality, they are to be brought to the market.

CHAPTER XIII

1. If a creditor holding a writing comes to seek satisfaction of the debt in the absence of the debtor, the court, if it can do so, sends a messenger to notify the debtor and to summon him to stand suit. But if the court cannot notify him speedily, the creditor is ordered to swear and allowed to take of the debtor's property, landed and movable, the possibility that the debtor is in possession of an acquittance being disregarded. This rule is an enactment of the Sages. It was designed to deter people from taking other people's money, going forth and settling in another province, with the result that the door would be closed to would-be borrowers.

2. Before a creditor may obtain satisfaction of his debt in the absence of the debtor, he must produce proof as to the following three matters: 1. that the writing is authentic; 2. that the debtor is in another province and is not available to stand suit; 3. that the property out of which he seeks satisfaction belongs to the debtor.

3. If a creditor holding a pledge comes to court and says, "This pledge belongs to such a one, and I wish to sell it and obtain therefrom the satisfaction of a debt which he owes me," the court need not say to the creditor, "Wait until the debtor comes and presents his plea," since the creditor, if he so wished, could say, "The thing is mine by purchase." He is, however, advised to sell the pledge

in the presence of witnesses in order that the debtor may know for how much it was sold.

Similarly, if a man lent money to his fellow on a pledge (and the debtor and the creditor died, whether the debtor predeceased the creditor or the creditor predeceased the debtor), he swears while holding a sacred object and takes what he claims, as do all those who swear and take what they claim, since he is seeking to obtain satisfaction from a thing in his possession with regard to which he could say, "It is mine by purchase." And why does he not swear the informal, instead of the formal, oath? Because he does not swear with regard to the pledge itself but with regard to the money he is claiming. If he were to say with regard to the pledge itself, "You sold it to me," or "You gave it to me by way of a gift," he would be required to swear the informal oath only and would be quit. But if there were witnesses who knew that the thing had been pledged but did not know for how much it had been pledged, he would be able to take what he claims is owing to him only after swearing the formal oath. Now that there are no witnesses he is similarly believed only after swearing the formal oath when he says, "So much is owing to me on the pledge," although he could say, "The thing is mine by purchase." For the inference of credibility is not resorted to to acquit one of an oath, but only to acquit one of paying money or surrendering property to another, as in this case, the pledgee, having the inference of credibility in his favor, is not required to surrender the pledge until he receives what he claims.

4. If a man lent money to his fellow on a pledge, and the pledge was lost or stolen without force—in which case the lender is liable for the value of the pledge as hereinabove stated—and the lender says, "I lent you a sela' on the pledge, and it was worth two denar," while the borrower says, "You lent me a sela' on it, and it was worth a sela'," the lender swears first the bailee's oath that the pledge is not in his possession, and then the borrower swears the informal oath that the value of the pledge was equal to the amount of the loan and is quit.

If the lender says, "I lent you a sela' on the pledge, and it was worth only a shekel," while the borrower says, "You lent me a sela' on it, and it was worth three denar," the lender swears first that it is not in his possession, and then the borrower, having made a partial admission, swears as to the value of the pledge and pays the one denar.

If the borrower says, "You lent me a sela' on the pledge, and it was worth two sela'," while the lender says, " I lent you a sela' on it, and it was worth a sela'," the lender swears that the pledge is not in his possession and includes in his oath an asseveration that the value of the pledge was equal to the amount of the loan.

If the borrower says, "You lent me a sela' on the pledge, and it was worth two sela'," while the lender says, "I do not know what its value was," the lender swears that the pledge is not in his possession, including in his oath an asseveration that he has no knowledge that it was worth even one pěruṭah more than the amount of the debt, and is quit, since he does not admit that he is liable in anything to the borrower.

But if the lender says, "I know that the pledge was worth more than the amount of the loan, but I do not know how much more," he pays all the borrower claims and is not entitled to subject the borrower to an oath. This is like the case where one litigant demands from the other 100 zuz and the other says, "That I owe you 50 zuz I know, but whether or not I owe you 50 more I do not know," in which case the party making the partial admission is subject to an oath but is unable to swear and must therefore pay, as hereinafter stated. But the lender may have the anathema proclaimed generally against him who makes a false claim.

5. If a man lent money to his fellow, fixing a time for repayment, he may not demand repayment before the end of the term, even though ḳinyan was not performed with regard to the term, regardless of whether it was an oral loan or a loan on a writing, a loan secured by a pledge or one not so secured, and of whether or not the debtor or the creditor died after the loan was made.

A loan in which no time of repayment is specified, whether

oral or on a writing, whether secured by a pledge or not, is made for 30 days.

If the lender stipulated that he may make demand at any time, he may do so even on the day the loan is made, because every stipulation in matters pecuniary is valid.

6. If the lender says, "Today is the end of the term I fixed for repayment," and the borrower says, "You fixed the time of repayment for 10 days hence," the borrower swears the informal oath—or the Pentateuchal oath, if there is one witness testifying that today is the end of the term—just as in the case of all other pleas. If the lender says that only five days of the term still remain, and the borrower says that 10 days still remain, we say to the lender, "Wait to the end of the five days when the borrower will be made to swear that five more days remain."

7. If the loan was made on a writing and the borrower pleads, "You fixed a specific time for repayment," it seems to me that the lender should swear the informal oath that he did not fix a specific time and should be entitled to receive payment immediately.

8. Demand for repayment of a loan may be made in any place. How is this to be understood? If a man lent money to his fellow in an inhabited place and made demand in the desert, the borrower may not dismiss him, but is bound to pay wherever the lender makes demand. But if the borrower offers to make payment in the desert the choice lies with the lender; if he wishes he accepts payment, and if not, he may say to the borrower, "I will not accept payment save in an inhabited place, just as I gave you the money in an inhabited place," and the money is to remain with the borrower until he pays the lender in an inhabited place.

CHAPTER XIV

1. He who *impairs* his writing by admitting receipt of partial payment, or holds a writing which is declared by one witness to have been discharged, or seeks to obtain satisfaction in the ab-

sence of the debtor, or seizes the debtor's property in the hands of a purchaser, or seeks to obtain satisfaction from the debtor's heir, whether minor or adult, may not obtain satisfaction save after taking a quasi-Pentateuchal oath. When he makes demand, he is told, "Take an oath and then you will receive what you claim." If, however, the debt had a specific date of maturity, and the lender made demand within the term, he may obtain satisfaction without previously taking an oath, and if the term was past, he may not collect save after taking an oath.

2. Where one demands of his fellow payment of a debt, and the borrower claims to have paid the writing, in whole or in part, while the owner of the writing says, "You have not paid anything on the writing," we say to the borrower, "Pay him what he claims." However, if the borrower says, "Let him first swear that I have not paid him and then he will receive what he claims," the lender is made to swear while holding a sacred object that the borrower has not paid him anything, or that he has paid him only so much, and he receives what he claims. But if the lender is a scholar the court will refuse to subject him to an oath.

3. Where one produces a confirmed writing, and the borrower pleads that the writing is forged and that he never wrote it, or that the indebtedness represents usury or quasi usury, or that the writing was made on trust, or that he wrote the writing intending to borrow on it but did not borrow—to state it generally, where the borrower pleads a plea which, if admitted by the lender, would render the writing void, and the lender stands on his writing, saying that the borrower's plea is false, and the borrower says, "Let him swear and he will receive what he claims"—there is a division of opinion among the Geonim as to what the rule should be. There is one authority who has taught that the lender must swear a quasi-Pentateuchal oath, such as he would be required to swear if the borrower pleaded that he had paid the debt. But my teachers have taught that the lender must swear only in the case where the borrower pleads that he discharged the writing—since the borrower admits the validity of the writing and since a writing is de-

signed to be paid—but in all of the aforementioned pleas the borrower will not be heard to avoid a confirmed writing. He must discharge the writing and then let him make a claim against the lender for as much as he desires, and if the lender will admit the claim, he will return what he received, and if he will deny it, he will have to swear the informal oath. And to this my own opinion inclines.

4. Where one produces a writing obligatory against his fellow, and the lender says, "I have not been paid anything on the writing," while the borrower says, "I have paid half of the amount," and witnesses testify that he has paid the entire amount, the borrower swears and pays half of the amount, since he has made a partial admission. He is not to be likened to one who restored lost property to its owner, because when he made the partial admission, he did so out of fear on account of the writing. The one half of the amount which the borrower admits is owing to the lender may be collected from the borrower's free property only, since purchasers of the borrower's property may say, "We stand upon the testimony of the witnesses who declared this writing to have been discharged in full."

5. Where one produces a writing obligatory which he is unable to have confirmed and the borrower says, "It is true that I wrote this writing but I paid it," or "It was made on trust," or "I wrote it intending to borrow money on it but did not borrow," and the like, he is believed, and he swears the informal oath and is quit, since the writing was confirmed but by the mouth of the borrower, who could have pleaded "No such things ever occurred." But if afterward the lender had the writing confirmed by a court, it is to be treated like all other writings.

6. Where one produces a confirmed writing, and the borrower says, "The writing is forged; I never wrote it," or "The writing was made on trust," while the lender says, "What you say is so, but I had another writing which was valid and which was lost," the lender does not collect anything on the writing—although it was

he himself who invalidated the writing which had been confirmed by a court and with regard to which he could have pleaded that it was not forged—the writing being considered like a potsherd.

7. A writing on which money was borrowed once and which was later discharged may not be used again for borrowing money, because the lien which it imports has already been canceled and it has become like a potsherd.

8. Where one produces a confirmed writing obligatory against his fellow, and the borrower says, "Did I not pay you the debt?" while the lender says, "What you say is so, but I returned the money to you by way of a second loan," the writing is void and considered like a potsherd. But if the lender says, "I returned the money to you and asked that it be exchanged, because it did not consist of good coin," the writing is not void and the lien which it imports remains valid.

9. Where one produces a confirmed writing obligatory for a mina against his fellow, and the borrower says, "Did I not pay you the debt in the presence of such a one and such a one," and the witnesses named come and testify that he paid him but that when making the payment, he made no mention of the writing, and the lender says, "It is true that you paid me, but the payment was made on account of another debt which you owed me," the writing is void.

This applies only where the witnesses testify that the borrower gave the lender the money by way of payment of a loan. But if they saw the borrower give money to the lender and did not know whether it was given by way of payment of a loan, by way of a deposit, or by way of a gift, then, if the lender says, *"No such things ever occurred,"* he is a proven liar and the writing is void, and if he says, "The money was given to me by way of payment of another debt," he is believed, and he swears and takes what is contained in the writing. Seeing that the borrower did not say in the presence of the witnesses that he was paying a debt, the lender is believed when he says that the money was paid on account of a debt other than the one contained in the writing, since he could say, "He gave me the money by way of a gift."

If the borrower says, "Does not this writing obligatory repre-sent the purchase price of an ox I purchased from you, and did you not collect out of the money that was realized from the sale of the meat?" while the lender says, "What you say is so, but I col-lected the money on account of another debt which you owed me," the writing is void, since the lender himself admits that the debt represents the purchase price of the ox and that he was paid out of the money realized from the sale of the meat. The creditor swears the informal oath and is quit, even though there are no witnesses testifying that he paid out of the money realized from the sale of the meat. And so it is in all similar cases.

10. Where one produces a writing obligatory attested by one witness, and the borrower pleads, "I have paid it," the borrower is liable to an oath but is unable to swear, and must therefore pay. If the borrower says, "Let him swear that I did not pay him," the lender must swear, for even where the writing is attested by two witnesses, and the borrower says, "Let him swear that I did not pay him," the lender is required to swear, as hereinabove stated.

11. Similarly, my teachers have taught, where one denies in court the receipt of an oral loan and one witness comes and testifies that he received the loan, he must take the Pentateuchal oath. But if he retracts and says, "It is true that I borrowed the money, but I paid it," or "He pardoned me the debt," or "He owes me money on another account," he is liable to an oath but is unable to swear, and must therefore pay.

12. Where one pleads that he paid a writing obligatory and says, "Let the lender swear and take what he claims," we say to him, "Bring the money," and then he will swear and take what he claims. If he has nothing with which to pay, he is made to swear, in accordance with the enactment of the Geonim, that he has noth-ing. And when he comes into money, he must pay the debt to his creditor, after the creditor swears that he was not paid.

13. If a man had a debt on a writing against his fellow, and the writing was lost but the witnesses are still available, and the borrower pleads that he paid the debt, he swears the informal oath and is quit, even though ķinyan was performed at the time the loan was made.

Moreover, my teachers have taught, even if the debt had a specified date of maturity which is not yet past, the borrower is believed and he swears the informal oath that he paid the debt and is quit. Since a writing was drawn up and given to the lender, and he does not have it in his hands, while the borrower pleads that he paid, a suspicion may be entertained that the borrower paid the debt and that therefore the writing was torn or burned up.

My teachers have further taught that even if the writing is in the hands of a third party, and the borrower pleads, "I dropped it after I paid it," he swears the informal oath and is quit, even though the date of maturity is not yet past, because, the writing not being in the hands of the lender, there is no presumption of nonpayment.

14. Where the lender and the borrower both hold the writing obligatory, and the lender says, "It is mine, and I took it out in order to obtain payment thereof from you," while the borrower says, "I have paid it, and after having obtained possession thereof, I dropped it," each one of them swears that he is entitled to no less than one half of the amount stated in the writing, and the borrower pays to the lender half of the amount stated in the writing, provided the lender is able to have the writing confirmed. But if the lender is unable to have the writing confirmed, the borrower swears the informal oath that he paid the debt and is quit.

15. If the plaintiff said to the defendant, "You owe me a mina," and the defendant said, "I do not owe you anything," or "I paid you what I owed you," whereupon the plaintiff said, "Swear the informal oath," to which the defendant replied, "You have a writing obligatory against me and you wish to subject me to an oath first and then you will produce the discharged writing and collect thereon," we say to the plaintiff, "Produce the writing." If the plaintiff says, "I never had a writing against him," or "I had a

writing and lost it," we say to him—so my teachers have taught—
"Annul every writing you may have ever had against him up to
the present time and then you will subject him to the informal
oath," or "Go and search until you find the writing."

CHAPTER XV

1. If a man lent money to his fellow in the presence of witnesses
and said to him, "Do not pay me save in the presence of witnesses,"
the borrower must pay in the presence of witnesses, whether the
lender told him so at the time he made the loan or afterward.

If the borrower said, "I did as you told me and I paid you in the
presence of such a one and such a one who have since departed
overseas or died," he is believed and he swears the informal oath
and is quit.

Similarly, if the lender said, "Do not pay me save in the presence
of scholars or physicians," and the borrower says, "I paid you in
the presence of such witnesses and they departed overseas or died,"
he is believed and he swears the informal oath and is quit. But if the
lender said to the borrower, "Do not pay me save in the presence
of such a one and such a one," and the borrower says, "I paid you
in the presence of other witnesses who have since died or departed
overseas," he is not believed. For it was to forestall such a plea that
the lender stipulated with the borrower, saying, "Do not pay me
save in the presence of Reuben and Simeon," who he knew
were going to stay in the locality where he was, in order that the
borrower should not be able to dismiss him by saying that he paid
in the presence of other witnesses who have since departed.

2. There are versions of the Gemara in which it is written: "If
a man said to his fellow, 'Do not pay me save in the presence of
witnesses,' and the borrower says, 'I paid you in the presence of
such a one and such a one who have since departed overseas,' he is
not believed." This is a scribe's error which misled those who have
taught in accordance with these books. I have investigated the old
versions and found therein that the reading is "He *is believed.*"

There has come into my hands in Egypt part of an old Gemara written on parchments, as they were wont to write approximately 500 years ago, and I have found two specimens of this proposition in these parchments, in both of which it is written, "And if he said, 'I paid before such a one and such a one who have since departed overseas,' he is believed."

Because of a similar error which occurs in some of the books, some of the Geonim have taught that if the lender said to the borrower, "Do not pay me save in the presence of such a one and such a one," and he paid him in the presence of others, he is not believed, even though he produces the witnesses in whose presence he paid. This too is a great error, the true rule being that if witnesses came and testified that the borrower paid the lender in their presence, the borrower is quit, and there is no room for any misgivings. This teaching of the Geonim, too, is based upon their books in which it is written with regard to one who said to his fellow, " 'Pay me in the presence of witnesses who are versed in legal propositions,' and he went and paid him in the presence of witnesses [who were not versed in legal propositions]." This too is a scribe's error, the version I have found in the parchments reading, "He went and paid him in privacy."

The above teaching is therefore contrary to the rule as it appears in the Gemara, where the reading is corrected in the manner stated above. Furthermore, this rule finds support in reason. For, what could the borrower do? The lender said to him, "Do not pay me save in the presence of witnesses," and he paid him in the presence of witnesses. Is he supposed to keep the witnesses in jail all their days so as to prevent them from departing? Again, if they died what should he do? Should he keep paying time and again forever until he is able to produce witnesses? If it were so, the testimony would become like testimony incorporated in a writing, and the loan in this case, where the lender said to the borrower, "Do not pay me save in the presence of witnesses," would be converted into a loan on a writing, something which was not contemplated by anyone. But certainly if the lender said, "Pay me in the presence of such a one and such a one," it is the borrower himself who causes loss to himself when he pays in the presence of others, and they depart. If, however, the witnesses in whose presence payment was made came and testified thereto, there is no room for any misgivings. Such is the rule according to which judgments should be rendered and which should be taught.

3. If the lender stipulated with the borrower that he should at all times be believed if he should say that he did not receive payment, the lender takes what he claims without an oath, even though the borrower pleads that he has paid. But if the borrower produces witnesses of payment the lender takes nothing.

4. If the borrower stipulated that the lender should be believed against him even as two witnesses, the lender collects without an oath, even though the borrower produces witnesses of payment, since the borrower gave the lender the credence accorded to two witnesses. Even if the borrower produces 100 witnesses who testify to payment, or to payment in their presence, the lender collects without an oath, two witnesses being like 100 witnesses.

If, however, the borrower said to the lender, "You shall be believed against me even as three witnesses," and the borrower paid him in the presence of four witnesses the debt is discharged, since the borrower referred to a specific number of witnesses.

If one has given the lender the credence accorded to two witnesses, what is his remedy? Let him cut up the writing when making payment, or let him have the lender make acknowledgment that he has canceled every writing he may have against the borrower, or let him have the lender make acknowledgment in the absence of the borrower that he has received payment of every debt the borrower ever owed him.

5. If the borrower paid the debt and the lender claimed that he had not been paid and the borrower paid him a second time by reason of the stipulation, the borrower may sue the lender, saying to him, "You owe me so much because I paid you twice." If the

lender confesses, he is to restore the excess payment, and if he denies, he is to swear the informal oath to the effect that the borrower paid him only once. And so it is in all similar cases.

6. If the borrower stipulated that he should be believed whenever he should say, "I have paid the debt," the lender may not collect on the writing either from the borrower's heir or from purchasers of the borrower's property. Even if the borrower says, "I have not paid the debt," the lender on such a writing may not *seize* property which formerly belonged to the borrower and is in the hands of purchasers from the borrower, there being a possibility that lender and borrower entered into a conspiracy against the purchaser's interests.

If the borrower on such a writing pleads, "I have paid part of the debt," and the lender says, "He has paid nothing," the borrower pays the part he confesses as owing and swears the informal oath as to the balance, since the lender has given him credence. And if he stipulated that he should be believed without an informal oath, he does not swear at all.

7. If the lender stipulated that he should collect without an oath, he collects from the borrower without an oath. But if he comes to collect from the borrower's heirs, he must swear before he collects. If, however, he stipulated that he should also collect from the heirs without an oath, he collects without an oath.

Similarly, if he stipulated that he should collect from the *best* of the borrower's property, he collects from such property, even from the borrower's heirs, for every stipulation with respect to matters pecuniary is valid. But if he comes to collect from a purchaser of the borrower's property, he may not seize the property save by an oath, since the borrower may not make a stipulation which will result in a pecuniary loss to his fellow.

CHAPTER XVI

1. The debt is at the borrower's risk until he has paid it into the hands of the lender or of the lender's messenger. If the lender said

to the borrower, "Throw the debt to me and be quit," and the borrower threw it, and it was lost or consumed by fire before it reached the lender's hands, the borrower is quit.

If the lender said, "Throw the debt to me as though it was a bill of divorce," then, if the money lodged nearer to the borrower it is still at his risk, and if nearer to the lender, the borrower is quit; and if it was equidistant from the lender and the borrower, and it was lost or stolen, the borrower pays one half thereof.

2. If Reuben who owed a mina to Simeon said to Levi, "Carry to Simeon this mina that I owe him," and thereafter he wished to retract, he may not do so, although he bears the risk of the loss of the mina until it reaches Simeon. If Levi returned the mina to Reuben, both of them bear the risk of its loss until the entire debt reaches Simeon's hands.

3. If Reuben owed Simeon a mina, and Simeon said to Reuben, "Give to Levi the mina you owe me," all three parties being present and Levi accepting, and it turned out that Reuben was poor and had no mina which Levi could collect, Levi may retract and collect his debt from Simeon, because he misled him. But if Levi knew that Reuben was poor, or if Reuben was rich then and became poor later, Levi may not retract, since he accepted.

If Levi claims that Reuben was poor and that Simeon misled him, while Simeon claims that Reuben was rich at the time and became poor later, it seems to me that Simeon must produce proof before he may be acquitted of the debt he owed to Levi. For Simeon's position is no better than it would be if he had an instrument of acquittance in his hands, in which case he would be told, "Have the instrument confirmed and you will be quit."

4. We have already stated in the Law of Purchase and Sale that if Reuben, who had nothing in the hands of Simeon and owed a mina to Levi, gave Levi an order on Simeon, the transaction is not binding, even though the order was given in the presence of all three parties. If Simeon so wishes, he may refuse to give the mina to Levi; but if he gave it to him, he may collect it from Reuben,

since he gave it to Levi upon Reuben's order. Similarly, if Levi wishes to retract and says, "I do not wish to collect from Simeon," he may do so and may insist upon collecting from Reuben. Even if he has already been paid part of the debt by Simeon, he may retract and insist upon collecting the balance from Reuben.

5. If a shopkeeper, who had been accustomed to supply to a householder all his needs on credit out of his shop, deferring payment until a cumulative account was made, was told by the householder, "Give a sela' to my workers or a mina to my creditor and I will reimburse you," and the shopkeeper says, "I disbursed the money as you told me," while the worker, or the creditor, says, "I did not receive the money," the worker, or the creditor, swears and takes his debt from the householder, and the shopkeeper also swears and takes from the householder what he claims to have disbursed to the worker, or to the creditor, since he was told by the householder to disburse the money.

The worker, or the creditor, swears in the shopkeeper's presence, and the shopkeeper swears in the worker's, or the creditor's, presence, in order that each may be abashed by the presence of the other. And so it is in all similar cases. This oath is administered by virtue of an enactment of the Sages and the party taking it must hold a sacred object while it is being administered, because it is an oath taken in support of a demand.

If, therefore, the shopkeeper died, the creditor takes without an oath, or if the worker or the creditor died, the shopkeeper takes without an oath, since the householder is required to make payment only once and, consequently, does not lose anything.

6. If the shopkeeper says to the householder, "You told me to disburse a mina to such a one," or "You ordered me to disburse a mina to such a one, if he should come and ask for it," and the householder denies it, the latter swears the informal oath and is quit and the shopkeeper sues the one to whom he made the disbursement.

Similarly, if the shopkeeper says to the householder, whose needs he has been accustomed to supply on credit, "There is an entry in my ledger that you owe me a mina," and the householder says, "I do not know," the latter swears the informal oath and is quit, in accordance with the rule which applies to all other claims made by a man against his fellow, the special enactment of the Sages not being applicable to such a case.

7. If Reuben produces a writing obligatory made by Simeon to Levi and claims that Levi transferred it to him by writing and delivery but that the deed of transfer was lost, or if Reuben claims that Levi transferred to him the writing obligatory by *transfer adjunct* to a transfer of land, he collects from Simeon the debt evidenced by the writing, because he holds the writing.

If Simeon claims to have paid the debt to Levi and says, "Let Levi swear to me," he must swear before Reuben may collect the debt.

If Levi admits receipt of payment from Simeon, he must pay to Reuben, and if he claims that he did not sell or give the writing obligatory to Reuben, he swears the informal oath and is quit.

8. If a depositary who was holding a writing obligatory in escrow produced the writing in court and said, "This writing has been discharged," he is believed, even though the writing be confirmed, since he could have burnt or torn the writing, had he wished to do so.

Similarly, if the depositary died and a note stating that the writing obligatory, which he was holding in escrow, had been discharged was found among his effects, it is deemed discharged, even though the note was not attested by witnesses. But if such a note was found in the lender's possession, even if it was written in his own handwriting, it is deemed to have been written in a manner not to be taken seriously.

9. If the note was attested by witnesses and a confirmation of their signatures appears thereon, the writing obligatory is deemed discharged. But if there is no confirmation on the note, the witnesses whose signatures appear thereon are to be examined, and

if they have no knowledge that the bond has been discharged, or if they are not available, the note of acquittance is of no effect, since it was found in the possession of the lender or of his heirs.

10. If the writing obligatory was found among the lender's discharged bonds it is deemed discharged, even though the writing of acquittance referring to it was not attested by witnesses. Similarly, if a notation appears on the body of the bond, whether on its face or on its back or even at its end, reading, "This bond has been discharged," or "So much has been paid on it," the notation is given effect, even though it is not attested by witnesses and even though it, together with the writing obligatory upon which it appears, was found in the possession of the lender, because it is assumed that he would not have made the notation on the body of the writing obligatory had he not been paid.

11. If a man finds a writing among his effects and does not know what its status is it is to remain until Elijah comes.

12. If a man said to his sons, "One of my writings obligatory has been paid, but I do not know which one it is," all his writings obligatory are deemed discharged. If, however, among these writings there are two, one in a larger sum and one in a smaller sum, made by the same debtor, the larger one is deemed discharged and the smaller one is deemed undischarged.

If a man said to his fellow, "A writing obligatory which I have against you has been discharged," and he happens to have against him two such writings, one in a larger sum and one in a smaller sum, the larger one is deemed discharged and the smaller one is deemed undischarged. If he said, "The indebtedness that I have against you is discharged," all the writings obligatory he has against him are deemed discharged.

CHAPTER XVII

1. If the creditor died and his heir comes to demand from the debtor the debt on the bond outstanding against him and the

debtor says, "I have paid the debt to your father," while the heir says, "I do not know," we say to the debtor, "Arise and pay him." If the debtor says, "Let him swear," the heir must swear while holding a sacred object saying, "Our father did not leave word to us through another, nor did he tell us by his own mouth, nor did we find written among his writings that this bond had been paid," whereupon he collects.

2. If the debtor died after the creditor's death and the creditor's heir comes and makes demand upon the debtor's heir, he may not collect save by an oath. We say to him, "First swear thus: 'Our father did not leave word to us, nor did he tell us, nor did we find written among his effects that this bond had been paid.' " Even if the creditor's heir was an infant in the cradle when his ancestor died, he swears and takes. If the creditor made a deathbed declaration that the bond had not been paid, his heir collects without an oath, even from the debtor's heir.

3. If the debtor died first and then the creditor died the creditor's heirs take nothing from the debtor's heirs. For at the time the debtor died the creditor became liable to an oath before he could collect the debt, as we have stated, and now that the creditor is dead the heirs cannot succeed him to the oath, because they cannot swear that their father had not been paid anything. If, however, the judge, in disregard of this rule, administered an oath to the creditor's heirs and they collected the debt, it may not be reclaimed from them.

Therefore, when the orphans of the creditor come to collect on a bond from the orphans of the debtor who predeceased the creditor, the bond is neither cut up nor is recovery had on it. Recovery is not had on it because a man's children cannot succeed him to an oath, as we have stated; and it is not cut up because another judge may some day render judgment and cause recovery to be had on it.

4. Even if there was a surety on the bond and the debtor predeceased the creditor, the creditor's heirs may not collect from the

surety. For if we were to say that the heirs could collect from a surety, the surety would, in his turn, collect from the debtor's heirs.

5. The above rule is not to be extended to similar cases by analogy. Thus, if a creditor impaired his bond, by admitting partial payment thereof, and died, his heirs swear, "Our father did not leave word to us, nor did he tell us, nor did we find written among his effects that this bond had been fully paid," and they collect the balance of the debt either from the debtor or from his heirs, although their father would not have been able to collect without an oath had he himself sued on the bond.

6. If the creditor's heirs come to collect from the debtor's heirs and the latter say, "Our fathers said to us, 'I did not borrow this money represented by this debt,'" the creditor's heirs collect without an oath, because he who says, "I did not borrow," is deemed to have said "I did not pay." Similarly, if the creditor comes to collect from the debtor's heirs and they say, "Our father said to us, 'I did not borrow this money represented by this debt,'" the creditor collects without an oath even though the creditor stipulated in the bond that the debtor should be believed if he should say, "I have paid," because he who says, "I did not borrow," is deemed to have said, "I did not pay."

7. If the creditor's heirs come to collect from the debtor on a bond which contains a stipulation giving credence to the debtor whenever he should say, "I have paid," the debtor swears the informal oath that he has paid the bond and is quit, even though the bond does not contain the phrase "And you shall be believed as against my heirs," because the condition of credence is of the very essence of the bond which was made on this condition.

If the creditor stipulated that the debtor should be believed without any oath whatsoever the debtor does not swear, even to the creditor's heirs.

8. If an heir who is a minor has a bond which he inherited from his father, and a release of the debt is produced for the first time after the creditor's death, the bond is neither canceled nor is re-

covery had on it until the orphan has reached majority, because the debtor's failure to produce the release during the creditor's lifetime gives rise to a suspicion that the release may have been forged.

9. If a man produces against his fellow a bond which was written in Babylon, he collects in Babylonian coin; if it was written in the land of Israel he collects in the coin current in the land of Israel. This rule does not apply in the case of a ketubbah. If the bond does not contain any place name and the creditor produces it in Babylon, he collects in Babylonian coin; if he produces it in the land of Israel he collects in the coin current in the land of Israel.

If the creditor demands payment in the coin of the place where he produces the bond and the debtor claims that the money he owes him is payable in a coin of smaller value, the creditor swears and takes what he claims. If the bond is for so many kesep, without further specification, the debtor may pay in any coin coming under that description.

From the above it may be deduced that a bond which does not contain the name of the place in which it was written is valid in every respect. The same is true of a bond which does not contain any mention of the time at which it was written. Such a bond is likewise valid, although it represents testimony incapable of refutation by *alibi testimony;* for in civil suits the court does not subject the witnesses to a strict inquiry and examination, as hereinafter stated, in order not to shut the door against would-be borrowers.

Therefore, a post-dated bond is valid, even though the testimony of the witnesses attesting it is incapable of refutation by alibi testimony, as will be stated in the proper place.

CHAPTER XVIII

1. If a man lent money to his fellow, without specification as to security for the loan, all of the debtor's property stands back of and is surety for the debt. Therefore, when the creditor comes to collect the debt he makes demand upon the debtor in the first instance.

If he finds property in his possession, whether movables or land, he collects therefrom with the debtor's consent, and if the debtor refuses to let him collect the court causes him to collect.

If the property in the possession of the debtor does not suffice to pay the full amount of the bond the creditor may collect from the landed property which once belonged to the debtor, even though it has been sold or transferred by way of gift to others. Since the debtor sold the property or transferred it by way of gift after he became obligated for the debt, the creditor may evict the purchasers or donees therefrom. He who obtains satisfaction of his debt in this manner is called a seizor.

This applies only to land which the debtor owned at the time when he borrowed the money, but property which he acquired after he borrowed the money and which, consequently, did not become obligated for the debt, the creditor may not seize. If, however, the creditor stipulated that all the property which the debtor should ever acquire should be obligated for the payment of the debt, and the debtor acquired property after he borrowed the money and then sold it, or transferred it by way of gift, the creditor may seize it.

2. All these rules apply only to land, but movables are not obligated for the payment of debts. Even the movables which the debtor had at the time when he borrowed the money and which he sold thereafter are not subject to seizure by the creditor.

If, however, the debtor conveyed to the creditor a security title to all of his movables by a transfer adjunct to the conveyance of such title to his land, the creditor may seize such movables, provided the debtor wrote in the bond, "I have given you title to my movables together with, and adjunct to, my land, not as an 'asmakta and not as a mere form of bonds."

Similarly, if the debtor wrote in his bond, "All property that I may acquire in the future, whether landed or movable, is obligated to you for the payment of the debt and title to the movables is hereby transferred to you together with, and adjunct to, my land as security for payment, not as an 'asmakta and not as a mere form of bonds," the creditor may seize even such movables as were acquired by the debtor after he borrowed the money, since every stipulation in matters pecuniary is valid.

3. If a man hypothecated his field to his creditor or to his wife for her kĕṭubbah—that is, if he wrote in the bond or in the kĕṭubbah, "From this field you shall collect"—and the field was struck by a blast, the creditor or the wife may collect from other property and may also seize such other property.

If the debtor stipulated with the creditor that the latter was to have no satisfaction of the debt except from the hypothecated field, the creditor may not collect the debt from other property.

Similarly, if the debtor specified that there was to be no obligation resting upon his property, the creditor may never collect from alienated property.

4. If a man hypothecated his field to his creditor or to his wife for her kĕṭubbah and thereafter sold it, it is sold; and when the time comes for the creditor to collect his debt he may seize the field, if he finds no free property belonging to the debtor. This applies only if the debtor sold the field temporarily, for as long as the creditor does not enforce the hypothec, but if he sold it in perpetuity it is not sold.

5. If a man hypothecated his bondman and thereafter sold him, the vendor's creditor may seize the bondman because the hypothecation of a bondman has publicity. But if a man hypothecated his ox and thereafter sold it, his creditor may not seize the ox. And so it is in the case of other movables because the hypothecation of movables does not have publicity.

6. If a master hypothecated his bondman and thereafter emancipated him the bondman is free, even though the bond contained a clause reading, "You shall have no satisfaction of your debt except from this bondman." The same rule obtains if the master hypothecated his bondman and thereafter dedicated him to the sanctuary because leavened matter, emancipation, and dedication to the sanctuary, break an obligation resting upon a person's

property. The creditor in such case is entitled to collect the amount of the debt from the debtor, who must execute a new bond for the amount of the debt, the obligation of which bond attaches to the debtor's property only from the date thereof.

And why is the debtor bound to pay? Because he indirectly caused a pecuniary loss to his fellow, and he who indirectly causes damage must pay, as we have stated in the proper place.

For the promotion of the general welfare the bondman's second master is compelled to emancipate him in order that he should not be able to say, when finding him in the market, "You are my bondman."

7. If a man dedicated his property to the sanctuary his creditor may not seize it from the sanctuary, because dedication to the sanctuary breaks an obligation resting upon property.

When the property is redeemed from the sanctuary an estimate is made of how much a man would be willing to pay for such property in order to be able to turn it over to a creditor for his debt or to a woman for her dower. Therefore, when the property has been redeemed and has become profane property in the hands of the purchaser from the sanctuary, the creditor, or the woman, may come and seize it for the debt, or for the kĕṭubbah, as we have stated in the Laws Concerning Valuations.

8. If a creditor comes to seize property in the hands of a purchaser from the debtor, such purchaser may prevent the creditor from seizing the property by paying him its value in money. The purchaser, in turn, may make demand upon the seller for the money so paid. If, however, the debtor hypothecated the property, the purchaser from the debtor may not prevent the creditor from seizing the property by paying him its value in money.

9. If Reuben who owed Simeon 200 zuz had two fields and sold one of them to Levi for a 100 zuz and then sold him the other one for another 100 zuz, and Simeon came and seized one of the fields for 100 zuz, representing part of his debt, and then came to seize the other field for the other 100 zuz, representing the balance

of his debt, and Levi tendered to him 200 zuz and said, "If you wish to have this field you have already seized appraised at 200 zuz, the amount of your debt, it is well, but if not take 200 zuz, the amount of your debt, and be thereby removed," Levi is within his rights. If Simeon chooses to remain in possession of the one field, Levi may make demand upon Reuben for 100 zuz only, even though Simeon accepted the field for 200 zuz.

10. If Reuben died and left a field worth 100 zuz and Simeon came and seized it and Reuben's orphans gave Simeon 100 zuz which they realized from the movables that their father left to them and removed him from the field, Reuben may again seize the field for the balance of his debt, since by giving Simeon the 100 zuz the orphans who are morally bound to pay their father's debts only performed a meritorious deed. But if the orphans said to Simeon, "We are paying this money for the field you have seized," Simeon may not seize the field again for the balance of his debt.

CHAPTER XIX

1. When the court proceeds to levy execution for a debt they are to levy upon the debtor's land of medium quality. By the rule of the Law a creditor should collect out of property of the poorest quality. For it is written *Thou shalt stand without, and the man to whom thou dost lend shall bring forth the pledge without unto thee* (Deut. 24: 11). What is customary for a man to bring forth? The poorest of his utensils. But the Sages have enacted that the creditor collect out of property of medium quality in order that the door should not be shut against would-be borrowers. This applies only if the creditor comes to seek satisfaction from the debtor himself, but if he comes to seek satisfaction from the debtor's heirs, whether minor or adult, the debt may be satisfied only out of property of the poorest quality.

2. No satisfaction may be had from alienated property, whether the alienation was by way of sale or by way of gift, where free property is available, even if the free property is of the poorest

quality and the alienated property is of medium or best quality. If the free property was struck by a blast the creditor may seize the alienated property, since unusable property is deemed nonexistent.

3. If Reuben sold all of his fields to Simeon and Simeon, in turn, sold one of these fields to Levi and Reuben's creditor came to effect seizure, he may effect it from either Simeon or Levi. This applies only where the field purchased by Levi was of medium quality, but if it was of best or poorest quality the creditor may not seize such field since Levi may say to him, "It was for the purpose of preventing seizure by you that I purchased a field not belonging to the class of property from which the Law makes debts collectible."

Similarly, if Levi purchased property of medium quality, leaving with Simeon other property of medium quality, the creditor may not seize Levi's property since Levi may say to him, "I left room for you to collect your debt."

4. We have already stated that the tortfeasee collects from property of best quality, a lender from property of medium quality, and a woman for her kĕṭubbah from property of poorest quality. If the debtor has property of best and property of poorest quality, the tortfeasee collects from the property of best quality and the lender and the woman collect from the property of poorest quality. If the debtor has property of best and property of medium quality, the tortfeasee collects from the best quality and the lender and the woman from the medium quality. If he has property of poorest and property of medium quality only, the tortfeasee and the lender collect from the property of medium quality and the woman from the property of poorest quality.

5. If the debtor sold all of his property to three parties at one and the same time they all take the debtor's place, so that the tortfeasee effects seizure out of the property of best quality, the lender effects seizure out of the property of medium quality, and the woman effects seizure out of the property of poorest quality. If the debtor sold his property piecemeal and at different times

to three different purchasers, they all effect seizure out of the property in the hands of the last purchaser. If this does not suffice seizure is effected out of the property in the hands of the second from the last purchaser, and if this still does not suffice seizure is effected out of the property in the hands of the third from the last purchaser. This is so even if the last purchaser was the one who purchased property of poorest quality, since the purchaser who preceded him may say to the creditor who comes to effect seizure, "I left room for you to collect your debt."

6. If the debtor sold his several parcels of property to the same purchaser at different times, the purchaser takes the place of the debtor. This applies only where the purchaser purchased the parcel of best quality last. If, however, he purchased the parcel of poorest quality last the creditors of all classes collect from the property of poorest quality, since the purchaser may say to him who comes to collect from the property which he purchased prior to the last purchase, "When I purchased this property I left sufficient other property in the hands of your debtor for you to collect your debt therefrom."

And why is not a creditor of any class, including a woman who comes to collect her dower or a lender who comes to collect his debt, allowed, by virtue of this rule, to collect from the property of best quality, if the purchaser purchased such property last? Because the rule is designed for the benefit of the purchaser, who may therefore say, "I do not wish to have this rule applied, but let each one of you collect from that which is appropriate to the class of his debt."

7. If the debtor sold his several parcels of property to another at different times, selling the property of best quality last, and the purchaser, in his turn, resold the property of poorest and the property of medium quality, leaving to himself property of best quality only, all classes of creditors collect from the property of best quality, since the first purchaser has no other property to which he could refer them. If he sold the property of best quality, leaving to himself the property of medium and the property of poorest

quality, the tortfeasee effects seizure out of the property of best quality in the hands of the second purchaser, and the lender and the woman for her dower, respectively, collect from the property of medium and poorest quality which the first purchaser left to himself.

8. If a man borrowed money from another and then sold some of his property to one party and some to another at different times and the lender gave to the second vendee a writing stating, "I have no lawsuit or claim against you," performing ḳinyan in connection therewith, the lender may not effect seizure out of the property in the hands of the first vendee, since the latter may say to him, "When I purchased this property I left sufficient property in the hands of your debtor for you to collect your debt therefrom, which property is now in the hands of the second vendee who purchased it after I purchased mine and it was you who occasioned a loss to yourself by removing yourself from the property in the hands of the second vendee." The same rule applies to a woman who comes to claim her dower and who gave a similar writing to the second vendee; she lost her dower and cannot effect seizure. But if they gave such a writing to the first vendee they may effect seizure out of the property in the hands of the second vendee.

If the borrower sold his field and the vendee resold it to another vendee and the lender gave to the first vendee a writing stating, "I have no lawsuit or claim against you," performing ḳinyan in connection therewith, the creditor seizes the field from the second vendee, the first vendee seizes it from the creditor by reason of the writing, the second vendee seizes it from the first vendee by reason of the sale, the creditor seizes it again from the second vendee, and so the process is repeated until they effect a compromise among themselves. And so it is also in the case of a woman's dower.

CHAPTER XX

1. If a man has many debts outstanding against him, the creditor whose debt is prior in time is prior in right to obtain satisfaction

from the property in the hands of the debtor himself, or in the hands of his vendees.

If a creditor who is subsequent in time obtained satisfaction before a creditor who is prior in time he is to restore what he took, because he who is prior in time is prior in right.

All this applies only with regard to landed property which the debtor owned at the time when he borrowed the money, but with regard to landed property which he acquired after he borrowed from several creditors, there is no right of priority even though the debtor wrote in the bond which he gave to each creditor, "What I may acquire in the future is obligated to you." All such creditors are equal, and if one of them obtained satisfaction before the others, that which he obtained is rightfully his, even though his debt is subsequent in time to those of the others.

2. If a man borrowed money and wrote in the bond which he gave to the creditor, "What I may acquire in the future is obligated to you," and then he acquired a field, and after he acquired it he borrowed money from another creditor, the field is obligated to the first creditor who is prior in right to obtain satisfaction therefrom. And so it is even if there be 100 creditors.

There is no right of priority in movables. If one of the creditors obtained satisfaction of his debt from movables before other creditors obtained satisfaction of their debts, that which he obtained is rightfully his, even though he is subsequent in time to the other creditors.

If a person other than a creditor seized some of the debtor's movables for the purpose of acquiring a right therein on behalf of one of the creditors, that which he seized does not rightfully belong to such creditor, because he who seizes movables on behalf of a creditor, where there is another debt outstanding against the debtor, does not acquire title on behalf of such creditor; but if there is no other debt outstanding against the debtor he does acquire a right on the creditor's behalf.

Also, if the debtor said to a person other than the creditor, "Acquire a right in this thing on behalf of such a one," such person acquires a right in the thing on behalf of the creditor named by the debtor and the other creditors cannot obtain satisfaction therefrom, since the first creditor on whose behalf it was seized acquired a right therein.

3. If several bonds were dated on the same day or in the same hour—in a place where hours are specified—the creditor who obtained satisfaction first, either from landed property or from movables, acquired a right to what he obtained.

4. If all such creditors come together to obtain satisfaction, or if creditors whose bonds are dated at different times come to obtain satisfaction from movables in which there is no right of priority, or if they come to obtain satisfaction from landed property which the borrower acquired after he borrowed from the last one of them, and there is not enough property for all of the creditors to obtain satisfaction therefrom, the property is divided among them.

How is the division made? If when the available money is divided by the number of creditors, the resulting quotient is equal to, or less than, the amount of the smallest debt, the available money is divided equally among the creditors. If, when all the money were to be divided equally, the creditor with the smallest debt would receive an amount exceeding the amount of his debt, they divide equally only so much of the money as will allow the creditor with the smallest debt to obtain the full amount of his debt, and the balance is divided among the remaining creditors in the same manner. How is this to be understood? If there are three debts outstanding against the debtor, one of 100 zuz, another of 200 zuz, and still another of 700 zuz then, if the amount of available money is 300 zuz, each one of the creditors receives 100 zuz. Similarly, if the amount of the available money is less than 300 zuz, the entire amount is divided equally among the creditors; if it is over 300 zuz they divide 300 equally, the creditor whose debt amounts to 100 zuz is removed from further participation, and the balance is divided between the remaining two creditors in the same manner. How is this to be understood? If the amount of available money is 500 zuz or less, 300 zuz is divided equally among the creditors, the one whose debt amounts to 100 zuz is removed from further participation, and the balance of 200 zuz or less is divided equally between the remaining two creditors. If 600 zuz is available, 300 is divided equally among all the creditors, the creditor whose debt amounts to 100 zuz is removed from further participation, and of the remaining 300 zuz 200 is again divided equally between the remaining two creditors, the creditor whose debt amounts to 200 zuz is removed from further participation, and the balance of 100 zuz is then turned over to the creditor whose debt amounts to 700 zuz, so that in the end he obtains 300 zuz only. And in this manner the division is made between the creditors when they all come at the same time to obtain satisfaction, even if they be 100 in number.

But some of the Geonim have taught that division of available property is made among the creditors in a ratio equal to that of their respective debts.

5. If Reuben and Simeon each have a bond against Levi, and Reuben's bond is dated on the fifth day of Nisan, while Simeon's bond is dated in Nisan without specification of the day, and Levi has a field which does not suffice to satisfy both debts therefrom, Reuben is put in possession of the field because it is possible that Simeon's bond was executed at the end of Nisan. By the same token Simeon cannot effect seizure out of property which was sold by his debtor on or after the first day of the month of Iyyar of the year in which his bond is dated, since the vendee may say to him, "It is possible that your bond was executed on the first day of Nisan, so that there is in Reuben's possession a field which was unencumbered at the time when your bond was executed, from which field you have a right to obtain satisfaction, and let Reuben, whose bond is subsequent in time to yours, come and effect seizure out of the property in my hands." If, therefore, the two creditors executed a power of attorney to each other they may, on every possibility, effect seizure out of property which was sold by the creditor on or after the first day of the month of Iyyar.

The same rule applies where a man sold a field to each of two parties and the deed of conveyance of one of these parties is dated in the fifth day of Nisan, while that of the other is dated in Nisan without specification of the day.

CHAPTER XXI

1. A creditor may obtain satisfaction out of the improvements of the property which accrued while the property was in possession of the debtor's vendee, whether they accrued as a result of expenditures made by such vendee or spontaneously, except that, while in the case of improvements which accrued spontaneously the creditor effects seizure out of the whole of the improvements, in the case of improvements which accrued through expenditures he may obtain satisfaction only out of the half thereof.

How is this to be understood? If Reuben had a debt of 200 zuz against Simeon and Simeon sold a field worth 100 zuz to Levi, who thereafter made expenditures thereon and improved it so that it is worth 200 zuz, Levi may effect seizure out of such field to the extent of 150 zuz, that is the whole of the original value plus one half of the value of the improvements. And if the improvements accrued spontaneously, as where the price of land rose or where trees sprouted forth spontaneously out of the land, the creditor may obtain satisfaction to the full extent of the improvements (Some great Sages have taught that the debtor's vendee is not to be put at a greater disadvantage than a squatter who is entitled to an appraisal of the improvements made by him, though *he has the lower hand*. If, therefore, the vendee improved the field to the extent of 100 zuz, through expenditures amounting to 50 zuz, he should obtain the entire amount of his expenditures plus one half of the excess of the improvements over the expenditures, and the creditor should effect seizure out of the other half of such excess together with the principal. And this teaching is sound in reason and in accordance therewith judgment should be rendered in practice.), and the vendee whose property was seized by the vendor's creditors may, in his turn, obtain satisfaction for his principal from the property of the vendor, even if such property was alienated by the vendor by way of sale or by way of gift, provided that it was so alienated subsequent to the time when he sold the property to such vendee. But the value of the improvements out of which the vendor's creditor effected seizure from the vendee, whether it be the whole or the half thereof, the vendee may collect only from the vendor's free property. For the general welfare requires that neither the value of improvements, nor the profits taken by a disseizor, nor that which is necessary for the maintenance of a man's widow or of his orphaned daughters should be collectible from alienated property, because these are things the extent of which is not ascertainable in advance.

It is one of the rules of leniency applicable to dower that a woman may not effect seizure on account of her dower out of the improvements made by a transferee of her husband's property.

Why does a creditor effect seizure only out of one half of the improvements which resulted from expenditures made by the debtor's vendee? Because the improvements came after the debtor borrowed from the creditor and after he sold the property to the vendee, so that the creditor and the vendee are both in the position of the debtor's creditors, and the improvements are to be treated as though they were property which came to the debtor after he borrowed from each one of the two, in which case the rule is that they divide the property between them, as we have stated.

If, therefore, Reuben borrowed 100 zuz from Simeon and gave him a writing containing a clause binding the borrower's future acquisitions for the payment of the debt, and then he borrowed from Levi 200 zuz and gave him a writing containing a similar clause, and thereafter he purchased a field which he later sold to Jehudah for 150 zuz and Jehudah improved the field through expenditures so that it is worth 300 zuz, Simeon and Levi effect seizure out of the principal which they divide equally between themselves, as we have stated, thus obtaining 75 zuz each, and then Simeon, Levi, and Jehudah divide the 150 zuz representing the value of the improvements, in the manner which we have explained, with the result that Simeon effects seizure from this field to the extent of 100 zuz, Levi to the extent of 137½ zuz, and Jehudah takes out of the improvements 62½ zuz. And in this manner the property is divided among them even if they be 100 in number.

2. Profits taken from the land by the debtor's vendee are not subject to seizure by the debtor's creditor, but fruit which is attached to the soil, even though it no longer requires nourishment from the soil, as in the case of grapes that are ripe to be cut, is subject to seizure by the creditor, just as improvements of the land are subject thereto.

3. If land was given away by the debtor as a gift and the donee made improvements thereon through expenditures, such improvements are not subject to seizure by the donor's creditor. An appraisal is made of how much the land was worth at the time the gift was made and the donor's creditor collects that much. If, however, the improvement occurred spontaneously the creditor collects to the full extent of the value of the land.

If the donor took upon himself a warranty of the gift his creditor collects from the improvements in the same manner as he collects from the debtor's land in the hands of a vendee.

Why does a creditor effect seizure out of half of the improvement of the land in the hands of his debtor's vendee, but does not collect anything from such improvements in the hands of the debtor's donee? Because the vendor writes to the vendee in the deed of sale, "I am obligated to you for the principal and for the labor you will expend and for the improvements you will make, and upon me rests the responsibility for all of it, and the vendee agreed and accepted this," so that the vendee takes possession upon condition that, if any improvements should be taken away from him, he would have recourse against the vendor. And even if this was not written in the deed of sale it is known that such is the rule between vendor and vendee. But in the case of a gift, where there is no such condition, the vendor's creditor does not collect anything from the improvements made by the donee through expenditures.

4. Similarly, if the debtor's orphans made improvements upon the property, the creditor does not collect anything from such

improvements; if the improvements occurred spontaneously the creditor collects to the full extent thereof.

5. After a creditor has effected seizure for his debt out of the principal, together with half of the improvements, in the hands of the debtor's vendee, the remaining land is disposed of in the following manner: If such land may still be profitably exploited by the vendee, as where the remainder consists of a parcel of land requiring nine ḳab for sowing in the case of a field or one half ḳab in the case of a vegetable garden, the creditor and the vendee take their respective shares of the land. But if the remainder to which the vendee is entitled is such that if the land were partitioned and the vendee given what is due to him, the share which he would obtain would no longer be in the same class of property as the land was before partition, the creditor is to pay to the vendee the value of his share in money.

6. If the field has been hypothecated the creditor takes it in its entirety, and as to the one half of the improvements the rule is as follows: if such half exceeds the total expenditures made by the vendee the latter takes from the creditor the amount of the expenditures, since the creditor may say to him, "It was my field in which the improvements occurred," and the remainder of the improvements he takes from the vendor; if the total expenditures exceed half of the improvements the vendee is entitled to obtain from the creditor who effects seizure only the value of one half of the improvements and to collect from the vendor the remaining one half of the value of the improvements seized.

7. If a creditor comes to effect seizure from the debtor's orphans and the orphans say, "The improvements were made by us," while the creditor says, "Perhaps they were made by your father," the orphans must produce proof. If they produce proof that they improved the property an appraisal is made of the improvements and of the expenditures, and whichever is smaller they take its value in money.

All this applies only where the debtor hypothecated the land, but if he did not hypothecate it the orphans may remove the creditor by paying him the value of the land in money or, if they wish, they may take a part of the land which is equivalent to the improvements they made.

CHAPTER XXII

1. The order of the collection of debts through legal process is as follows: when the creditor produces the writing obligatory in court and it is confirmed, the court says to the debtor, "Pay," and they do not take possession of the debtor's property for the purpose of satisfying the creditor therefrom until the creditor has made demand upon the debtor.

If the judge erred and gave the creditor possession of the debtor's property before the creditor made demand upon the debtor, the creditor is to be removed from the property.

If the debtor said, "I am willing to pay, but give me time, so as to enable me to borrow from another or to pledge my property or sell it, and I will bring the money," the court gives him 30 days' time without compelling him to give a pledge, because if he had movables the court would immediately proceed to collect the debt therefrom. But if the creditor so wishes the anathema is proclaimed generally against him who has money or movables, but pretends to have none. Nor is the debtor compelled to produce a surety to guarantee payment before the end of the period.

If after the expiration of the 30-day period the debtor does not produce the money the court issues a writ of execution against his property.

If at the time the creditor made demand upon him the debtor said, "I will not pay," the court issues a writ of execution against his property immediately without giving him an extension of time.

Similarly, in the case of an oral debt or of a confession, the court issues a writ of execution against the debtor's free property.

2. If the debtor makes a claim saying, "This writing obligatory which has been confirmed before you is forged; I will produce

proof by such a one and such a one, witnesses, who are in such a place, to the effect that it is void," then, if it appears to the judges that there is substance in his words, they fix a time for him to produce his witnesses, and if it appears to them that he only seeks pretenses and makes empty claims, they order him to pay and to return when he has the proof available. But if the creditor is a powerful man, defiant of the Law, from whom the debtor may not be able to reclaim the money, it is placed in the hands of a third party depositary.

3. If a time was fixed for the debtor to produce proof that the writing obligatory was void and he did not come forward with the proof at the time fixed, the court, nevertheless, suspends action for a period of time embracing a Monday, a Thursday, and another Monday. If he does not come then, the court issues a writ of excommunication against him and he remains under the ban of excommunication for 90 days, during which period no further action is taken against him. The first 30 days, it is assumed, he is endeavoring to borrow money, the middle 30 days he is endeavoring to sell his property, and the last 30 days a vendee to whom he has sold his property is endeavoring to procure the purchase money.

If after the expiration of the 90-day period he does not come forward with the money the court issues a writ of execution against his property, dissolving, at the same time, the ban of excommunication against him.

4. A writ of execution may not be issued before the debtor has been given notice thereof, provided he is in a place which is only two days or less distant from the court. If he is in a more distant place it is not necessary to give him notice.

All this applies only where the debtor, during the 90-day period, was continually parrying by saying, "I will presently produce proof that the writing obligatory is void," but if he said, "I will not come to court," a writ of execution is issued against his property, landed and movable, immediately.

Similarly, if the writing evidences a deposit there is no suspension of 90 days, but a writ of execution is issued immediately against the property of the party against whom the writing is produced.

5. When we said that if the debtor does not come forward at the end of the 90-day period a writ of execution is issued by the court, we had reference to a writ against the debtor's landed property. In the case of movable property, however, the creditor is not given possession by the court, even after the 90-day period, so long as the debtor says, "I will presently produce proof that the writing obligatory is void." This is so because of the possibility that the creditor will, in the meantime, consume the movables and when the debtor will produce proof that the writing obligatory is void he will find nothing to retake from the creditor. The rule is so even if the creditor has landed property, because of the possibility that it will lose its fertility or become blasted.

6. How is the writ of execution worded? If execution is issued against the debtor's free property the writ states: "Such a one having become bound by judgment to pay so much to such a one and having failed to pay voluntarily, we have issued this writ of execution against such a field belonging to him." Thereafter, three appraisers assess so much of the field as is necessary to satisfy the debt, causing proclamation to be made as often as to them appears expedient, until no higher bids are received, and possession of so much of the field as is assessed for the amount of the debt is given to the debtor, and his writing obligatory, if there be one, is torn up. If the debtor has no free property the writ of execution is written thus: "Such a one having become bound to such a one for so much on a writing which he holds in his hands and having failed to pay his debt, we, having found no free property belonging to him and having torn up the writing, have given permission to such a one to inquire and investigate and lay his hands on all of the debtor's property which he may find, and he may collect his debt out of all the landed property which the debtor sold after such a date."

7. After the writ of execution is issued the creditor goes out in search for the debtor's property. If he finds property belonging to

the debtor an assessment is made of so much thereof as is necessary to satisfy the debt, and if he finds no free property but only such as was alienated by the debtor after the date of the writing obligatory, he may effect seizure therefrom. The writ of execution is then torn up and a writ of seizure is drawn up.

8. How is the writ of seizure worded? "X, son of Y, having been adjudged to be entitled to effect seizure for a debt which Z owes him and which amounts to so much, out of such a field which A purchased from Z on such a date, we, having torn up the writ of execution which he held in his hands, have authorized him to effect seizure for so much."

9. After the writ of execution is drawn up, three experienced men are brought to the field and so much thereof as is equivalent to the amount of the debt is assessed by them, which assessment is made out of the principal and half of the improvements, as we have stated, and proclamation is caused to be made for a period of 30 days, in the same manner as it is made when property belonging to orphans is sold.

10. Thereafter, if the debtor is present in the locality he is subjected to an oath, in accordance with the enactment of the Geonim, that he has nothing with which to pay the debt. The seizor is also subjected to an oath while holding a sacred object that the debt was neither paid, nor released, nor sold by him to a third party. Thereafter, the seizor is given possession of the vendee's property, in accordance with the assessment made, and a writ of transfer of possession is drawn up.

11. How is this writ worded? "After having made an assessment in favor of such a one, by virtue of a writ of assessment which he had in his hands, after having caused proclamation to be duly made for a period of 30 days and after having subjected this seizor and the debtor, respectively, to an oath, we have given him possession of such a field, that he may make use thereof in the manner in which man makes use of his property."

12. From what point of time does the seizor take the profits from the field? From the time when the days of proclamation have come to an end.

13. A writ of execution which does not contain the clause, "We have torn up the writing evidencing the loan," is not valid; a writ of seizure which does not contain the clause, "We have torn up the writ of execution," is not valid; and a writ of assessment which does not contain the clause, "We have torn up the writ of seizure," is not valid.

14. If three appraisers came to assess property and one of them assessed it at 100 zuz, while the other two assessed it at 200 zuz, or one at 200 zuz and the other two at 100 zuz, the opinion of the lone dissenter is null because he is in the minority.

If one of the appraisers assessed the property at 100 zuz, another at 80 zuz, and the third one at 120 zuz, the assessment is taken at 100 zuz. If one of them assessed it at 100 zuz, another one at 90 zuz, and the third one at 130 zuz, the assessment is taken at 110, and in this manner a composite assessment is reached.

15. If the court assessed a vendee's property for the benefit of a seizor and it erred in the assessment, however slight the error, the sale made pursuant to such assessment is void because the court is deemed agent for the seizor and for the vendee and, like every other agent, it has authority only to act to the principal's advantage and not to his disadvantage. On this, there is universal agreement among the authorities.

16. If the court assessed property to a creditor, whether the property was at the time in the hands of the debtor himself or of his vendee, and thereafter the debtor or the seizee, or their respective heirs, came into money and tendered to the creditor the amount of his debt, the creditor is removed from the property, the rule being that property assessed for the satisfaction of an obligation always reverts back to its owner. For it is said *And thou shalt do that which is right and good* (Deut. 6:18).

17. If the property, after having been assessed to a creditor, was assessed to the creditor's creditor, it reverts back to the original owner, because the power of the second creditor cannot be greater than that of the first creditor.

If the creditor sold the property, gave it away by way of gift, or had it assessed for the benefit of his creditor voluntarily, or if the creditor died leaving the property to his heirs, it does not revert back to the original owner.

If property was seized for the benefit of a woman, or taken away from her by assessment, and thereafter she married, the husband is deemed a purchaser; he neither has a right of redemption, nor can such a right be asserted against him.

CHAPTER XXIII

1. Writings obligatory which are antedated are invalid because, if they were held to be valid, the creditor would sometimes be able to effect seizure unlawfully out of property in the hands of the debtor's vendees. It was for this reason that the Sages established a penalty against the holder of an antedated writing and declared that the debt evidenced by such a writing is collectible only from the debtor's free property, lest the creditor effect seizure thereon out of property sold by the debtor during the period between the ostensible date of the writing and the actual date thereof.

2. Postdated writings obligatory are valid, since the holder of such a writing can only effect seizure thereon out of property sold by the debtor after the ostensible date thereof, and his power is thus impaired rather than augmented. Even though it is not stated in the writing that it is postdated, it is valid.

3. A writing which was drawn up during the day and signed during the night next following is invalid because it is antedated. But if they were engaged in the matter all the time until night descended, when the writing was signed, it is valid, even though ḳinyan was performed at night.

4. A writing which is dated on the Sabbath or on the tenth day of Tishri (Yom Kippur) is taken to be postdated and is therefore valid. It is not to be feared that the writing is antedated and that it was written on Sunday or on the eleventh day of Tishri, there being a presumption in favor of the validity of the writing. Since it is a matter of common knowledge that they do not write on the Sabbath the writing is taken to be postdated.

5. A writing may be drawn up at the instance of the debtor, even though the creditor is not present with him at the time; but it may not be written at the instance of the creditor unless the debtor is present with him. This applies only to a writing which contains a clause reciting that ḳinyan was performed in connection therewith, since the debtor's property becomes obligated for the payment of the debt from the moment ḳinyan is performed; but if the writing does not contain such a clause it may not be drawn up, even at the instance of the debtor, unless the creditor is present with him at the time so that the debtor may deliver the writing to the creditor in the presence of the witnesses. This is so because of the possibility that the debtor will have the writing drawn up with the intention of borrowing money from the creditor in the month of Nisan, but will not borrow it until the month of Tishri next following, and the creditor will then be in a position to effect seizure on the writing unlawfully out of property sold by the debtor after the month of Nisan, though the writing will not have reached his hands until the month of Tishri next following.

6. If the witnesses performed ḳinyan from the hand of the debtor or the vendor and the like, and the writing of the instrument was delayed a long time, then, if the witnesses know the day on which ḳinyan was performed the instrument is dated on that day, even though it is not the day of the signing, and they need not state in the instrument, "And the writing of the instrument was delayed until such a day," and if they do not know the day when ḳinyan was performed they date the instrument on the day of the writing thereof.

Similarly, if authorization to bear witness to a certain transaction was given to witnesses in one locality and they wrote the instrument in another locality, it is not necessary to mention in the instrument the place where the authorization was given but only the place in which the instrument was signed by the witnesses.

7. An instrument of purchase and sale which was not written on the day it is dated, even if it is postdated, is invalid, because if it were deemed valid it would be possible by means thereof to dispossess an owner from his property unlawfully. How? If the vendor should purchase the property back from the vendee before the date of the postdated instrument, the vendee would be able to produce the postdated instrument and say, "I purchased the property from you a second time," and would thus be in a position to dispossess the owner unlawfully.

And why, in the case of a postdated writing obligatory, do we not take into consideration a similar possibility, namely, that the debtor will discharge the bond before the day on which it is dated, receiving from the creditor a release, and that the creditor will then produce the postdated writing obligatory and effect seizure thereon unlawfully? Because he who writes a postdated writing obligatory has the remedy of having the release written without a date, so that the release may be effective against the writing obligatory at any time it is produced; and if the debtor fails to do so, and has the release dated on the day he discharges the debt, any loss that he may suffer will have been occasioned by himself.

8. If a man sold a field under duress and made a declaration to that effect or if, anticipating duress, he sold or gave away the field to another before he sold it to the vendee who subjected him to duress, the money which such vendee gave to the vendor is deemed on oral loan and the vendee cannot effect seizure on the instrument of conveyance which he holds, because this instrument is illegal in its inception, having been written only because of the duress. And so it is in all similar cases.

9. It is possible for one to obtain by legal process, without a written instrument but by virtue of oral testimony only, possession

of property in the hands of another. How? Where a man has witnesses testifying that his father was forcibly dispossessed from the property, he may reclaim it by virtue of such testimony although there is no writing. Also, if witnesses testify that his father was adjudged to be entitled to effect seizure out of the property of such a one for so much and from such a time, and his father died without having effected seizure, he may do so by virtue of such testimony.

10. Therefore, it is not permissible to write two deeds of purchase for the same vendee purchasing the same property, lest the vendee enter into a conspiracy with the heir of the vendor's creditor and effect seizure unlawfully. How? The heir of the vendor's creditor will come and effect seizure out of the property in the hands of the vendee without a writing, but only by virtue of oral testimony to the effect that his father was adjudged entitled to seizure. The vendee will then effect seizure, on one of the deeds of purchase which he will produce, from another vendee of some of the same vendor's property whose deed of purchase will have been dated subsequently to his, and the first vendee's deed of purchase will be torn up. The first vendee will then be allowed, by conspiracy with the heir of the vendor's creditor, to retake possession of the property that will have been seized from him. The heir of the vendor's creditor will then come and seize the same property again by virtue of oral testimony to the same effect as above. Finally, the first vendee will produce his second deed of purchase and will unlawfully effect seizure from still another vendee of some of the same vendor's property whose deed of purchase will have been dated subsequently to his.

If so, then, what is to be done in the case of a vendee who has lost his instrument of conveyance if the witnesses who attested it are still living and present? A second instrument is to be written which is to contain the following recital: "This instrument is not valid for the purpose of collecting thereon either from alienated property or from free property, it having been written only for the purpose of protecting the possession of the vendee against the vendor or his heirs."

11. In the case of writings obligatory it is not so. If the creditor comes and says, "I have just lost the instrument," or "It has just been destroyed by fire," it is not permissible to write for him another instrument, even though the witnesses are present and kinyan was performed in connection with the making of the instrument, because of the possibility that the instrument has been discharged or released. Even if the debt had a definite date of maturity and the claim of loss or destruction of the instrument was made by the creditor before the date of maturity, he cannot collect anything on the strength of the witnesses' testimony alone, unless the creditor entered a plea of "no such thing ever occurred," in which case the falsity of the plea is deemed established by the witnesses' testimony, as hereinafter stated.

12. He who holds a writing obligatory which is decaying and about to become blotted out, must invite witnesses to bear witness to the contents of the instrument. He then comes to court and they prepare for him a confirmation of the instrument. The witnesses who attested the instrument, however, may not write another instrument for him, even though the first instrument became blotted out in their presence; they must come to court and a confirmation must be made by the court.

13. How is such an instrument confirmed? Another instrument is written in which it is stated: "Before us, the court, consisting of X, Y and Z, there was produced by A, the son of B, a blotted-out instrument dated on such a day and attested by C and D." And if they wrote in addition, "And we examined the witnesses and their respective testimonies were found to be in agreement," the holder of the instrument may collect thereon without a further confirmation; but if they did not write so the holder of the instrument must produce proof with respect to the first witnesses to confirm their attestation.

14. A writing obligatory which was torn is valid. If it was blotted out or blurred it is similarly valid, provided the traces of the writing are still discernible. A writing obligatory which was torn by *judicial incision* is invalid. What is a *judicial incision?* One made lengthwise and crosswise.

15. He who has paid part of his debt may have his bond exchanged for another bond, which is to be written by the court for the balance of the debt and dated on the day the original bond was dated. But the witnesses who attested the original bond may not write the substituted bond. If the debtor so desires he may have instead a release written for the amount paid by him.

16. If a man comes to pay his debt and the creditor says, "I have lost the bond," the latter is to write a release and the debtor is to pay the entire debt. The debtor may, however, have the anathema proclaimed generally against him who conceals his bond and claims that it has been lost.

My teachers have taught: If the debtor makes a *claim certain* saying, "He has the bond in his possession and has just put it in his pocket," the creditor must swear the informal oath to the effect that he lost the bond, whereupon the debtor is to pay the debt and the creditor is to write a release.

17. If a man produces a bond for 100 zuz and says, "Make for me two bonds of 50 zuz each instead of this one," it is not permissible to make such two bonds, because it is to the debtor's advantage to have the entire debt contained in one bond, in that if he should make partial payment thereon the creditor would find himself holding an impaired bond.

Similarly, if the creditor produces two bonds of 50 zuz each and says, "Make for me one bond for 100 zuz instead," it is not permissible to make such bond, but the confirmation is to be made by the court for each bond separately, because it is to the advantage of the debtor to have two bonds, instead of one, so that the creditor may not compel him by law to pay the entire debt at once.

18. If the creditor produces a bond for 100 zuz and says, "Tear up this bond and write for me another one for 50 zuz," no heed is to be paid to him, because it is possible that the debtor paid the entire debt and the creditor wrote to him a release of the bond for 100 zuz, and when the creditor produces the bond for 50 zuz and the debtor produces his release, the creditor will say, "This is a different bond."

CHAPTER XXIV

1. We have already stated that a bond, the making of which is accompanied by ḳinyan, may be drawn up at the instance of the debtor, even though the creditor is not present with him.

Similarly, an instrument of conveyance may be written for the vendor, even though the vendee is not present with him. A release may be written at the creditor's instance, even though the debtor is not present with him; a release of dower may be written at the wife's instance, even though her husband is not present with her; and a bill of divorce may be written at the husband's instance, even though his wife is not present with him.

But instruments of betrothal and marriage, instruments of letting on shares or for a fixed rental, an instrument of selection of judges or an instrument of the pleading of litigants, and all other judicial instruments may be written only with the consent of both parties, and one must exercise as great care in the preparation of these instruments, as in the preparation of all other instruments.

2. Who pays the scribe's fee? The debtor pays for the instrument of indebtedness, the vendee pays for the instrument of purchase and sale, the woman pays for the bill of divorce, the groom pays for the instrument of betrothal or marriage, the lessee for a fixed rental, and the lessee on shares and the hired person pay for their respective instruments. But in the case of an instrument evidencing the selection of judges or containing the pleadings of the litigants both parties pay the fee.

3. Whether an instrument is such that it may be written at the instance of one party and in the absence of the other, or whether it is such that it may only be written with the consent and in the presence of both parties, as, for example, an instrument that is written at the instance of the creditor or of the vendee, it is necessary that the witnesses know the names contained in the instrument, that this one is X, the son of Y, and that one A, the son of B. This requirement is designed to forestall the possibility of two parties entering into a conspiracy, changing their names for the names of other parties, and making acknowledgments to each other.

4. If a person has been known in the town by a certain name for a period of 30 days, the possibility that he has another name which he changed for the purpose of deceiving others and of entering into a conspiracy is disregarded, because otherwise there would be no end to this matter of suspicion. Therefore, if a person who has not been known in the town for a period of 30 days comes and says, "Write an instrument that I owe this one or to that one so many denar," the instrument may not be written unless he produces proof that his name is what he says it is or unless he has been known by that name for the required period of time.

5. Whenever an instrument is produced before us and the debtor makes a claim saying, "I am not indebted in anything, perhaps a deceiver other than this one adopted my name and made acknowledgment to him," or if he says, "I am not indebted in anything," or "It is not to this man that I am indebted but to another, and this one is a deceiver who adopted the name of my creditor," his words are disregarded, if there is no other individual in the town known by the same name as the plaintiff, since there is a presumption that witnesses will not sign an instrument unless they know those whose names are mentioned therein.

There is also a presumption that witnesses will not sign an instrument unless it is known to them that those who made the declaration contained in the instrument are adults and of sound mind.

6. Witnesses may not sign an instrument unless they know how to read and to sign. If witnesses who do not know how to sign had blank paper traced for them and they signed on the tracing, they are to be punished with *lashes of disobedience* and the instrument is invalid.

7. If the chief of the court who was familiar with the matter contained in an instrument had it read before him by his scribe, he may sign it, although he himself did not read it, since he has confidence in the scribe, who would be afraid to mislead him. But the rest of the people may not do so. A witness may not sign unless he has read the instrument word by word.

8. If there are in a town two persons named Joseph, son of Simeon, neither may produce a bond against the other, nor may anyone else produce a bond against either of them, unless the witnesses to the bond appear personally and say: "This is the instrument we attested and this is the man about whom our attestation was made."

Similarly, they may not divorce their wives save in the presence of each other.

If there is found among a man's documents a release stating that the bond of Joseph, son of Simeon, has been discharged, and the same man happens to be indebted to each one of the two men so named on a separate bond, both bonds are deemed discharged.

What, then, is to be done by those whose names and father's names are the same? Let them state the names of their grandfathers; if the names of their grandfathers were also the same, let them state their distinguishing marks; if they are alike in appearance, let them state their lineage; and if both of them are Levites or Priests, let them state (their) genealogies.

9. If a man produces a bond in which it is written, "I, X, son of Y, have borrowed from you a mina," he collects thereon, even though the name of the creditor is not mentioned therein, and the debtor may not dismiss him by saying, "This bond belongs to another who dropped it."

Similarly, if there are two persons by the name of Joseph, son of Simeon, living in a town, and one of them produces a bond against one of the inhabitants of the town, the debtor may not dismiss him by saying, "I am indebted to the other Joseph, son of Simeon, who dropped his bond." He who produces the bond collects thereon and the possibility of its having been dropped by his namesake is disregarded.

10. If each of two persons produces a bond against the other, the one who holds the bond dated last may not say to the one who holds the bond dated first, "If I was indebted to you at the time, how did it happen that you borrowed from me?" but each one of the two collects his debt.

If each of the two bonds is for the amount of 100 zuz and each of the two debtors has property of best, or of medium, or of poorest quality, no action is taken by the court, each one of the two retaining what he has. If one of them has property of best or of medium quality, and the other one has property of poorest quality, the one collects out of the property of medium quality and the other collects out of the property of poorest quality.

11. If a man produces a bond against another, and the party against whom the bond is made out produces a deed evidencing the sale of a field to him by the party who produces the bond against him, then, if they are in a place where it is customary for the vendee to hand the money to the vendor before the deed is written, the bond is deemed void, because the party against whom the bond is produced may say to him who produces it, "If I had been indebted to you, you would have kept the money in satisfaction of your debt," and if they are in a place where it is customary to write the deed of conveyance before the purchase money is handed to the vendor, the bond is valid since the vendor may say to the vendee, "I sold you the field in order that you might have property from which I would be able to collect my debt."

CHAPTER XXV

1. If a man lent money to another and thereafter a third party said to the creditor, "I am guarantor," or if a man sued his debtor at law and a third party said to him, "Let him go, and I am guarantor," or if one was attempting by physical force to compel his debtor to pay the debt and a third party said to him, "Let him go, and I am guarantor," the guarantor is not liable in anything, even if he said, "I am guarantor," before a court. But if ḳinyan was performed to confirm that he is guarantor for the money, he is bound in all of the above cases, whether he assumed the guarantee before a court or privately between himself and the creditor.

2. If at the time the creditor handed the money to the debtor a third party said to the creditor, "Lend him the money, and I am guarantor," the guarantor is bound and ḳinyan is not required. Similarly, if the court constituted one a guarantor—as where the court was about to cause a debt to be satisfied out of the debtor's property, and a third party said to them, "Let him go, and I am guarantor"—he is bound, even though ḳinyan was not performed. Seeing that he derived pleasure from the confidence which the court reposed in him, it is assumed that because of such pleasure he determined to bind himself.

3. He who lends money to another on a guarantee may not demand payment from the guarantor in the first instance, although the latter becomes bound to him. He must demand payment from the debtor in the first instance, and only if the debtor does not pay him may he have recourse to the guarantor to obtain satisfaction from him.

This applies only where the debtor has no property; if he has property the creditor may not obtain satisfaction from the guarantor at all, but only from the debtor. If the debtor is a man defiant of the law and the court is unable to cause collection to be made from him, or if he fails to appear in court, the creditor may obtain satisfaction from the guarantor in the first instance, whereupon the guarantor may sue the debtor and obtain satisfaction from him, if he can, or may have the court place him under the ban of excommunication until he pays.

4. Even if the creditor stipulated with the guarantor, saying, "On condition that I may obtain satisfaction, at my option, either from you or from the debtor," he may not obtain satisfaction from the guarantor if the debtor has property. But if he said "On condition that I may obtain satisfaction, at my option, either from you or from the debtor in the first instance," or if the third party was a ḳabbĕlan, he may make demand upon the guarantor or the ḳab-bĕlan, in the first instance, and may obtain satisfaction from him even though the debtor has property.

5. Who is a guarantor and who is a ḳabbĕlan? If the third party said to the creditor, "Give to him, and I will give to you," the third party is a ḳabbĕlan from whom the creditor may obtain satis-faction in the first instance even though he did not specifically say, "On condition that I may obtain satisfaction, at my option, either from you or from the debtor." But if the third party said, "Lend to him, and I am guarantor," "Lend to him, and I will pay," "Lend to him, and I will be indebted," "Lend to him, and I will give," "Lend to him, and I am ḳabbĕlan," "Give to him, and I am ḳab-bĕlan," "Give to him, and I will pay," "Give to him, and I will be indebted," "Give to him, and I am guarantor"—all these phrases import a guarantee and the creditor may not make demand upon the third party in the first instance, nor may he obtain satisfaction from him where the debtor has property unless he specifically said, "I may obtain satisfaction, at my option, either from you or from the debtor."

6. A guarantor on a keṭubbah is quit of payment, even though ḳinyan was performed in connection with the guarantee, since the guarantor intended only to perform a meritorious deed and since he did not occasion a pecuniary loss. But if the husband's father became guarantor for the keṭubbah of his son and ḳinyan was performed in connection with the guarantee, he is liable. A ḳabbĕlan on a keṭubbah is similarly liable.

7. If Reuben sold a field to Simeon, and Levi came and took upon himself the warranty thereof, Levi is not bound, because this is 'asmaḵta. But if ḵinyan was performed to the effect that Levi was guarantor for the payment of the purchase price of the field whenever Reuben should demand payment from Simeon, Levi is liable. So my teachers have taught.

8. Also, if the guarantor or the ḵabbĕlan obligated himself conditionally, even though ḵinyan was performed, he is not bound, because it is 'asmaḵta. How is this to be understood? Where the guarantor said to the creditor, "Give to him, and I will give to you, if such an event occurs," or "if such an event does not occur," the guarantor is not bound, because he who undertakes on obligation which he does not owe and makes it dependent upon the occurrence, or the nonoccurrence, of an event, does not bind himself with that finality of determination which is required by law.

9. If two persons borrowed on one instrument or made one purchase, or if a member of a partnership borrowed or purchased something on behalf of the partnership, they are guarantors for each other, even though it was not so specifically stipulated.

10. If two persons entered as guarantors for another, the creditor may, at his option, obtain satisfaction from either of them when such satisfaction is due from the guarantors. If one of the guarantors does not possess sufficient property to satisfy the entire debt, the creditor may turn to the second guarantor and make demand upon him for the balance of the debt.

11. If one person entered as a guarantor for two debtors, he must, when making payment, advise the creditor as to the identity of the debtor whose debt he is paying in order that he may have recourse against that debtor.

12. If a man says to another, "Enter as a guarantor for such a one for so much, and I am your guarantor," it is as though he said to him, "Lend to him, and I am guarantor," and just as the guarantor becomes bound to the creditor so the second guarantor becomes

bound to the first guarantor. The rules applicable between the first guarantor and the second guarantor are the same as those applicable between the guarantor and the creditor.

13. If the guarantor did not specify the extent of his guarantee, as where he said, "Give to him all you may wish, and I am guarantor," or "Sell to him, and I am guarantor," or "Lend to him, and I am guarantor," he is bound for everything, according to the opinion of some Geonim, even if the person to whom the guarantee was given sold to the other property worth 10,000 zuz or lent to him 10,000 zuz. It seems to me, however, that the guarantor is not obligated in anything because, having been ignorant of the extent of the obligation he was undertaking, his mind was not definitely set upon the matter and, therefore, he did not become bound. And the discerning will recognize that this opinion is grounded in reason.

14. If a man said to another, "Lend to him, and I am guarantor for the debtor's body, that is, I am not guarantor for the money itself, but I will bring the debtor to you at any time you may so desire," or if he said to the creditor, after the latter had lent the money to the debtor and made demand upon him, "Let him go and I will bring him to you at any time you may so demand," and ḳinyan was performed in connection therewith, the guarantor, according to some of the Geonim, is bound to pay if he does not bring the debtor. There were, however, others who taught that even if the guarantor stipulated saying, "If I do not bring him, or if he dies or absconds, I shall be liable to pay," it is 'asmaḳta and he is not bound. And to this my own opinion inclines.

CHAPTER XXVI

1. If a man lent money to another on a bond and, after the witnesses attested the bond, a guarantor came and gave a guarantee for the debtor, the creditor, when he comes to obtain satisfaction out of the guarantor's property, may not seize such property in the

hands of the guarantor's transferees, even though ḳinyan was performed in connection with the guarantee and the guarantor thus became bound to pay, as we have stated.

If the guarantor is mentioned in the body of the bond before the witnesses' signatures, then, if it is stated in the bond, "Such a one is guarantor," the creditor may not collect out of the guarantor's alienated property, since the latter is not conjoined with the debtor in the loan, and if it is stated in the bond, "Such a one borrowed from such a one so much *and* such a one is guarantor," the creditor may obtain satisfaction out of the guarantor's alienated property, since the guarantor is conjoined with the debtor in the bond and ḳinyan was performed by the guarantor before the witnesses signed the bond.

2. If the creditor made demand upon the debtor and found no property in his possession, he may not compel satisfaction of the debt by the guarantor before the expiration of a 30-day period from the day when the guarantor became liable to pay; for the power of the guarantor ought not to be of a lesser extent than that of the debtor himself. So my teachers have taught. But if the creditor made a specific stipulation with the guarantor with regard to this matter, such stipulation governs.

3. If the creditor made demand upon the debtor and found no property in his possession, the debtor may not dismiss him by saying, "Go to the ḳabbĕlan from whom you may demand payment in the first instance." It is the creditor who has the option of demanding payment in the first instance either from the debtor or from the ḳabbĕlan. But if the ḳabbĕlan took the money out of the hands of the creditor and handed it to the debtor, the creditor has no claim against the debtor.

If the debtor is in a province where the creditor can neither reach him nor send notice to him, or if the debtor dies and leaves orphans who are minors—whose property is immune from judicial process—the creditor may demand payment from the guarantor in the first instance, since the debtor is not available.

4. If the creditor made demand upon the debtor and discovered that he was poor, the creditor may not obtain satisfaction from the guarantor unless the debtor swears, in accordance with the enactment of the later Sages, that he has nothing, lest the creditor and debtor enter into a conspiracy against the guarantor.

5. If a man guaranteed payment of an oral loan and the creditor came to make demand upon the guarantor, the debtor having departed overseas, the guarantor may say to him, "Produce proof that the debtor did not discharge the debt, and I will pay you."

6. If the guarantor paid a debt to the creditor before the latter made demand upon the debtor, the guarantor, in his turn, collects from the creditor all he paid, even though the debt arose out of an oral loan or out of a loan without any witnesses at all.

This applies only where the debtor said to him at the time he became a guarantor, "Enter into a guarantee for me and pay." But if he became a guarantor or a ḳabbĕlan of his own accord, or if the debtor said to him, "Enter into a guarantee for me," but did not authorize him to pay, and he paid, the debtor is not liable to pay him anything.

Similarly, if a man paid another's bond without his knowledge, even if the debt was on a pledge, the debtor is not liable to him in anything, and takes the pledge without paying therefor, the party who paid thus losing his money, because it is possible that the debtor would have induced the creditor to release the debt to him.

If the debtor died and the guarantor paid the debt before he notified the heirs, then, if it is known that the debtor did not discharge the bond before he died, as where he admitted before his death that he still owed it, or where he was placed under the ban of excommunication for failure to pay and died while under the ban, or if the debt was not yet due when he died, the guarantor collects from the heirs everything he paid.

If the creditor was a heathen the heirs are not liable to pay to the guarantor, since it is possible that their father, knowing that it is customary for the heathen to demand payment from the guarantor in the first instance, gave the entire amount of the debt to the guarantor, and that therefore the guarantor paid the creditor of his own accord without notifying the orphans. But if the guarantor notified the heirs that the heathen was demanding payment of him and that he was going to pay him, they are liable to pay.

7. A guarantor who comes to take what he paid, whether from the debtor's heirs or from the debtor himself, is required to produce proof of payment, and the presence of the bond in the guarantor's hands is not deemed to be such proof, since it is possible that the bond was dropped by the creditor and that the guarantor did not pay anything thereon.

8. If a man says to another, "You guaranteed payment to me," while the other says, "I did not guarantee," or if the guarantor says to the debtor, "You authorized me to enter into a guarantee for you and to pay," while the debtor says, "You entered into the guarantee of your own accord," or "You did not enter into a guarantee at all," or if the guarantor says, "I paid the debt in your presence," while the debtor says, "You did not pay," or "You paid, and I reimbursed you," or if the creditor says, "You guaranteed payment of 200 zuz," while the guarantor says, "I only guaranteed payment of 100 zuz"—in all of these and in similar pleas the rule that he who claims anything from his fellow must produce proof is applicable. If no proof is available, the defendant swears the informal oath or, if he made a partial admission, the Pentateuchal oath, exactly as in all other claims of a pecuniary nature.

9. If a bondman or a married woman borrowed money or entered into a guarantee for others and became liable to pay, the bondman must pay when he becomes emancipated and the woman when she is divorced or becomes a widow.

10. A minor who borrowed money is liable to pay when he reaches majority. However, no bond may be written for such a debt which is deemed an oral loan, even though ḳinyan was performed, the performance of ḳinyan by a minor being a nullity.

11. If a minor entered into a guarantee for others he is, according to the teaching of the Geonim, not liable to pay at all, even when he reaches majority, the creditor, who gave the money on the minor's guarantee having occasioned his own loss, since a minor does not possess sufficient mental capacity to bind himself for something he does not owe or to give a guarantee and the like. And this is a true rule in accordance with which judgment should be rendered in practice.

12. If a woman borrowed money on a bond or entered into a guarantee on a bond and thereafter married, she is liable to pay. However, if the debt arose out of an oral loan she does not pay until she is divorced or becomes a widow, since the possession of the husband is deemed like the possession of a vendee, as we have stated in several places. But if the money she received as a loan is still in her possession *in specie* it must be returned to the creditor.

CHAPTER XXVII

1. An instrument that is written in any language and in any script, if it was prepared in accordance with the formal requirements of instruments used in Israel which cannot be forged or added to or diminished from, and the witnesses thereto are Israelites who know how to read it, is valid and collection may be made thereon even from alienated property.

But instruments which are signed by heathen as witnesses are invalid. An exception, however, is made in the case of instruments of purchase and sale and of indebtedness, provided the money was handed over in their presence and the instrument recites, "In our presence such a one counted to such a one so much, being the amount of the purchase price or of the debt," and provided further that the instrument was made in their courts. But if the instrument was made in the place of assembly of their courts, without the judge's confirmation, it is of no avail. It is also necessary that Israelite witnesses testify that the heathen who attested the instrument, and the judge who confirmed their attestation, are not known as bribe-takers.

If an instrument prepared by the heathen lacks any one of these requisites it is deemed like a potsherd. Similarly, instruments of recognizance, gift, compromise, or release which are attested by their witnesses, even though the instruments possess all the requisites we have enumerated, are deemed like potsherds.

My teachers have taught that even an instrument of indebtedness, which was prepared by them after the money loaned was handed by the creditor to the debtor in their presence, is invalid, my teachers having ruled valid only an instrument of purchase and sale which was prepared after the purchase money was handed by the vendee to the vendor in their presence. However, I do not agree with them.

If the Israelite judges do not know how to read an instrument which was prepared in the courts of the heathen they give it to two heathen who read it, each in the absence of the other, so that each one of them may be considered like a witness who speaks in the integrity of his mind, without being aware that his statement will be used as testimony.

Collection on such an instrument prepared by the heathen may be made only out of free property, seizure not being allowable thereon, since it is not accompanied by publicity and the obligor's vendees are not presumed to have known what was done by the heathen.

2. If an instrument attested by heathen witnesses was delivered by the debtor to the creditor, or by the vendor to the vendee, in the presence of two Israelite witnesses, collection may be made thereon out of free property, even though it was not prepared in a court of the heathen and lacks the requisites we have enumerated, provided the witnesses in whose presence it was delivered knew how to read it and did read it when it was delivered in their presence, and provided further that it was prepared in accordance with the formal requirements of instruments used in Israel, which cannot

be forged, or added to, or diminished from. And why may not collection be made thereon out of alienated property? Because such an instrument is not accompanied by publicity.

3. The formal requirements of instruments used in Israel are as follows: in all instruments it is necessary that the last line be repetitious of the matter contained in the instrument, since that which is written on the last line is not to be taken into account in construing the instrument. For it is possible that the witnesses' signatures were distant from the body of the instrument by a space which was sufficient to write a line thereon, and that the party who holds the instrument committed a forgery by inserting the last line in such space.

4. If the witnesses' signatures were distant from the writing by a space sufficient to write two lines thereon the instrument is invalid; if by less than that it is valid.

In measuring the two-line space it is the witnesses' handwriting that is to be taken into consideration, and not that of the scribe, because he who commits a forgery does not use a hand like that of the scribe but like that of the witnesses. Also to be taken into consideration in measuring this two-line space is a certain amount of space between the two lines, such as would be sufficient to write thereon the letter L over the letter K.

If the witnesses' signatures were distant from the writing by a space of more than two lines and such space was filled with the signatures of witnesses that were unqualified or related to one of the parties, the instrument is valid, since it cannot be forged. But if such space was filled with ink scratches the instrument is invalid, because it is possible that the witnesses signed with respect to the scratches, and not with respect to the body of the instrument.

If the entire instrument together with the signatures of the witnesses thereto was contained in one line, the instrument is valid.

5. If the entire instrument was written on one line and was followed by the witnesses' signatures on the next line, it is invalid, because it is possible that the witnesses' signatures were removed by

a one-line space from a valid instrument, which had been cut off, and the proffered instrument was written on the blank one-line space above the witnesses' signatures, making it appear that the witnesses signed with respect thereto.

Similarly, if the entire instrument together with the signatures of two witnesses was written on one line and the signatures of two other witnesses were written on the next line, and the party who proffered the instrument said, "I intentionally had the instrument attested by many witnesses," the instrument may not be confirmed through the witnesses whose signatures appear below on the second line, but through the witnesses whose signatures appear above, because it is possible that the instrument together with the signatures of the first two witnesses was written on a blank one-line space of another instrument which had been cut off.

6. The judicial confirmation of an instrument must appear immediately next to the witnesses' handwriting or next to the body of the instrument laterally, or on the back of the instrument opposite the writing. If there is a one-line space between the confirmation and the body of the instrument it is invalid, because of the possibility that the confirmation, together with the one-line space, will be cut off and a new instrument, together with the signatures of two witnesses, will be forged on the blank one-line space, with the result that a forged instrument will appear over the confirmation.

7. If the confirmation is removed from the body of the instrument by a space of more than two lines, which is filled with ink scratches, the confirmation is valid, since there would be no opportunity for forgery in such case, and since the possibility that the court's confirmation refers to the ink scratches, rather than to the body of the instrument, may be disregarded.

8. All erasures must be confirmed at the end of the instrument by saying, "Such a letter or such a word or such a line is written on an erasure or is suspended, and everything is valid."

If an erasure is found in the place where the phrase *firm and valid* usually appears, and is of the size of such phrase, the instrument is invalid, even though the erasure was again confirmed, because it is possible that the phrase "firm and valid" was erased and that in its place something was added by forgery and was confirmed in the space between the body of the instrument and the witnesses' signatures.

9. If the entire instrument was written, and the witnesses signed on an erasure it is valid, and if the objection should be raised that erasure may have followed upon erasure, the answer would be that that which has been erased twice is different in appearance from that which has been erased only once. And if the further objection should be raised, that it is possible that the place where the witnesses' signatures appear was erased twice, and that after the body of the instrument had been written it was erased and in place thereof the holder of the instrument wrote new matter at will—with the result that the appearance of the body of the instrument and of the witnesses' signatures is the same, both having been written on a double erasure—the answer would be that the Sages have already enacted that witnesses may not sign an instrument written on an erasure, unless the erasure was made in their presence.

10. If the body of the instrument and the signatures of the witnesses thereto are written on an erasure, while the confirmation underneath is written on unused paper, the instrument is not to be confirmed through the confirmation witnesses but through the witnesses whose signatures appear above the confirmation, because it is possible that the confirmation was far removed from the body of the instrument, that the space was filled with ink scratches and that the holder of the instrument cut off the body thereof, erased the ink scratches and wrote a new instrument, together with the witnesses' signatures, on the erasure.

11. If the instrument is written on unused paper and the witnesses are signed on an erasure, the instrument is invalid, lest the body of the instrument be erased and a new instrument forged,

with the result that the instrument, together with the signatures of the witnesses thereto, will be written on the erasure. But if the witnesses wrote, "We, the witnesses, have signed on an erasure, whereas the body of the instrument has been written on an unused paper," it is valid. This notation, however, must be written between the signature of one witness and that of the other, in order to prevent forgery.

12. If the body of the instrument is written on an erasure and the signatures of the witnesses thereto are written on unused paper, the instrument is invalid, even though the witnesses wrote, "We, the witnesses, have signed on unused paper, whereas the instrument has been written on an erasure," because the holder of the instrument may erase the writing a second time and substitute therefor anything at will. Since the whole instrument will have been erased twice it will not be possible to discern the second erasure, a second erasure being discernible only by contrast, where the same instrument has been erased twice in one place and only once in another.

It is one of the rules governing the preparation of instruments that one must be very cautious with the letters for W and Z that they should not be crowded between the words, in order not to give rise to a suspicion of forgery through addition; nor should these letters be too far removed from the other letters in the same word, in order not to give rise to a suspicion that a letter such as that for H or for $Ḥ$ was partly erased leaving one stroke which has the appearance of a W. The same caution must be exercised in similar matters in every tongue and in every script.

13. No number between 3 and 10 may be written at the end of a line, lest an alteration be made through forgery, changing the 3 (*šlš*) to 30 (*šlšym*) and the 10 ('*śr*) to 20 ('*śrgm*). But if one of these numbers happens to come out at the end of a line, the number should be repeated several times in the body of the instrument until the number comes out in the middle of a line.

14. If the instrument contains the sum of 100 zuz in the earlier part thereof and the sum of 200 zuz in the later part, or vice versa,

the sum that appears last in the instrument governs. And why does
not the lesser of the two sums govern? Because one sum is not
made dependent upon the other. If it were written in the instrument, "A hundred, that is, two hundred," or "Two hundred,
that is, a hundred," the holder of the instrument would collect
only 100, but in the case of two recitals which are independent of
one another the one appearing last in the instrument governs.

If the instrument contains one name in the earlier part thereof
and another name, similar to the first one, in the later part, the
name appearing last in the instrument governs. If so, then, why
should the earlier name have been written? In order to make it
possible to infer the correct reading of the later name from the
reading of the earlier one, in case *one* of the letters in the former
becomes blurred, as, e.g., where the earlier name reads *Hanani* or
Anani and the latter one reads *Hanan* or *Anan,* it may be taken for
granted that the earlier name is the correct one. But two letters
in the later name may not be inferred from the earlier one.

15. If the instrument contains the word *sepel* in the earlier part
thereof and the word *ḳepel* in the later part, the word appearing
last in the instrument governs, ḳepel being less than sepel. If the
word ḳepel is contained in the earlier part of the instrument and
the word sepel in the later part thereof, regard is had to the possibility that a fly may have removed the foot of the letter for Ḳ
which thus became like the letter for S, and the holder of the instrument collects only a ḳepel, which is the smaller measure. And
so it is in all similar cases, because the holder of the instrument
has the lower hand.

It once happened that an instrument contained the sum of 600
and a zuz, and it was doubtful whether what was meant was 601
zuz or 600 *'istera* and one zuz. The Sages said "Let the holder of the
instrument take 600 'istera and a zuz," because he has the lower
hand.

If so, then, why should we not say that the holder of the instrument take 600 pĕruṭahs and a zuz? Because the scribe usually
sums up the pĕruṭahs into zuz before writing down the amount.

So also in all similar cases, the known practice of the time and place should always be followed.

16. If the instrument contains the words "an 'istera, a hundred ma'ah" or "a hundred ma'ah, an 'istera," the lesser one of the two sums governs and the holder of the instrument collects only one 'istera, because it is he who has the lower hand, by reason of his being a claimant who takes only that which is not subject to doubt. Therefore, in the case of every instrument which contains a recital with two different meanings, one referring to a greater sum and the other referring to a lesser sum, the holder of the instrument collects only the lesser sum. But if he seized the greater sum it may not be reclaimed from him without clear proof.

17. If the instrument contains the words "gold coin," it is not less than one gold denar; "gold denars" or "denars gold," it is not less than two gold denar; "gold in denars," it is not less than the value of two silver denar in gold. And so it is in all similar cases.

TREATISE IV

LAWS CONCERNING PLEADING

Involving One

Affirmative Commandment

To Wit

To administer the Law with respect to claims, confessions, and denials.

An exposition of this commandment
is contained in the following chapters.

CHAPTER I

1. If a defendant, against whom a claim concerning movables is made, makes a partial admission, he must pay what he admits and swear the Pentateuchal oath as to the balance. For it is written *Whereof one saith: "This is it," the cause of both parties shall come before God* (Exod. 22:8).

Similarly, if the defendant denies everything saying, "No such thing ever occurred," while one witness testifies against him, he must swear the Pentateuchal oath. From the *oral tradition* it has been learned that wherever the testimony of two witnesses subjects a party to liability to pay, the testimony of one witness subjects him to liability to swear. From the oral tradition it has also been learned that *One witness shall not rise up against a man for any iniquity, or for any sin* (Deut. 19:15), *but that he shall rise up to subject the man to an oath* (B. Shebu 40a).

2. None but the following three parties is liable to a Pentateuchal oath: a. he who makes a partial admission of a claim touching movables; b. he against whom one witness testifies that he is liable to pay; c. the bailee, with regard to whom it is said *The oath of the Lord shall be between them both* (Exod. 22:10). The bailee's oath we have already explained in the Laws Concerning Hiring.

Every one of these three swears and is quit of payment. But all those who swear and take, such as the hired man, the party who sustained a personal injury, he who impaired his writing, and the like, as well as those who swear by reason of a claim doubtful on the part of their respective adversaries, such as partners and tenants on shares, swear only by virtue of an enactment of the Sages.

All of these oaths, like the Pentateuchal oath, are performed while the party swearing holds a sacred object, although these oaths are derived only from the words of the Scribes.

3. If a man makes a claim touching movables against his fellow, and the defendant denies everything saying, "No such thing ever occurred," or if the defendant makes a partial admission and im-

mediately tenders to the plaintiff that which he admits, saying, "You have nothing in my hands save this, and here it is," or if the defendant says, "It is true that you had with me that which you now claim, but you later pardoned it to me," or "You gave it to me by way of gift," or "You sold it to me," or "I returned it to you," or if the plaintiff claims that the defendant owes him wheat and the defendant makes an admission with respect to barley—in all of these cases the defendant is quit of the Pentateuchal oath.

But the Sages of the Gemara have enacted that in all of these cases the defendant swears an informal oath, and is quit. This oath is unlike the Pentateuchal oath, the party taking it not being required to hold a sacred object during the performance thereof.

We have already explained in the Laws Concerning Oaths the manner in which the Pentateuchal oath and the informal oath are administered.

4. He who has become liable to a Pentateuchal oath swears and is quit, and if he does not wish to swear resort is had to his property out of which the plaintiff's claim is collected, since the plaintiff may say to the defendant, "I stand upon the rule of the Law; either swear or pay." But the defendant may, before making payment, have the anathema proclaimed generally against him who claimed anything from the defendant untruthfully.

But he who has become liable to a Rabbinical oath, if he is one of those who swear and take, may not shift the oath to the defendant, since the defendant may say to him, "Swear and take, in accordance with the Rabbinical enactment." And if he does not wish to swear, let him go without recovery.

My teachers have taught that if the plaintiff says, "I do not wish to avail myself of the enactment of the Sages which was intended for the benefit of those who are in my position, but I wish to be treated like all other plaintiffs," he may subject the defendant to an informal oath, and if the defendant wishes to shift this oath to the plaintiff, the plaintiff must either swear or go without recovery.

5. If a man who has become liable to a Rabbinical oath and who is one of those who swear and are quit—as where he is liable to an

oath by reason of the assertion of a claim doubtful on the part of his adversary or is liable to an informal oath—does not wish to swear, the ban of excommunication is pronounced against him for a period of 30 days. If he does not come to have the ban dissolved he is subjected to lashes of disobedience—he who has been under the ban of excommunication for a period of 30 days is subjected to lashes of disobedience and the ban against him is dissolved—but no resort may be had to his property, since he is not liable to an oath by the rule of the Law.

6. He who has become liable to an informal oath may, if he wishes, shift the oath to the plaintiff who swears the informal oath and takes.

In no case does the party seeking recovery swear an informal oath, except where such oath has been shifted to him by his adversary; and no oath may be shifted except on informal oath. But the Pentateuchal oath or the Rabbinical oath, which is quasi-Pentateuchal, may not be shifted.

7. One may be subjected to the informal oath only by reason of a *claim certain,* and he against whom a claim doubtful is asserted is quit of such an oath. How is this to be understood? If the plaintiff says, "It seems to me that I have a mina with you," "I loaned you a mina, and it seems to me that you have not paid me," "My father told me that he had a mina with you," "My father left word to me in the presence of witnesses that he had a mina with you," "Such a thing was stolen from my house while there was no one there but you, and it seems to me probable that you stole it," "I counted my money and found a deficiency therein; perhaps you deceived me in the accounting you made to me," while the defendant says, "You have nothing in my hands," the defendant is quit even of an informal oath. And so it is in all similar cases.

8. If the plaintiff says, "I know with certainty that I have a kor of wheat in your hands," while the defendant says, "I do not know, what you say may, or may not, be true," the defendant swears the informal oath to the effect that he does not know and is

quit, since he does not admit liability with certainty. And so it is in all similar cases.

If the plaintiff says, "I know with certainty that I have a kor of wheat in your hands," while the defendant says, "I do not know whether it is wheat or barley," the defendant swears the informal oath to the effect that he does not know and pays the value of the barley. And so it is in all similar cases.

9. If the plaintiff says, "I know with certainty that I have a mina in your hands," while the defendant says, "Yes, you did have a mina in my hands but I do not know whether or not I have returned it to you," the defendant is liable to pay and the plaintiff is not required to swear at all, even the informal oath, since he knows that the defendant is liable to him and asserts his claim with certainty, while the defendant is in doubt whether or not he has discharged his liability. And so it is in all similar cases.

But if no demand is made upon a party and he, of his own accord, makes an admission saying, "I robbed you of a mina," or "You lent to me a mina," or "Your father deposited a mina with me and I do not know whether or not I have returned it to you," he is not liable to pay. But if he wishes to discharge his duty to heaven he must pay.

10. "I have a mina in your hands," "You have nothing in my hands," "Swear the informal oath and go quit," "You swear the informal oath and take," "I do not wish to swear"—the defendant may insist that the plaintiff either swear and take or go without recovery, no further shifting of the oath being allowable. But the plaintiff may have the anathema proclaimed generally against him who is liable to him and would not pay.

11. My teachers have taught that he who has become liable to an oath, whether Pentateuchal, Rabbinical, or informal, may, before swearing, have the anathema proclaimed generally against him who claims from him something for which he is not liable in order to subject him to an oath unnecessarily, and the party at whose instance the oath is to be taken must answer *amen*. This is

a desirable rule designed to cause litigants to refrain from making false claims, thus causing the name of heaven to be pronounced in vain, and to prevent the making of idle claims.

12. Whenever a party has become liable to an oath, whether Pentateuchal or Rabbinical, the party at whose instance the oath is to be taken may, if he wishes, cause the party who is to take the oath to swear, by accumulation, with respect to any claim which, if it were admitted by the latter, would subject him to pecuniary liability.

How far does the force of accumulation reach? To the extent that the party at whose instance the oath is to be taken may even say to the party who is to take the oath, "To be included in this oath is an asseveration that you have not been sold to me as a Hebrew bondman and that you are not now my bondman."

We have already stated that the rule with respect to an oath by accumulation does not apply to a hired man.

13. If a man became liable to an oath, even an informal oath, and the plaintiff began to present against him other claims, which he did not present before, for the purpose of subjecting him to an oath by accumulation, whereupon the defendant said, "I do not wish to swear, but I will rather pay you the first claim for the denial of which I became liable to an oath," no heed is to be paid to him. Rather he is told, "Either pay to the plaintiff all the claims he has presented against you or swear with respect to all of them and be quit."

14. If many claims are presented by a man against his fellow, the defendant is not subjected to a separate oath with respect to each claim but swears only one oath with respect to all of the claims.

If a party has become liable to two oaths, a light one and a strict one, with respect to two claims, he is to be subjected to the strict oath in which everything else is to be included.

15. If the plaintiff makes a claim which, if it were admitted by the defendant, would not subject him to liability to pay, the de-

fendant is not to be subjected either to the informal oath or to the general anathema, even though he denies the claim. How is this to be understood? If the plaintiff says to the defendant, "You said that you would give me a mina," and the defendant answers, "No such thing ever occurred," the defendant is not to be subjected either to the informal oath or to the general anathema, since he would not be liable to anything, even if he were to admit the claim; or if the plaintiff says to the defendant, "You cursed me," or "You cursed or defamed me," and the defendant answers, "No such thing ever occurred," the defendant is not to be subjected to the anathema. And so it is in all similar cases.

16. If the plaintiff says to the defendant, "You inflicted personal injury upon me," and the defendant says, "No such thing ever occurred," the defendant is to swear the informal oath, for while the defendant, if he were to admit the plaintiff's claim, would not render himself liable to a penalty by his own admission, he would render himself liable to pay the plaintiff for his idleness, for medical expenses, and for subjecting him to shame.

If the plaintiff says to the defendant, "You put me to shame," and the defendant says, "No such thing ever occurred," the defendant is subjected to the informal oath, if he is sued in a place where the courts are authorized to impose penalties, since he would be liable to pay for subjecting the plaintiff to shame if he were to admit his claim.

17. The rule that he who made an admission with respect to a penalty is quit applies only where he admitted the claim which made him subject to the penalty, as where he said, "I inflicted personal injury upon this man." But if he said, "I inflicted personal injury upon this man and he produced witnesses against me in court and I was adjudged liable to pay him so much for his injury," he is liable to pay.

If, therefore, the claimant says, "You were adjudged by the court liable to pay me 100 denar because of the injury you had inflicted upon me," and the party against whom the claim is asserted says, "No such thing ever occurred," he is liable to the informal oath. And so it is in all similar cases.

CHAPTER II

1. He who is *suspect* with regard to an oath may not be subjected to an oath, whether Pentateuchal or Rabbinical or informal. Even if the plaintiff wishes to have the defendant who is so suspect subjected to an oath, no heed is to be paid to him.

2. One is suspect with regard to an oath, whether he swore falsely an *oath of utterance,* an *oath of testimony,* a *bailee's oath,* or a *vain oath.* Also, he who is incompetent as a witness by reason of a transgression he has committed, whether the incompetence be Pentateuchal, as in the case of usurers, those who eat meat of animals not slaughtered in accordance with the rules of the ritual, or robbers, or whether the incompetence be Rabbinical, as in the case of dice players or pigeon flyers, is deemed suspect with regard to an oath and may not be subjected thereto.

3. A man does not become suspect until witnesses come and testify that he has committed a transgression which disqualifies him. But if one confesses by his own mouth that he is suspect and that he has committed a transgression which disqualifies him, although his confession may not be altogether disregarded and it is improper to constitute him a witness *at the outset,* if he has become liable to an oath he is subjected thereto, since we may say to him, "If what you say is true, swear, the fact that you have committed a transgression notwithstanding, there being no prohibition against you to swear to the truth; and if what you say is false, make an admission to your adversary." But he who has become suspect through testimony of witnesses may not be trusted to swear.

4. The Sages have enacted that if a defendant who has become liable to a Pentateuchal oath by reason of a claim certain is suspect, the plaintiff swears a Rabbinical oath and takes. If both are suspect,

the oath reverts back to the one who is liable thereto, that is to the defendant, and since he is unable to swear he must pay.

If the suspect is a bailee who claims that the deposit was lost or stolen, his adversary cannot swear and take since he does not make a claim certain that the bailee converted the deposit to his own use.

If, therefore, the bailor makes a claim, saying, "The bailee misappropriated the deposit or committed an act of negligence with regard thereto in my presence," the plaintiff swears, in accordance with the enactment of the Sages, and takes.

5. If a suspect has become liable to a Rabbinical oath in a case where the oath falls upon the party seeking recovery, he may not swear and take, but his adversary, the defendant, swears the informal oath and is quit.

Similarly, if a creditor who has impaired his writings and the like is suspect and the debtor, claiming that he has paid the indebtedness, says, "Let him swear," the debtor swears the informal oath and is quit of the writing.

6. If a suspect has become liable to an oath by reason of the assertion of a claim doubtful by his adversary, neither he nor the adversary swears. The adversary does not swear because the suspect is not liable to the oath by virtue of a rule of the Law and also because he is not making a claim certain to which he could swear.

7. If a suspect has become liable to an informal oath his adversary does not swear and take, since the informal oath itself is a remedial enactment and it was not intended that another remedial enactment, namely, that the plaintiff should swear, instead of the defendant, be engrafted upon it. The defendant therefore is quit without an oath.

8. If the defendant has become liable to an informal oath and the plaintiff is suspect, the defendant may not shift the oath to the plaintiff since the latter is unable to swear. The defendant must either pay or swear the informal oath, and will not be allowed to

make his liability to the oath or to payment depend upon something which is impossible of performance. It is as though he attempted to shift his oath upon a minor, in which case no heed would be paid to him, but he would be required either to swear the informal oath or pay.

9. If a man who had become liable to an oath, whether Pentateuchal or Rabbinical, swore and took, or swore and went quit, and thereafter witnesses came and testified that he was suspect, his oath is not accounted for anything; his adversary may either recover from him what he took or swear and take from him, as the case may be.

The suspect is forever judged in accordance with these rules until he has received lashes in court.

10. If witnesses testify that he has received lashes and has repented he is restored to his competence, whether for the purpose of giving testimony or of taking an oath.

11. If a claim was made against a man and he denied it under oath, whether Pentateuchal or informal, and thereafter witnesses came and testified that he swore falsely, he must pay, and his status of suspect with regard to an oath is established. We have already stated in the Laws Concerning Oaths that he who swore falsely with regard to his fellow's property, and thereafter repented, is liable to payment of an addition of one fifth of the value of such property.

12. If the plaintiff claimed that the defendant owed him a debt which had been contracted in the presence of witnesses and by the performance of ḳinyan and the defendant said, "Yes, I contracted the debt, but I have paid you," or "I do not owe you anything," and swore thereto, and thereafter the witnesses to the ḳinyan came, or the plaintiff produced the instrument and had it confirmed, the defendant must pay, but he does not become suspect since the witnesses did not testify that he did not pay the debt, nor did he say "No such thing ever occurred." And so it is in all similar cases.

CHAPTER III

1. He who makes a partial admission is not liable to a Pentateuchal oath, unless the admission is with respect to one pĕruṭah or more and the denial with respect to two ma'ah of silver.

How much is a pĕruṭah? The weight of one half of a grain of barley in pure silver. How much are two ma'ah? The weight of 32 grains of barley in pure silver.

2. All references to kesep̄ (silver) mentioned in Scripture imply the sacred shekel which was 20 ma'ah, and all instances of kesep̄ mentioned by the Rabbis are to be reckoned in the coin of Jerusalem, where the sela' was one eighth silver and the remainder copper, as we have stated. But the ma'ah was of pure silver even in Jerusalem, and that is what was called the kesep̄ of Jerusalem.

Since the requirement that the denial of a claim be made with respect to two kesep̄ is Rabbinical, they made it two kesep̄ of Jerusalem, that is two ma'ah, and did not make it two shekel, reckoned in the sacred shekel. Such is the plausible way of reckoning the standard required for the denial of a claim. But my teachers have taught that the standard applicable to the denial of a claim is the weight of nineteen and a half grains of silver. However, I have a number of proofs to refute the method which they have adopted in arriving at this figure, and it seems to me that it is erroneous.

3. If the plaintiff says, "I have two ma'ah and a pĕruṭah in your hands," while the defendant says, "You have but a pĕruṭah in my hands," the defendant is liable to an oath. But if the defendant says, "You have but two pĕruṭah in my hands," he is quit of an oath because his denial is with respect to less than two ma'ah.

"I have a ma'ah in your hands," "You have but a half a pĕruṭah in my hands"—the defendant is quit because he who makes an admission with respect to less than a pĕruṭah is deemed as though he made no admission at all.

4. "I have 100 dates in your hands," "You have but 90 dates in my hands"—an estimate is made of the value of the 10 dates which

the defendant denies and if they are worth two ma'ah, he is liable
to an oath, and if not, he is quit.

"I have five or six nuts in your hands," "You have but one nut
in my hands," an estimate is made of the value of the one nut and
if it is worth a pĕruṭah, the defendant is liable to an oath, and if
not, he is quit. And so it is in all similar cases.

5. All this applies to money, wares, fruit, and the like, but in the
case of utensils no estimate is made of the value thereof, and even
if 10 needles are being sold at a pĕruṭah and the plaintiff claims
two needles, while the defendant makes an admission with respect
to one and a denial with respect to the other, he is liable to an
oath. For it is written *Kesep or utensils* (Exod. 22: 6)—all utensils
are deemed like kesep.

If the plaintiff claims money and utensils and the defendant
makes an admission with respect to the utensils and a denial with
respect to the money, the defendant is liable to an oath if the denial
comprises a pĕruṭah. And so it is in all similar cases.

6. If one witness testifies against the defendant, even if the defendant's denial is with respect to a pĕruṭah only, he is liable to an
oath, because wherever two witnesses subject a party to liability
to pay, one witness subjects him to liability to swear.

How is this to be understood? If the plaintiff says, "I have a
pĕruṭah or a pĕruṭah's worth in your hands," while the defendant
says, "You have nothing in my hands," and one witness testifies
that the plaintiff has in the defendant's hands what he claims, the
defendant is liable to an oath. A similar rule prevails with regard
to the bailee's oath: even if the bailor deposited with the bailee only
a pĕruṭah or a pĕruṭah's worth and the bailee claims that it has
been lost, he is liable to an oath. But anything less than a pĕruṭah
is not deemed property and the court will not take jurisdiction with
regard thereto.

Similarly, all those who swear and take do so only with respect to
claims involving a pĕruṭah or more.

7. My teachers have taught that in the case of those who swear
and take it is not necessary that the claim be with respect to two

keseḇ. But I say that it is necessary that the defendant make a denial with respect to two ma'ah before the plaintiff may be allowed to swear, by virtue of the enactment of the Sages, and take. Since, in the case of those who swear by reason of the assertion of a claim doubtful on the part of the adversary, the requirement that there be a denial with respect to two ma'ah applies, a similar requirement should apply in the case of those who swear and take.

8. He who makes a partial admission is not liable to an oath, unless the admission relates to the claim. How is this to be understood? If the plaintiff says, "I have a kor of wheat in your hands," while the defendant says, "You have but a *leṭek* of wheat in my hands," the defendant is liable to an oath; but if he says, "You have but a kor of barley in my hands," he is quit, because what the plaintiff claims the defendant does not admit, and what the defendant admits the plaintiff does not claim.

"I have a denar of gold in your hands on deposit," "You deposited with me but a denar of silver," "I deposited with you a silver ma'ah," "You deposited with me only a pĕruṭah"—the defendant is quit because the plaintiff claims a thing in specie and the defendant makes an admission with regard to something of a different kind.

Similarly, if the plaintiff says, "I deposited with you 10 Egyptian denar," and the defendant says, "You deposited with me 10 Phoenician denar," he is quit. And so it is in all similar cases.

9. If the plaintiff says, "I have a large candlestick in your hands," while the defendant says, "You have but a small candlestick in my hands," the defendant is quit. But if the plaintiff claims a candlestick of 10 *liṭra,* and the defendant makes an admission with respect to a candlestick of five liṭra, it is a partial admission because the candlestick may be scraped and reduced to five liṭra.

Similarly, if the plaintiff claims a large belt and the defendant says, "You have but a small belt in my hands," he is quit. But if the plaintiff claims a sheet of 20 ells and the defendant makes an admission with respect to a sheet of 10 ells, the defendant is liable to an oath, because the sheet may be cut and reduced to 10 ells. And so it is in all similar cases.

10. If the plaintiff says, "I have a kor of wheat in your hands," while the defendant says, "You have a kor of barley in my hands," the defendant is quit even of the value of the barley, because with the plaintiff saying, "I have no barley in your hands," the situation is similar to the case in which a man said to his fellow in court, "You have a mina in my hands," and his fellow said to him, "I have no mina in your hands," in which case the party who made the admission would not be adjudged liable to anything by the court. But if the plaintiff seized the value of the barley, it may not be reclaimed from him.

11. If the plaintiff claims two kinds of things and the defendant makes an admission with respect to one, it is an admission relating to the claim and the defendant is liable to an oath. How is this to be understood? Where the plaintiff says, "I have a kor of wheat and a kor of barley in your hands," while the defendant says, "You have but a kor of wheat in my hands," the defendant is liable to an oath. If the plaintiff began by saying, "I have a kor of wheat in your hands," and before he had an opportunity to complete what he was going to say, namely, "I have a kor of barley in your hands," the defendant said, "You have a kor of barley in my hands," then, if it appears to the judge that the defendant resorted to a ruse, he is liable to an oath, and if the defendant acted with integrity he is quit of an oath.

12. If the plaintiff said, "I have a kor of wheat in your hands," and the defendant said "Yes," whereupon the plaintiff continued, "and a kor of barley," and the defendant said, "You have no barley in my hands," the defendant is quit of an oath and is not deemed to have made a partial admission, unless the plaintiff said to him simultaneously, "I have a kor of wheat and a kor of barley in your hands," and he said, "You have but a kor of barley in my hands." And so it is in all similar cases.

13. If the plaintiff said, "I have 10 jugs full of oil in your hands," and the defendant said, "You have but 10 jugs without oil in my hands," he is quit of an oath, since the plaintiff claimed oil and the

defendant made an admission with respect to jugs. But if the plaintiff said, "I have 10 jugs with oil in your hands," and the defendant said, "You have but 10 empty jugs in my hands," the defendant is liable to an oath, since the plaintiff claimed jugs and oil and the defendant made an admission with respect to the jugs. And so it is in all similar cases.

14. If the plaintiff said to the defendant, "I have a mina with you on loan," and the defendant said, "No such thing ever occurred; I have never borrowed any money from you, but you have 50 denar in my hands on deposit or as damages for a tort and the like," the defendant, according to the opinion of my teachers, is deemed to have made a partial admission and is liable to an oath. Since the plaintiff claimed that the defendant was liable to him for 100 denar and the defendant admitted that he was liable for 50 denar, what does it matter whether he is liable by reason of a loan, a deposit, or damages for a tort? And to this my own opinion inclines.

15. If the plaintiff said, "I have a mina and a utensil in your hands," and the defendant said, "You have but a utensil in my hands, and here it is," the defendant is quit of an oath and swears only the informal oath to the effect that the plaintiff has nothing in his hands except what he has admitted.

If the plaintiff said, "This is not my utensil," the defendant is to include in his oath an asseveration to the effect that this is the plaintiff's utensil. If the defendant admitted that it was not the plaintiff's utensil and that he mistook it for another utensil he is liable to an oath.

Wherever in treating of this subject we said that the defendant is quit, we meant quit of a Pentateuchal oath but liable to an informal oath, as we have stated several times.

CHAPTER IV

1. He who makes a partial admission is not liable to a Pentateuchal oath unless his adversary claims something which is meas-

urable, weighable, or numerable, and the admission is likewise made with respect to something which is measurable, weighable, or numerable.

How is this to be understood? "I have 10 denar in your hands," "You have but five denar in my hands"; "I have a kor of wheat in your hands," "You have but a letek in my hands"; "I have two litra of silk in your hands," "You have but a rotel in my hands"—the defendant is liable to an oath. And so it is in all similar cases.

But if the plaintiff says, "I delivered to you a purse full of denar," and the defendant says, "You delivered to me but 50 denar," or if the plaintiff says, "I delivered to you 100 denar," and the defendant says, "You delivered to me but a pouch with denar, without counting them in my presence, and I do not know what was therein, and what you put there you will receive," the defendant is quit of an oath. And so it is in all similar cases.

2. If the plaintiff says, "I delivered to you a house full of grain," and the defendant says, "You delivered to me but 10 kor of grain"; or if the plaintiff says, "I delivered to you 10 kor of grain," and the defendant says, "I do not know how much there was, since you did not measure it in my presence, but what you put there you will receive," the defendant is quit of an oath.

3. If the plaintiff says, "I delivered to you *this* house full of grain up to the projection from the door frame," and the defendant says, "Only up to the window," he is liable to an oath. And so it is in all similar cases.

4. He who makes a partial admission is not liable to an oath, unless the admission is made with respect to something which he could deny. How is this to be understood? If the plaintiff said, "You owe me 100 denar, 50 on *this* writing and 50 without a writing," and the defendant said, "I owe you but 50 denar on the writing," the defendant is not deemed to have made a partial admission, because a denial of the debt on the writing, by which all of the defendant's property is bound, would have availed nothing to the defendant, since he would have been liable to pay even if

he had denied the debt. Therefore, he swears only the informal oath with respect to the 50 denar.

5. If a creditor produced a writing referring to "sela's" without mentioning the number thereof, and the creditor said, "I have five sela' in your hands," and it is to these five sela' that the writing refers, while the debtor said, "You have but three sela' in my hands, and it is these three sela' that are referred to in the writing," the defendant is quit of an oath—although on the strength of the writing alone he could have been adjudged liable to pay two sela' only, so that the third sela' constitutes an admission on his part of something that he could have denied—because he is deemed a *restorer of lost property,* and the Sages have enacted that he who restores lost property should not be subjected to an oath, as we have stated in the proper place.

Similarly, if a man said to his fellow, "My father told me that I have a mina in your hands," and his fellow said to him, "You have but 50 denar in my hands," he is a restorer of lost property and is quit even of the informal oath. And it is needless to say that if the debtor, of his own accord, made an admission saying, "Your father had a mina in my hands and I gave him 50 denar, leaving a balance of 50," he is quit even of the informal oath.

But if an heir made a claim saying, "I know with certainty that my father had a mina in your hands," or "in your father's hands," and the debtor said, "He had but 50 denar in my hands," or "in my father's hands," he is deemed to have made a partial admission and is liable to an oath.

6. If the creditor said, "I have a mina in your hands on this pledge," while the debtor said, "You have but 50 denar in my hands thereon," he is deemed to have made a partial admission and is liable to an oath.

If the pledge is worth only 50 denar or less, he swears and pays the 50 denar which he has admitted. If the pledge is worth 100 denar or more, the creditor, seeing that he could have made a claim with respect to the pledge up to the full value thereof, swears and takes what he claims out of the money which may be realized from the pledge.

If the pledge is worth 80 denar, the creditor swears that the debtor owes him not less than 80 denar and takes the 80 denar out of the money which may be realized from the pledge, while the debtor swears the Pentateuchal oath with respect to the 20 denar which he has denied.

If the debtor made a complete denial saying, "This is not a pledge but a deposit, and I owe him nothing," the creditor swears that the debtor owes him not less than 80 denar, and the debtor swears the informal oath with respect to the 20 denar.

7. If the creditor said, "I have a mina in your hands," and the defendant said, "I know with certainty that you have 50 denar in my hands, but as to the other 50 denar I do not know whether I owe them to you or not," the defendant is liable to an oath because he has made a partial admission, but is unable to swear with respect to the part which he has denied, since he claims lack of knowledge with respect thereto, and therefore he pays the mina and does not swear. And so it is in all similar cases. But he may proclaim the anathema "Against him who claims from me something which he does not know with certainty that I owe him."

8. If the plaintiff said, "I have a mina in your hands," and produced one witness who testified to that effect, while the defendant said, "It is so, but you owe me a mina against the mina I owe you," he is liable to an oath, but is unable to swear and must therefore pay. And why is he unable to swear? Because he admitted what the witness testified to, and one does not swear by reason of the testimony of one witness unless he contradicts the witness and denies the truth of his testimony, in which case he swears to the denial. Therefore, if the plaintiff produced a writing attested by but one witness and the debtor claimed that he had paid the debt, or if one witness testified against a defendant whose dishonesty had been established and the defendant claimed that he had paid the debt or returned the deposit, the defendant is liable to an oath, but is unable to swear and must pay.

It once happened that a man forcibly seized a silver bar from his fellow in the presence of one witness. Afterward he said, "I did seize, but what I seized was mine," and the Sages said, "He is liable to an oath, but is unable to swear and must therefore pay." And so it is in all similar cases.

9. If the plaintiff said, "I lent to you a mina," while the defendant said, "No such thing ever occurred," and thereafter the plaintiff produced one witness who testified that the loan was made in his presence, the defendant is liable to an oath by reason of the testimony of the one witness, since wherever two witnesses subject a defendant to payment, one witness subjects him to an oath, and since the defendant's dishonesty would have been established and he would therefore have been liable to pay, had there been two witnesses instead of one. But if the defendant retracted his former plea and said, "I paid the debt," he must pay without an oath, as we have stated.

10. If the plaintiff said, "I have a mina in your hands," while the defendant said, "You do not have anything in my hands," and witnesses testified that the plaintiff still had 50 denar in the defendant's hands, all the Geonim have held that the defendant must pay 50 denar and swear with respect to the balance, since no greater effect is to be attributed to the defendant's admission than to the testimony of witnesses.

CHAPTER V

1. According to the rule of the Law, no oath may be imposed upon a defendant with respect to the following: a. Landed property; b. Bondmen; c. Bonds; d. Property belonging to the sanctuary.

Even though the defendant made a partial admission, or there was one witness testifying against him, or, in the case of a bailee, he entered the bailee's plea, he is quit. For it is written *If a man deliver unto his neighbour* (Exod. 22:6)—property belonging to the sanctuary is thus excluded; *money or utensils* (*ibid.*)—landed property and bondmen, which have been likened to landed property, are thus similarly excluded. Likewise excluded are bonds which, unlike money and utensils, have no inherent value and are designed to be used only for the evidence they contain.

Only the informal oath may be imposed upon the defendant with respect to all these, if a claim certain is asserted by the plaintiff, except in the case of property belonging to the sanctuary, where the Sages have enacted that, although one is not liable to a Pentateuchal oath with respect thereto, a quasi-Pentateuchal oath be imposed in order to discourage disrespect for property belonging to the sanctuary.

2. If the plaintiff said, "You sold me two fields," while the defendant said, "I sold you but one," or if the plaintiff said, "I have two bondmen," or "two bonds in your hands," while the defendant said, "You have but one bondman in my hands," the defendant swears the informal oath.

Similarly, if the plaintiff made a claim saying, "This house or this bondman or this bond, which is in your hands, belongs to me, you having sold it to me," and the defendant said, "No such thing ever occurred," whether the plaintiff produced one witness or not, the defendant swears the informal oath and is quit.

Similarly, in a case involving injury to a field through the digging of pits, ditches, and cavities, for which damages lie, whether the plaintiff said that the defendant did the digging and the defendant said that he did not do the digging, or the plaintiff said that the defendant dug two cavities and the defendant said, "I dug but one," or one witness testified that the defendant did the digging and the defendant said, "I did not do any of the digging," the defendant swears the informal oath.

3. If the plaintiff claimed utensils and landed property, whether the defendant admitted the plaintiff's claim with respect to all of the landed property and denied it with respect to all of the utensils, or admitted it with respect to all of the utensils and denied it with respect to all of the landed property, or admitted it with respect to some of the landed property and denied it with respect to some of

the utensils—in all of these cases the defendant swears the informal oath.

But if he made an admission with respect to some of the utensils and a denial with respect to the balance thereof, together with the landed property, seeing that he is liable to an oath with respect to the balance of the utensils which he denied, he also swears with respect to the landed property which the plaintiff claimed together with the utensils, because it is all one claim. The same rule applies where the plaintiff claimed utensils and bondmen or utensils and bonds.

4. If the plaintiff claimed grapes which were about to be cut, or grain which was about to be harvested, and the defendant made an admission with respect to some of them and a denial with respect to the balance, he is liable to an oath just as in the case of other movables, provided the grapes, or the grain, no longer require nourishment from the soil, because that which is ready to be cut is deemed, with respect to admission and denial, as though it has already been cut. But if the grapes still require nourishment from the soil they are considered as landed property in every respect, and only the informal oath may be imposed with respect to them.

5. If the plaintiff made a claim saying, "You dwelt two months in my house and you owe me two months' rent," and the defendant said, "I dwelt there but one month," the defendant comes within the rule concerning partial admission, and if the rent for one month, with respect to which he made a denial, amounts to two keseр̄, the defendant is liable to an oath, because the claim does not relate to the corpus of the landed property but only to the rent thereof, which is movable property.

6. If the plaintiff said, "I delivered to you a bond evidencing a debt of 10 denar in my favor," and the defendant said, "No such thing ever occurred," he swears the informal oath.

If the defendant shifts the oath to the plaintiff, the latter swears the informal oath to the effect that the bond contained evidence of a debt of 10 denar in his favor and that with the loss of the bond he lost the 10 denar, and takes.

But if the defendant said, "It is true that you delivered the bond to me, but it was lost," he is quit even of the informal oath. For even if the bond was lost through the defendant's negligence he would be quit of liability, as we have stated in the Law Concerning Injuries.

7. If a man says to his fellow, "A writing which you have in your possession contains evidence of rights belonging to me," and his fellow says, "I do not find the writing," or "I do not know whether it contains any evidence of your rights," the holder of the writing is compelled to produce it.

8. If the defendant claims that the writing was lost, the general anathema is proclaimed with respect to him. If the plaintiff claims that he knows with certainty that the writing containing evidence of his rights is in the defendant's possession, the defendant swears the informal oath to the effect that the writing has been lost and that it is not in his possession. So my teachers have taught.

9. One may not be subjected to an oath by reason of a claim asserted against him by a deaf-mute, a mentally incompetent, or a minor, whether the claim is made by the deaf-mute, the mentally incompetent, or the minor as the original owner thereof, or by derivation through his father, because he who makes a partial admission to a minor is deemed like a restorer of lost property.

Similarly, if the defendant made a complete denial, and one witness came and testified in favor of the minor, the defendant is not liable to an oath, because while there is one witness against the defendant, there is no claimant against him, the claim of a minor not being a true legal claim.

It follows therefore that if a minor says to an adult, "I have a mina in your hands," or "My father had a mina in your hands," while the defendant says, "You have but 50 denar in my hands," or "You do not have anything in my hands," and one witness testifies that he has in his hands what he claims, the defendant is quit of the Pentateuchal oath.

But if the defendant is a bailee for the minor and he claims that the thing bailed was lost, he swears the bailee's oath, because the bailee does not swear in support of a denial of his adversary's allegation.

If a man admitted that he was the partner of a minor, or his guardian, the court appoints a guardian over the minor, and the partner, or the like, swears by reason of the assertion by his adversary of a claim doubtful.

10. My teachers have taught that although one may not be subjected to a Pentateuchal oath by reason of a claim asserted against him by a minor, he may be subjected to an informal oath by reason of such a claim.

Even if the minor is not quick in matters pertaining to business one may be subjected to an informal oath by reason of a claim asserted by such a minor. This rule is designed to prevent men from taking away property belonging to others while the owners are minors and going away free. To this rule my own opinion inclines, and I hold it to be conducive to the promotion of the general welfare.

It follows therefore that if a minor claims anything against an adult, whether the defendant makes a partial admission or a complete denial, whether there is one witness testifying against the defendant or not, the defendant swears the informal oath, and he cannot shift it to the minor, since a minor may not be subjected to an oath at all; nor can the minor take upon himself even a general anathema, because he does not know the nature of the punishment for a false oath.

11. If an adult asserts a claim against a minor with respect to something from which the minor derived a benefit, such as a claim arising out of a business transaction, and the minor makes an admission, the claim may be collected out of the minor's property, and if he has no property the plaintiff waits until the

minor acquires property and pays. If the minor makes a denial he is to be subjected to the informal oath upon reaching majority.

But if the plaintiff makes a claim against the minor with respect to something from which the minor derived no benefit, such as claims arising out of torts and personal injury, the minor is quit, even if he makes an admission and has the means of paying, and he is not to be subjected to liability therefor even after he has reached majority.

If the plaintiff is one of those who swear and take, as, for example, a hired man who conferred a benefit upon a minor by his labor, he swears and takes from the minor. But a shopkeeper, who ordinarily would be allowed to swear and take that which is entered upon his books of account, is not allowed to swear and take from the minor, since the minor, being in any event liable to pay the workers who swear and take, would derive no benefit from paying to the shopkeeper. The shopkeeper is deemed to have caused the loss to himself by advancing his money at the request of a minor. And so it is in all similar cases.

12. No action may be taken by the court to order a light oath—and needless to say a strict oath or payment—on a claim involving a deaf-mute or a mentally incompetent, whether he makes a claim against others or others make one against him.

But a blind person is treated, with regard to these matters, as normal in every respect. He may be subjected to every manner of oath, and others may be subjected to an oath by reason of a claim asserted by him.

CHAPTER VI

1. If litigants came to court and one of them said, "I have with this man a mina which I lent to him," or "deposited with him," or "which he took from me unlawfully," or "which he owes me as hire," and the like, and the defendant answered, "I do not owe you anything," or "You do not have anything in my hands," or "You are making a false claim," it is not a proper answer.

The court will say to the defendant, "Make answer to his claim and be as specific in your answer as he was in his claim; say whether you borrowed money from him or you did not borrow, whether he deposited anything with you or he did not deposit, whether you took anything from him unlawfully or you did not take, whether you hired him or you did not hire," and so with respect to other claims.

And why is such an answer not acceptable? For fear that the defendant errs in his opinion and that he may thus unwittingly come to swear to a falsehood, since it is possible that the plaintiff lent the money to the defendant, as he claims, and that the defendant returned the debt to the plaintiff's son or wife, or made a gift to the plaintiff equivalent to the debt, and that he thinks that he has thereby been discharged of the debt.

The defendant is therefore told, "How can you say you are not liable in anything, when it is possible that you are liable at law to pay without your knowing it; inform the judges of the specific meaning of your words and they will advise you whether or not you are liable."

Even if the defendant is a great scholar he is told, "You will incur no disadvantage by answering the plaintiff's claim and by informing us as to why you are not liable—whether because no such thing ever occurred or because you paid what you owed—since we always apply the inference of credibility."

Similarly, if the plaintiff made a claim saying, "This man owes me a mina," or "I have a mina with this man," he is told, "How? Did you make a loan to him? Did you make a deposit with him? Or did he cause injury to your property? Tell us how he became liable to you"—since it is possible that the plaintiff thinks the defendant is liable to him when he is not, as where the plaintiff suspects the defendant of having stolen something from him, or where the defendant told the plaintiff that he would give him a mina, and the like.

If the plaintiff claimed that he had lent the defendant a mina and the defendant answered by saying, "No such thing ever occurred," and thereafter the plaintiff produced witnesses who testified that the loan was made in their presence, whereupon the defendant retracted and said, "What the witnesses say is true; I borrowed the money, but I paid it afterward," his plea is not accepted; his dishonesty is deemed established and he must pay.

But if he answered, "I am not liable," or "You do not have anything in my hands," or "You are making a false claim," and the like, and thereafter the plaintiff went and produced witnesses who testified that the loan was made in their presence, whereupon the defendant said, "What the witnesses say is true, but I have returned the deposit or paid the debt," his dishonesty is not deemed established and he swears the informal oath and is quit.

2. If witnesses saw a man count money and give it to another, but they did not know what the money represented, and thereafter the first man sued the second man at law saying to him, "Give me the money I lent to you," and the second man said, "You gave me the money as a gift or in payment of an indebtedness," he is believed; he swears the informal oath and is quit. But if he said, "No such thing ever occurred," and thereafter witnesses came and testified that the plaintiff counted the money and gave it to the defendant in their presence, the defendant's dishonesty is deemed established.

A man's dishonesty is never deemed established unless he makes a denial in court and two witnesses come and contradict his denial.

3. If the plaintiff said, "I lent you a mina," and the defendant made a denial in court saying, "No such thing ever occurred," and thereafter two witnesses came and testified that the defendant borrowed a mina from the plaintiff but had since paid it to him, and the plaintiff said, "I have not been paid," the defendant is liable to pay. For where one says "I did not borrow," and then witnesses come and testify that he did borrow, it is as though he said, "I did not pay." The result is that while the witnesses testified that the defendant had paid, the defendant himself said, "I did not pay," and, the admission of a litigant being as good as the testimony of 100 witnesses, the defendant is liable to pay to the plaintiff and,

the defendant's dishonesty having been established, the plaintiff is not even liable to an oath.

Similarly, if the plaintiff produced against the defendant a note of hand evidencing a debt, and the defendant said, "No such thing ever occurred, and this is not my handwriting," then, if the defendant's handwriting has been judicially established, or if witnesses came and testified that it was his handwriting, his dishonesty is deemed established and he must pay.

4. If the plaintiff said, "I lent to you a mina and you still owe it to me," and the defendant said, "Did I not pay you in the presence of such a one and such a one?" and thereafter the witnesses named came and said, "No such thing ever occurred," the defendant's dishonesty is not deemed established—because witnesses remember only that which they are called upon to witness—and he swears the informal oath and is quit.

Similarly, if the plaintiff said, "Give me the mina I lent to you while you were standing near that pillar," while the defendant said, "I have never stood near that pillar," and thereafter witnesses came and testified that he did stand near the pillar, the defendant's dishonesty is not deemed established, because one does not put his mind on things which do not matter. And so it is in all similar cases.

5. If the plaintiff said, "Give me the mina I lent to you in the presence of witnesses who are ready to testify thereto," and the defendant said, "I paid you in the presence of such a one and such a one," the defendant is told, "Produce the witnesses and be quit." If the witnesses do not come forth, or if they died or departed abroad, the defendant swears the informal oath that he paid and is quit, because when we tell the defendant to produce the witnesses it is only for the purpose of allowing him to establish, by their testimony, the truth of his allegation so as to dispense even with an oath on his part, there being no requirement that a loan made in the presence of witnesses be repaid in the presence of witnesses, as we have stated.

6. If a man said to another in the presence of witnesses, "I have a mina in your hands," and the other said, "Yes, you have," and on the morrow the former sued the latter, producing the witnesses, and the defendant said, "I was only jesting with you; you do not have anything in my hands," the defendant swears the informal oath that the plaintiff has nothing in his hands and is quit. This is so even if the defendant said, "No such thing ever occurred," since the defendant did not say to the witnesses, "Ye be my witnesses," and what is not done by attestation a man might not remember. Therefore the defendant's dishonesty is not deemed established if he said, "No such thing ever occurred."

7. Moreover, even if the plaintiff had witnesses concealed behind a fence when he said to the defendant, "I have a mina in your hands," and the defendant said to him, "Yes, you have," and the plaintiff said, "Do you wish to have such a one and such a one bear witness to what you have just said," and the defendant said, "Perhaps tomorrow you will attempt to compel payment at law and I will have nothing to give to you," and on the morrow the plaintiff sued the defendant, producing the said witnesses, the defendant, whether he said, "I was only jesting with you," or "No such thing ever occurred," swears the informal oath and is quit. For a loan is not deemed to have been attested by witnesses unless the borrower said to the witnesses, "Ye be my witnesses," or the lender said so in the borrower's presence and the latter remained silent. But by an attestation, like the one described above, the defendant's dishonesty is not deemed established.

It once happened that a man was called a "potful of debts," that is, that there were many debts outstanding against him, and he said, "To whom but to such a one do I owe money?" and the party named by him came and demanded payment, whereupon the man who was called a "potful of debts" said that he did not owe anything to the man who demanded payment, and the Sages said, "Let him swear the informal oath and be quit."

There was also once a man who was talked of as being wealthy.

Before he died he said, "If I had money would I not pay to such a one and to such a one?" Upon his death, the parties named by him came and demanded payment, and the Sages said, "They shall not have anything," because a man may sometimes wish to create the appearance that he is not wealthy and that he is not leaving great wealth to his children. And so it is in all similar cases.

8. Although when witnesses are concealed what they hear is not deemed an attestation—and the same is true if a man, of his own accord, made an acknowledgment to his fellow while witnesses were listening, or if a man said to another before witnesses, "I have a mina in your hands," and the other said, "Yes"—nevertheless, in all of these cases, when the parties come to court, the judges say to the defendant, "Why do you not pay to the plaintiff what he has with you?" If the defendant says, "He does not have anything with me," he is told, "Did you not say in the presence of these witnesses thus and so?" or "Did you not make an acknowledgment of your own accord?" If he pays, all is well, and no plea will be made for him, if he himself does not plead. But if the defendant pleads saying, "I was jesting with you," or "No such thing ever occurred," or "It was my intention only to create the appearance that I was not wealthy," he swears the informal oath and is quit, as we have stated.

CHAPTER VII

1. If a man acknowledged before two witnesses that such a one had a mina with him, making his declaration in the manner of a recognizance and not in the manner of a casual conversation, even though he did not say, "Ye be my witnesses," and even though the cognizee was not present, it is a valid recognizance. If the cognizee demanded payment at law, and the cognizor said, "No such thing ever occurred," his plea is disregarded and he must pay on the strength of the testimony of the witnesses to the recog-

nizance—and if only one witness was present when he made his declaration he must swear—since the declaration was made in the manner of a recognizance.

If, when the witnesses came and testified, the defendant made a plea saying, "I made the recognizance for the purpose of creating the appearance that I was not wealthy," he is believed and swears the informal oath. But if the cognizee was present at the time when the cognizor made the recognizance before the witnesses, he may not plead that he made it for the purpose of creating the appearance that he was not wealthy. If, however, he pleaded payment, he is believed and swears the informal oath.

2. He who made a recognizance in the presence of two persons —and needless to say if he made the recognizance in the presence of three persons—may not retract and say "I was jesting with you." He is adjudged liable to pay by the confession of his own mouth, since he who makes a declaration in the manner of a recognizance is deemed as though he said, "Ye be my witnesses."

But the witnesses may not reduce the recognizance to writing, unless the cognizor said to them, "Write, sign, and deliver to him." And the witnesses must consult the cognizor, as we have stated.

Also, if the cognizor made a recognizance in court after having been summoned, as hereinafter stated, it may be reduced to writing, provided both parties are known to the court, which shall thus be satisfied that no false indebtedness is being created by ruse against a third party.

3. If a court of three was in regular session at its appointed place and the plaintiff came and made a complaint before them, whereupon they sent a messenger to the defendant and he appeared before them and acknowledged the plaintiff's claim, they may reduce the recognizance to writing and give it to the plaintiff.

But if the court was not in regular session and they did not summon the cognizor, then, even if the cognizor assembled the judges and made a recognizance before them, saying, "Ye be judges," and thereafter the cognizee came and said, "Write down his recognizance for me," the judges may not reduce the recognizance to writing, because it is possible that after the cognizor has paid to the cognizee what he acknowledged to him, the cognizee will again make a demand on the basis of the writing.

All this applies only to movables. But if the cognizor made a recognizance with respect to land, even if it was made before two persons only, and even if ḳinyan was not performed and the cognizor did not say to the persons present, "Write and give," they may reduce the recognizance to writing and give it to the plaintiff, since here there is no room for fear that, after the cognizor has given to the cognizee what he acknowledged to him, the cognizee will make a second demand upon the cognizor.

4. If a writing of recognizance is produced, and it does not contain the clause, "He said to us: 'Write, sign and deliver to him,'" it is valid, because there is a presumption that if the cognizor had not said to them, "Write, sign and deliver," they would not have delivered the writing to the cognizee.

If the writing contains a clause stating, "Such a one acknowledged before us, the court," but it is not stated therein that they were three, and the writing does not contain words from which it may be inferred that they were three, a doubt may be entertained that only two were present and that they erred thinking that a recognizance before two is a recognizance before a court, and therefore the instrument is not to be accorded the force of a writing.

5. We have already stated that a recognizance before a court, or testimony of witnesses in court, is deemed like a debt on a writing and therefore the recognizance, or the court's judgment, may be reduced to writing and given to the cognizee, or to the plaintiff. This applies only where the adversary did not of his own accord submit to the jurisdiction of the court before they sent for him and he was brought before them, as we have stated.

But if two litigants came to court and one of them made a demand upon the other saying, "I have a mina in your hands," and the defendant said, "Yes, you have," and the judges said to the defendant, "You are liable to pay him," or "Go forth and pay him," and the defendant went out and later said, "I have paid," he is believed and swears the informal oath that he has paid.

If, therefore, the plaintiff came back and said to the judges, "Write down his recognizance for me," it may not be reduced to writing, because it is possible that the defendant has already paid.

Similarly, if one was adjudged liable to an oath by a court and he went out and later said, "I have taken the oath," he is believed and may not be subjected to an oath to the effect that he has already taken the oath.

If witnesses testified that he did not take the oath, his dishonesty is deemed established with respect to that oath and he is never believed when he says, "I have taken the oath," unless his adversary makes an admission to that effect, or he produces witnesses in whose presence he took the oath.

6. If two litigants came before a court and one of them was adjudged liable to the other, and the judges said to him, "Go forth and pay," and he went out and then returned and said, "I have paid," but witnesses testified that he did not pay, his dishonesty is deemed established with respect to that money.

If the judges said to him, "You are liable to pay," and he went out and then returned and said, "I have paid," but witnesses testified that he did not pay, his dishonesty is not deemed established because he may have been seeking to be evasive until the judges have given further deliberation to his case.

If, therefore, he returned a second time and claimed to have paid the money, to which he was adjudged liable before the judges, and there were no witnesses to contradict him the second time, he swears the informal oath that he has paid and is quit.

It was therefore the custom among the well-informed in Spain that when the defendant made an acknowledgment or was adjudged liable to an oath in court, his adversary would say to him, in the presence of the court, "Ye be witnesses that he must not pay me or swear save in the presence of witnesses."

7. If the defendant made an acknowledgment in court that he was liable to the plaintiff for a mina and thereafter said, "I now recall that I have paid him the debt which I have just acknowledged," and there are witnesses testifying in support of the defendant's plea of payment, the testimony is effective and judgment is to be rendered in accordance therewith, since the defendant's plea does not contradict the testimony of his witnesses, and he is therefore unlike one who said, "I have never borrowed any money from him."

8. A pleader in court may withdraw his original plea, and plead a different plea which contradicts the original plea, and his last plea may be relied upon, even though he gave no explanation for his original plea. Even if he left the courtroom he may, upon his return thereto, retract and change all his pleas at will, until witnesses have come and testified.

But after witnesses have come and contradicted his last plea, upon which he relied, he may not change it to a different plea unless he gives an explanation for the plea upon which he relied, and unless this plea is consistent with his latest plea. This applies only if he did not leave the courtroom. But if he left the courtroom he may not change his plea after the witnesses have come and testified, because a suspicion may be entertained that wicked people have taught him how to make false pleas. And so it is in all similar cases.

CHAPTER VIII

1. All movables are in the seizin of him in whose hands they are, even though the plaintiff produces witnesses who testify that the movables are known to have belonged to him. How is this to be understood? If the plaintiff says, "This garment or this utensil which is in your hands, or in your house, is mine; I deposited it with you, or lent it to you, and here are witnesses who know that it was formerly in my possession," while the defendant says, "It is

not so; you sold it to me, or gave it to me by way of gift," the defendant swears the informal oath and is quit.

2. If the defendant claims that he holds the thing as a pledge he may claim against it up to its full value, and he swears while holding a sacred object and takes, as we have stated.

3. All this applies only in the case of things which are not designed to be lent or rented out, such as garments, food, household utensils, merchandise, and the like. But things which are designed to be lent or rented out, even though they are in the hands of the defendant, and even though he did not borrow or hire them in the presence of witnesses, are in the seizin of the original owner.

How is this to be understood? If Reuben had a utensil which was designed to be lent and rented out and has witnesses to the effect that it is known to have belonged to him, and the utensil is now in the hands of Simeon, who, Reuben claims, borrowed or hired it from him, and Simeon makes a claim, saying, "You sold it to me, you gave it to me as a gift, you pledged it with me," Simeon is not believed. Reuben swears the informal oath and recovers the utensil. Even if Simeon died, Reuben recovers the utensil. But the Geonim have taught that Reuben must swear the informal oath, because we plead for the heir.

4. The above applies only where the utensil was seen in the hands of Simeon. But if Reuben made a claim, saying to Simeon, "I have such a utensil which I rented to you, in your hands; bring it forth and give it to me, as I have witnesses to the effect that it is known to have belonged to me," and Simeon said, "You sold it to me, you gave it to me as a gift," he is believed. He swears the informal oath and is quit. Seeing that he could have said, "No such thing ever occurred; you do not have anything in my hands," he is believed when he says, "I have the thing in my hands but you sold it to me."

5. All the above does not apply except where the original owner of the utensil makes a claim saying, "I deposited it with you," or "I lent it to you." But if he claims that the utensil is his and that it

was stolen or lost or forcibly taken from him, and he produces witnesses to the effect that it is known to have belonged to him, while the one who holds the utensil in his hands says, "I do not know; but others sold it to me or gave it to me as a gift," even though the thing is one of those which are designed to be lent or rented out, it is to remain in the hands of the one who holds it, and he does not even swear at all since his adversary does not contradict his plea.

6. But if a report was current that the original owner's utensils had been stolen, he who holds the utensil swears while holding a sacred object as to how much he paid therefor, is reimbursed, and returns the utensil to the original owner, as we have stated in the Laws Concerning Theft.

If the person holding the utensil makes a claim saying, "You sold it to me, you gave it to me as a gift," he swears the informal oath, and the utensil remains in his possession, if it is one of those designed to be lent or rented out, even though a report was current that utensils had been stolen from the original owner.

From the above it may be deduced that wherever one has in his possession movables against which a claim is asserted by the original owner, although he could claim that he had purchased them and he would be quit after swearing the informal oath, yet if he says to the claimant, "They are yours; but you owe me so much," he must swear while holding a sacred object before taking what he claims, as is the rule with regard to all those who swear and take.

7. If a man has in his possession utensils which are designed to be lent or rented out, even though he made an admission to the original owner saying, "I know that these utensils once belonged to you, but such a one sold them to me, or gave them to me as a gift," the utensils are not to be taken away from him who holds them, even if the original owner produces witnesses to the effect that they are known to have belonged to him, because it is not unlikely that a man should sell his utensils.

8. If the plaintiff made a claim saying, "I rented," or "I lent the utensils to you," they are to be taken away from the defendant. But if they are of the things designed to be lent or rented out, the defendant swears the informal oath that he did not borrow or rent the utensils, but that he purchased them from the plaintiff, and they remain in his hands.

9. Do not err by confusing things that are designed to be lent or rented out with things that are fit to be lent or rented out, as many great men have erred. For all things are fit to be lent; even a man's shirt, his bedding, and bed are fit to be lent. But things designed to be lent and rented out are those utensils which the people of a given locality originally make for the purpose of lending or renting them out and receiving hire therefor. They are to the owner like land. Just as he eats the fruit of the land, while the corpus remains, so in the case of these utensils the main purpose of making them is to derive profit from renting them out, as in the case of large copper kettles which are used for cooking at banquet halls, or gilded copper ornaments which are rented out to a bride for adornment. These utensils are not made for sale or for use by the owner in his own household, but for the purpose of lending them to others in order to receive in return an equivalent benefit, or renting them out and receiving hire therefor.

Similarly, if a man had a utensil not belonging to the class just described, but produced witnesses that he always lent or rented it out and that it was known (*huḥzak*) in the community that the utensil was used by him for lending and renting out, it is deemed like a utensil which is designed to be lent or rented out.

10. If a utensil is such that its deterioration in use is greater than the hire therefor, and people are generally minded not to lend it, as, e.g., a knife for slaughtering animals, it is presumed not to be designed to be lent or rented out. Therefore, even if people came and testified that the owner lent or rented out the utensil the presumption is thereby not annulled, and the utensil is deemed like all other utensils.

Support for our view may be found in the fact that *Raba*

ordered the recovery of a pair of scissors used for shearing shaggy woolen stuff, and of a book of Aggada by virtue of the rule concerning things designed to be lent or rented out, and if it had not been proved before him by witnesses that these articles were of the things designed to be lent or rented out, he would not have ordered the recovery thereof from the hands of orphans. But all other scissors and books are not within this rule, although they are fit to be lent or rented out.

This matter is a fundamental principle in the Law; it is grounded in reason and should be relied upon in rendering judgment; it is clear to those who have found knowledge, and it is fitting that the judge always keep it in mind so that he may not err.

CHAPTER IX

1. A craftsman has no seizin in the utensils which are in his hands, whether or not they are designed to be lent or rented out. How is this to be understood? If a man saw a utensil belonging to him in the hands of a craftsman and produced witnesses who knew that the utensil was his, and made a claim saying, "I gave you the utensil for repair," while the craftsman said, "This utensil came into my hands by way of sale or gift," or if he pleaded, "You gave it to me," or "You sold it to me after it had come into my hands for repair," the owner of the utensil is believed, even though he delivered the utensil to the craftsman without the presence of witnesses. The utensil is taken away from the craftsman and the owner swears the informal oath in support of his claim.

There were, however, some Geonim who ruled that even if the claimant did not produce witnesses that the utensil was his, and the craftsman admitted that the utensil once belonged to the claimant but claimed that the latter sold it to him, the claimant is believed; but if the craftsman said, "No such thing ever occurred; the utensil is mine," he is believed and swears the informal oath; and if the claimant produced witnesses that the utensil was known to belong to him, the craftsman is not believed. And this rule is a wonderment in my eyes.

2. If the claimant did not see the utensil in the hands of the craftsman but made a claim saying, "I gave him such a utensil for repair," and the craftsman said, "You later sold it to me," or "You later gave it to me by way of gift," the craftsman swears the informal oath and is quit, since he could have said, "No such thing ever occurred." And even if the claimant delivered the utensil to the craftsman in the presence of witnesses, the craftsman is believed, since he could have said, "I returned it to you," the rule being that he with whom anything is deposited in the presence of witnesses is not required to return it in the presence of witnesses. Therefore, the craftsman swears the informal oath and is quit, and he is not ordered to produce the utensil.

But if the craftsman produced the utensil, seeing that it is manifestly in his hands, the claimant may produce witnesses that it belongs to him and he will be adjudged entitled to take it, even though he delivered it to the craftsman without the presence of witnesses, as we have stated.

Therefore, if the craftsman made a claim saying, "You stipulated with me for two denar as my compensation," while the owner said, "I stipulated with you for only one denar," then, if the utensil was seen in the hands of the craftsman, the owner swears while holding a sacred object with regard to the stipulation, as we have stated in the Law Concerning Hiring, and pays, since the craftsman has no seizin in the utensil and cannot claim that it is his by purchase; and if the utensil was not seen in the craftsman's possession, the craftsman may claim up to the value of the utensil and he swears while holding a sacred object and takes, in the manner of all those who swear and take, as we have stated, since he could have claimed, "The utensil is mine by purchase," and would have been believed.

3. A craftsman, who has ceased practicing his craft, and the son of a craftsman are like all other men: they have seizin in all movables, in the manner we have stated.

4. If a man entered a house in the presence of the householder and then went out with utensils concealed under his garments, wit-

nesses seeing him, and thereafter the householder made a demand upon him saying, "Return to me the utensils I lent to you, and here are the witnesses," while he said, "The utensils have come to me by purchase," he is not believed. The householder swears the informal oath in support of his claim that he neither sold the utensils nor gave them by way of gift to the person in possession thereof, and the court orders the utensils returned to the householder.

All this applies only where the householder is one who is not likely to sell his utensils, and the person who carried out the utensils under his garments is not accustomed to conceal utensils which he carries, and the utensils are such that it is not customary for people to carry them concealed. The person who carried out the utensils is bound to return them to the householder, because he concealed them only for the purpose of denying the householder's ownership thereof.

But if the householder is one who is likely to sell his utensils, even though the person in possession thereof is not accustomed to carry utensils concealed, and even though the utensils are such that it is not customary to conceal them under the garment, the person in possession thereof swears the informal oath that they have come to him by purchase.

Similarly, if the person in possession of the utensils carried them out openly in the presence of witnesses, even though the householder is one who is not likely to sell his utensils, he is believed when he says, "They have come to me by purchase"—since it is possible that the householder was in need of money and sold the utensils—provided, however, that the utensils were not of the things designed to be lent or rented out.

But utensils designed to be lent or rented out are always in the seizin of the original owner, as we have stated. Even if such utensils were carried out openly and even if the householder is one who is likely to sell his utensils, seeing that the original owner has witnesses that the utensils were designed to be lent or rented out, and that they are known to have belonged to him, they are, under all circumstances, to be taken away from the person in possession thereof, unless he produces witnesses that the original owner sold or gave them to him, the rule governing such utensils being the same as that governing landed property.

5. Even if the person who had the utensil in his possession died, it is to be taken away from his heir without an oath on the part of the claimant. For just as the father would not have been heard to claim that he purchased the utensil or that he held it as a pledge, so his heir will not be heard to demand an oath on the part of the claimant.

But if the heir made a claim certain saying, "The householder gave it to my father or sold it to him in my presence," the householder, like all other parties who are subject to an oath under similar circumstances, swears the informal oath.

We have already stated that there was one authority who taught that, in any event, the householder must swear the informal oath before he may obtain the utensils from the heir. But my own opinion does not incline to this.

6. If a man took an axe and said, "I am going to cut off the date tree belonging to such a one, which he sold to me," and he did cut off the tree, it is in his seizin, because a man does not possess the effrontery to cut off a tree which does not belong to him. And if the original owner claims that he did not sell the tree, he who cut it off swears the informal oath that it belongs to him and is quit, because once the tree has been cut off it is like all other movables.

Similarly, if a man entered the field of his fellow and took the profits therefrom for a year or two, and the owner of the field claims that he entered without permission as a robber and took the profits unlawfully, and he produces witnesses to the effect that the defendant took such profits, while the defendant says, "I entered the field with your permission to take the profits therefrom," the defendant is believed and he swears the informal oath in support of his plea. For there is a presumption that a man does not possess the effrontery to take the profits which do not belong to him, and though the land is in the seizin of the owner, the profits are not, because a man does not sell the profits from a field by deed, and hence we cannot say to the defendant, "Produce your deed." And it is needless to say that if the defendant took the profits from the field for many years, he is believed when he says, "I entered the field lawfully to take the profits therefrom," and swears the informal oath, since he could say that the field was his by purchase.

7. If two persons were holding a utensil or riding on a beast, or if one was riding and one was leading the beast, or if they were sitting beside a pile of wheat which was piled in an alley, or in a courtyard belonging to both of them, and one of them said, "It is all mine," each one of the two swears while holding a sacred object that he has in the thing not less than one half thereof, and it is divided between them. And this oath was enacted by the Sages in order that one should not seize the cloak of his fellow and keep it without an oath being required of him.

8. If one of them said, "The whole of it is mine," while the other said, "The half of it is mine," he who said, "The whole of it is mine," swears that he has therein no less than three parts, and he who said, "The half of it is mine," swears that he has therein no less than one quarter, and the former takes three parts and the latter takes one part.

Form this it may be inferred that all those who swear and take, whether it be a light oath or a strict oath, do not swear with regard to what they claim but only with regard to what they take, even though they claim more.

9. If two persons were holding a cloak in their grasp and one of them said, "The whole of it is mine," and the other said, "The whole of it is mine," each one takes so much of the cloak as is within his grasp and the remainder is divided between them equally after each one swears. And each one may have the other swear, by accumulation, that what he took he took lawfully.

10. If one was holding the fringes of a cloak on one side and the other was holding the fringes on the other side, the cloak is divided between them equally after each one takes an oath.

What is meant by division here is that the value of the thing in money shall be divided, and not that the thing itself shall be divided, which would result in the destruction of the utensils or of the cloak or in the death of the animal.

11. If one of them was holding the whole of the cloak and the other was grappling with him, endeavoring to take hold of it, it is in the seizin of the one who was holding the whole of it.

12. If the two came before us holding the cloak in their grasp and one of them removed it from the grasp of the other in our presence and the other one remained silent, it is not to be taken away from the first one, even though the second one protested thereafter, because his original silence is deemed an admission. But if thereafter the second one, in his turn, seized it from the first one it is divided between them, even though the first one did not protest at all from the beginning to the end.

13. If the two came before us holding the cloak in their grasp and we said to them, "Go forth and divide its value in money between yourselves," whereupon they left and then returned with the cloak in the possession of one of them, who claimed that the other had admitted his ownership of the cloak and removed himself therefrom, while the other said, "I sold it to him," or "He overpowered me and seized it from me," the rule that he who claims anything from his fellow must produce proof applies, and if the latter does not produce proof, the former swears that the cloak belongs to him and is quit.

CHAPTER X

1. A domestic animal which walks around and grazes in all places unguarded, is not in the seizin of the one who has possession thereof, if it is known to have belonged to another. How is this to be understood? If the plaintiff produces witnesses to the effect that the animal is known to have belonged to him, and the defendant, having the animal in his possession, makes a plea saying, "You gave it to me or sold it to me," he is not believed, because the

animal's being in his possession is no proof in view of the possibility that it walked into his domain by itself. If, therefore, he does not produce proof, the animal is to be returned to its original owner who is to swear the informal oath in support of his claim.

2. If the animal was guarded or if it was under the care of a shepherd, it is in the seizin of the one who has possession thereof—even though the original owner produces witnesses to the effect that the animal is known to have belonged to him—and if he makes a claim saying, "You sold it to me," or "You gave it to me," he swears the informal oath and is quit.

3. Therefore, if a man has possession of his fellow's animal, which was guarded or under the care of a shepherd, and the owner makes a claim saying, "The animal left my domain and came into yours by itself," or "It came into your hands by way of deposit or loan," and the person in possession makes a plea saying, "It is so; the animal is not mine, but you owe me so much," or "You caused damage to me for which you are liable to pay so much," his plea is good up to the value of the animal, since he could say, "The animal is mine by purchase." He therefore swears while holding a sacred object and takes.

4. Similarly, bondmen who are able to walk are not in the seizin of the person having possession of them. If, therefore, the plaintiff produces witnesses to the effect that the bondman is known to have belonged to him, while the defendant having possession of the bondman pleads, "You sold him to me," or "You gave him to me by way of gift," the latter is not believed and the bondman is to be returned to his original owner who swears that he neither sold him or gave him away by way of gift.

If, however, the defendant produces witnesses to the effect that the bondman has been with him continually for three years to the day and that he has been serving him in the manner in which bondmen serve their masters, seeing that the plaintiff did not protest during all these years, the defendant is believed and, after he swears the informal oath that he purchased the bondman from the plaintiff, or that the plaintiff gave him to him by way of gift, the bondman is confirmed in his possession.

But a young bondman who is unable to walk on his feet by reason of his youth is like other movables and is in the seizin of the one who has possession of him, and the rule that he who claims aught from his fellow must produce proof applies.

5. If the plaintiff said, "This garment or beast or bondman that you have in your possession is mine; I lent him to you," or "You robbed me of him," "I entrusted him to you," or "You hired him from me," while the defendant said, "It is not so; the thing is my property and inheritance," and the plaintiff produced witnesses who testified that the thing or the bondman or the beast was known to have belonged to the plaintiff, whereupon the defendant retracted his previous plea and said, "Yes, it is yours, but you gave it to me by way of gift," or "You sold it to me, and when I said, 'It is my inheritance,' I did not mean that I inherited it from my ancestors, but that it is mine as though I inherited it," the defendant is believed and swears the informal oath, since, as we have stated, a pleader may change his plea if the change is a plausible one.

6. If two persons were disputing the ownership of a ship and the like, one of them saying, "The whole of it is mine," and the other saying, "The whole of it is mine," and they came to court and one of them said to the court, "Take it into your possession until I produce witnesses," the court may not take it into its possession. But if the court took possession and then the party at whose instance the ship was taken into possession by the court, having failed to find witnesses, said, "Leave it between us and the one who will gain the upper hand over the other will take it, in accordance with the rule which would have been applicable if the ship had not been taken into possession by the court," no heed is to be paid to him, and the court is not to relinquish possession of the ship unless one of them produces witnesses, or there is an admission by one of them, or they voluntarily make a division thereof and each one takes an oath, as we have stated.

CHAPTER XI

1. All landed property which is known to have belonged to a certain owner, even though it is now in the possession of others, is the seizin of the owner. How is this to be understood? If Reuben was using a court in the manner in which people generally use their courts, to wit, was living in it or renting it to others or was building and taking apart, and after some time Simeon came and presented a claim against Reuben saying to him, "This court which is in your possession is mine, and you are in possession as a lessee or as a borrower," and Reuben made answer saying, "It was yours but you sold it to me," or "You gave it to me by way of gift," then, if Simeon has no witnesses that the court is known to have at one time belonged to him, Reuben swears the informal oath and remains in possession of the property; but if Simeon produces witnesses to the effect that the court at one time belonged to him, it is in Simeon's seizin, and we say to Reuben, "Produce proof that he sold it to you or gave it to you," and if Reuben fails to produce such proof, he is removed from the property and Simeon is given possession thereof, even though Reuben does not admit to Simeon that the property was his, since Simeon has witnesses that it was his.

2. What has been said above concerning Reuben, namely, that he must either produce proof or vacate the property, applies only if he was not using the property for a long time. But if he produces witnesses that he took the profits of the land for three years in succession and derived benefits from the whole of it in the manner in which every man derives benefits from that type of land—provided it was possible for the original owner to know that he was thus in possession and the original owner did not protest—Reuben is confirmed in the possession of the property, and he swears the informal oath that Simeon sold it to him or gave it to him and is quit, because we say to Simeon, "If what you say, namely, that you did not sell or give the property to him is true, why did you not

protest against him when he was using your land year after year, while you had neither a writing of letting nor a writing of gage against him?" If he answers saying, "Because I was in a distant land and the information did not reach me," we say to him, "It is not possible that the information should not have reached you in three years, and once it reached you, you should have protested in the presence of witnesses, declaring to them, 'Such a one robbed me, and on the morrow I will sue him at law,' and since you failed to protest you occasioned the loss to yourself."

If, therefore, it was a time of war or of unsafe roads between the place where Reuben was and the place where Simeon was, the property is taken away from Reuben and restored to Simeon, even if Reuben took its profits for 10 years, because Simeon may say, "I did not know that he was using my land."

3. If Reuben produces witnesses that Simeon was coming every year and staying for 30 days or more in the locality, we say to Simeon, "Why did you not protest on one of the occasions when you came to the locality? Because you failed to protest, you have lost your right." If Simeon pleaded saying, "I was preoccupied in the market and I did not know that this man was in possession of my court," it is a good plea, because a man is likely to be preoccupied in the market for a period of 30 days. But if he stayed there for more than 30 days and failed to protest, he has lost his right. And it seems to me that this rule applies only to villages, where the people are preoccupied in the markets.

4. Why do we not say to Reuben, "If it is true that he sold you the property or gave it to you as a gift, why were you not cautious with your writing"? Because ordinarily a man is not cautious with his writings all his days. There is a presumption that a man is not cautious with a writing after the lapse of three years. When he sees that no one is protesting against him, he is no longer cautious.

5. If Simeon protested in a distant land, why is not Reuben allowed to make a plea saying, "I did not hear of his protest and therefore was not cautious with my writing"? Because we say to

him, "Your friend has a friend and your friend's friend has a friend, and the presumption is that the information has reached you, and having known that he protested within the three-year period you occasioned the loss to yourself, if in truth you had a writing and were not cautious with it."

6. If, therefore, Simeon made protest in the presence of witnesses and said to them, "Do not utter this matter," it is not good protest. But if the witnesses, of their own accord, said, "This matter will not be uttered by us," it is good protest, because a matter concerning which a man is not under instructions is likely to be uttered by him inadvertently.

Similarly, if the protesting party instructed the witnesses, saying to them, "Do not inform him," or if the witnesses, of their own accord, said, "We will not inform him," it is good protest. For even if the witnesses themselves will not inform him other people will, and the matter will reach him.

7. How is protest made? The protesting party says in the presence of two persons, "Such a one, who is using my court or my field, is a robber and I am going to sue him at law."

Similarly, if the protesting party said, "He is holding the property as a lessee or as a gagee and if he should claim that I sold it to him or gave it to him by way of gift I would sue him at law," or the like, it is good protest, even though protest was not made in the same province in which the land is situated.

But if he said to them, "Such a one, who is using my court, is a robber," it is not good protest, since Reuben may say, "When I heard this I said to myself, 'Perhaps he was just insulting me,' and therefore was not cautious with my writing."

8. Protest before two persons is good protest and may be reduced to writing, even though the protesting party did not say to them, "Write it down." Once protest is made during the first year, it is not necessary to repeat it year after year, but it is necessary to protest at the end of every three-year period. And if protest was made, and thereafter the party against whom it was made re-

mained in possession for three full years, and only then protest was made anew, it is not good protest.

9. If Reuben produces witnesses that Simeon, the original owner of the field, gathered its fruit and gave it to him, the field is to remain in Reuben's possession, even if he pleads that Simeon sold it to him or gave it to him by way of gift on the same day only; for if Simeon had not sold or given it to Reuben, he would not have done service to Reuben, gathering the fruit of the field for him.

10. If Simeon pleads saying, "It is true that I gathered the fruit for him because I let the field to him for its fruit, but I did not sell him the corpus of the field," he is believed, and the field is to be restored to Simeon unless Reuben took its profits in Simeon's presence for a period of three years and Simeon failed to protest against him, as we have stated.

CHAPTER XII

1. The three years we have mentioned must be complete to the day. Even if they lack one day the party in possession does not acquire seizin and may be removed from the property.

All this applies only to landed property which produces profits continually, such as houses, courts, cisterns, trenches, vaults, shops, inns, bathhouses, dovecotes, olive presses, irrigated fields which are continually watered, sown, and planted, vegetable gardens, and orchards, as well as bondmen who are able to walk, as we have stated.

But in the case of an unirrigated field, which is watered by the rain alone, and a field planted with trees, it is not three years to the day; but once the party in possession took the profits of three crops of one kind, it is like three years.

How is this to be understood? If it was a field planted to dates or grapes or olives and he reaped three harvests, he acquired seizin. Even if the trees were closely planted, without the necessary distance between them, so that they were bound to dry up, he acquired seizin in the field if he took the profits of three harvests.

2. If the party in possession produces witnesses to the effect that he dwelt in the apartment house for three years, or that others to whom he had let it dwelt therein for three years, it is good seizin. If the original owner pleads saying, "Perhaps he did not dwell therein day and night," or "Perhaps those to whom he had let the property did not dwell therein day and night," we say to the party in possession, "You must produce witnesses that these years were complete, day and night, or you must vacate the premises."

Even if witnesses come and say, "It was to us that he let the property and we dwelt therein day and night," and the original owner pleads saying, "Let them produce witnesses to the effect that they dwelt therein day and night," the lessees must produce proof that they dwelt therein continually, because this matter relates to an assertion made by themselves, and not to one made by the party claiming seizin which they could support by their testimony.

3. If the party in possession, or the witness who dwelt therein, is an itinerant merchant who makes the rounds of neighboring villages or the like, the question of continual possession is raised at the very outset, and when he produces witnesses of his seizin, we say to him, "Produce witnesses that you were in possession day and night."

All this applies to courts, houses, and the like, which are designed for continual dwelling. But in the case of shops and the like, which are occupied only during the day, if the party in possession stayed there during the daytime for three years, it is good seizin.

4. The three years we have mentioned must be consecutive, one after the other. If a person took possession of a field, sowed it during one year, and let it lie fallow during the following, sowed it again, and let it lie fallow again—even if he did so for many years—he did not acquire seizin.

If it was customary for the people of that locality to let their fields lie fallow, even though some of the people sowed year after year and others sowed one year and let the fields lie fallow the following, it is good seizin because the party in possession may say, "I let the field lie fallow only for the purpose of reaping a richer harvest the following year."

5. If two tenants in common were in possession of a field for six years, the first one having taken its profits during the first, third, and fifth years, and the second one during the second, fourth, and sixth years, neither of them acquired seizin, since the original owner of the land may say, "I did not protest, because I neither saw nor heard that one man was in possession of the land year after year."

If, therefore, the tenants in common had executed a writing between themselves that one should occupy the field one year and the other should occupy it the following year, and so on, they acquired seizin at the end of three years, because a writing is accompanied by publicity and the original owner lost his right by his failure to protest. The same rule applies to a bondman of whom two individuals took possession and of whose services they availed themselves in succession; if they had executed a writing between themelves they acquired seizin.

6. If the party who took possession of the field took its profits for one year, then sold it and the vendee took its profits for the second year, and then the first vendee sold it to a second vendee who took its profits for a third year—the sales having been made by writing—the three periods of possession are added together and it is good seizin, because the original owner failed to protest.

But if the sales took place without a writing, it is not good seizin, because the original owner may say, "Since no one man remained in the field for three years, it was not necessary for me to protest."

7. If a father took the profits of a field for one year and his son for two years, or the father for two years and the son for one year, or the father for one year, the son for one year, and the son's vendee for one year, it is good seizin, provided the vendee purchased the field by a writing.

8. If the party in possession took profits against a father, who was the original owner of the property, for one year and against his son for two years, or against the father for two years and against the son for one year, or against the father for one year, against the son for one year, and against the son's vendee for one year, it is good seizin, provided the son sold the field together with other fields belonging to him, so that the party in possession did not become aware of the sale and therefore was not cautious with his writing. But if the son sold the field separately, there is no greater protest than that.

9. If the party in possession only broke the ground of the field year after year—even for many years—it is not good seizin, since he did not benefit therefrom. Similarly, if he only opened the water channels and cleared the field it is not good seizin, since he did not take the profits therefrom.

10. If he sowed the field and did not gain anything, having sown a kor and gathered a kor, he did not acquire seizin, since he did not benefit therefrom.

11. If he only took grass, he did not acquire seizin. But if it was customary in the locality to sow to grass, because of its high price, it is good seizin.

12. If the party in possession took the profits in 'orlah, or during a Sabbatical year, or in diverse kinds, it is good seizin, although he derived his benefit through the transgression of a religious precept.

13. If the property of which he took possession was stony or rocky and unfit for sowing, he must derive a benefit therefrom in a manner appropriate to the property, such as spreading out fruit or keeping an animal there, and the like, and if he did not derive any benefit from the property during the three years in a manner appropriate thereto, he did not acquire seizin.

14. If a man was wont to keep an animal, to raise chickens, or to put an oven, a stove, a handmill, or manure in a definite place in his

fellow's courtyard, whether he put up a partition or not, and was using the place for these purposes, and the like, for a period of three years, day and night, and made a claim against the owner of the courtyard saying, "You gave me that place or you sold it to me," it is good seizin.

15. If a field was surrounded by a fence and a man came and took possession thereof, sowing outside of the fence, and took the profits from the part of the field which was unguarded, it is not good seizin, even though he took such profits for three years, because the original owner may make a claim saying, "Since I saw that he was sowing in an abandoned place, I said to myself: whatever he is sowing will be consumed by the beasts of the field, and therefore I did not protest." The same rule applies whenever one sows in a place which is unguarded against the foot of the beast and the hand of man.

16. If the party in possession took profits from the whole of the field except a stretch of one quarter of a ḳaḇ, he acquired seizin in the whole of the field except that stretch of one quarter of a ḳaḇ from which he took no profits. Even if there was a rock in the midst of the field, he did not acquire seizin therein if he did not use it in a manner appropriate thereto.

17. If one person took possession of the trees and took profits therefrom, while another person took possession of the land, sowed it, and took profits therefrom, and each one of the two claims, "The whole of it is mine; I purchased it," he who took possession of the trees and took the profits therefrom for three years shall have the trees and so much of the soil as is necessary, that is, the space around each tree required for the gatherer and his basket; and he who took possession of the land shall have the remainder of the land.

18. Similarly, if a man took all the profits from a tree for three years and then made a claim against the original owner of the tree saying, "You sold to me this tree together with its soil," he

shall have so much of the soil as corresponds to the thickness of the tree, down to the depth of the earth.

19. If a field planted with trees contained 30 trees within an area of three sĕ'ah and a man took the profits from 10 of the trees in the first year, from 10 others in the second year, and from the remaining 10 in the third year, he acquired seizin in all of them, provided that the 10 trees from which he took the profits were scattered throughout the area of the three sĕ'ah, and that the other trees did not bear any fruit. But if the other trees bore fruit and he did not take profits therefrom, he did not acquire seizin except in those trees from which he took profits.

20. All this applies only where he took some of the fruit and the remainder was taken away by trespassers. But if he left some of the fruit on the trees, even though he did not gather all of its fruit, seeing that he took the fruit of one tree here and of one tree there throughout the field, he acquired seizin in the entire field.

CHAPTER XIII

1. The following are not to be confirmed in their possession of landed property, even though they took the profits therefrom for three years: craftsmen, tenants on shares, guardians, tenants in common, a husband in his wife's property, a wife in her husband's property, a son in his father's property and a father in his son's property, because in each of these cases the one party does not mind the taking of profits by the other, and therefore such taking of profits does not constitute proof, even though the owner did not protest. The property is to be restored to the owner who produces proof that the property is known to have belonged to him, and he is to swear the informal oath that he neither sold the property nor gave it away by way of gift, as we have stated.

2. The taking of profits by the exilarchs of Talmudic times did not then, as the taking of profits by a robber or by a heathen does not now, constitute proof, because they were men of might.

The taking of profits by a deaf-mute, a mentally incompetent, or a minor does not constitute proof, because an assertion of a claim by the deaf-mute, the mentally incompetent, or the minor is without legal effect. He is therefore not to be confirmed in possession of the land, but the land is to be restored to its original owner.

Similarly, the taking of profits from the property of the deaf-mute, the mentally incompetent, or the minor, by a person who took possession thereof, does not constitute proof.

3. How is the above rule concerning those who are not to be confirmed in their possession—despite their having taken profits during the required period—to be understood? If Reuben took the profits from Simeon's field for the period required to constitute seizin and claimed that the field had come into his hands by purchase, and Simeon produced witnesses to the effect that the field was known to have belonged to him, and also produced witnesses that Reuben was known to have held the field together with him by tenancy in common or to have been his tenant on shares or his guardian, and claimed that for that reason he had made no protest, the field is to be restored to Simeon, who is to swear the informal oath that he neither sold it nor gave it away by way of gift. The same rule applies to all the others.

But if Simeon did not produce proof that Reuben had held the field together with him by tenancy in common, or that he had held it as tenant on shares, and Reuben admitted this but said, "He subsequently sold the field to me," he is believed, like any other man would be believed, since, having taken the profits for the period required to constitute seizin, he could have said, "Reuben was never a tenant in common together with me."

4. How is the above rule with regard to craftsmen to be understood? Where the craftsmen were building upon the land or making repairs thereon for many years (they have no seizin). But if the craftsmen ceased practicing their craft and thereafter took the profits of the land for three years, they have seizin.

5. How is the above rule with regard to tenants on shares to be understood? Where the party in possession had been a tenant on shares for the father of the owner of the field or for other members of his family, in which case it may be said that the owner's failure to protest was due to the fact that the party in possession had been a tenant on shares for his family. But if the party in possession had been a tenant on shares for the owner, he is confirmed in his possession once he took *all* the profits of the field during the period required to constitute seizin, and we say to the original owner, "How come that he took the profits year after year and you did not protest?"

6. If a family tenant on shares let the field to other tenants on shares under him, he acquired seizin. For no man will remain silent when he sees that his property is being let on shares by his tenant on shares. But if he only apportioned the profits to other tenants on shares in the field, he has no seizin, since it is possible that he was made foreman over the tenants on shares.

If a tenant on shares terminated his tenancy and thereafter took the profits of the field for three years, he acquired seizin.

7. How is the above rule with regard to guardians to be understood? Whether the party in possession was a guardian over the field in question or over other property, whether he was appointed by the court or by the father of the orphans, and the orphans allowed him to remain on the property after they had reached majority, or whether a man appointed him guardian with respect to his expenditures and income, seeing that he used the property with the consent of its owner, he has no seizin. But if the guardian's office was terminated and thereafter he took the profits of the property for three years, he acquired seizin.

8. How is the above rule with regard to tenants in common to be understood? If one of two tenants in common was in possession of a field to which the rule of compulsory partition does not apply, the field remains in the seizin of both tenants in common, even though

the one in possession of the field took *all* the profits therefrom for many years.

But if the field is one to which the rule of compulsory partition applies, and one of the tenants in common took all the profits therefrom for the number of years required to constitute seizin, he acquired seizin therein, because he may say to the other tenant in common, "If it be true that you did not sell or give the property to me, how come that I took all the profits therefrom and you remained silent, without making formal protest, throughout the three-year period?"

Similarly, if the husband took the profits from his wife's property for the number of years required to constitute seizin, even though he had stipulated with her that he was to take no profits from her property, or if the husband took the profits from the wife's property, built, and took apart, even though he had stipulated with her while she was his betrothed that he was not to inherit from her, or if the wife took the profits from her husband's property and used such property at her pleasure for many years, even though the husband had designated to her a certain field for her maintenance and she took the profits from other fields—such taking of profits does not constitute proof.

9. But a son who went to live apart from his father, and a wife who was divorced, even if the divorce be of doubtful validity, are like all other people.

10. The taking of profits by the exilarchs who flourished in the days of the Sages did not constitute proof, because they had power to chastise the people. So, too, in the case of a private person who took possession of their property and took profits therefrom for many years, such taking of profits did not constitute proof, because the exilarch's failure to protest was assumed to have been due to the power they possessed to remove the occupant at any time.

However, the informal oath of no sale and no gift was required of the exilarchs if a private person was in possession of their property, and of a private person if they were in possession of his property.

11. How is the above rule with respect to a robber to be understood? If the party in possession of a field was established to have at one time been a robber with respect to that field, or if his ancestors were established to have been murderers for money, he did not acquire seizin, even though he took the profits from the field for many years, and the field is to be restored to its owner.

CHAPTER XIV

1. If any one of those whose taking of profits does not constitute proof produces witnesses that the original owner sold the field to him or gave it to him by way of gift, it is good proof, with the exception of a robber or of a husband with respect to the property of his wife, that is the property classified as iron sheep, or a field which the husband had designated to the wife for collection of her kĕtubbah, or a field which he had deeded to her in her kĕtubbah, or a field which he had given to her to be included in the appraised property which she brought with her at the time of the marriage. But with respect to property classified as *mĕloğ*, the husband may produce proof, as we have stated in the Laws Concerning Marriage.

2. How is the rule that the robber's proof is not good proof to be understood? Once a party in possession of a field has been established to have been at one time a robber with respect to that field, he must restore it to the original owner without receiving anything in return, even though he produces proof that the original owner admitted in the presence of witnesses that he had sold the field to him, if the original owner says to the party in possession, "I did not sell the field to you, but I made the admission out of fear."

But if the witnesses testify that the party in possession counted off so much money to the original owner in their presence, the field is to be taken away from the robber and the original owner is to return to him the money, as we have stated in the Laws Concerning Robbery.

3. The son of the craftsman or of the tenant on shares or of the guardian who took the profits from the field for the number of years required to constitute seizin, has seizin therein, if he claims that the original owner sold it to him or gave it to him by way of gift. But if he claims that the field came to him by way of inheritance from his father who had taken the profits therefrom for the number of years required to constitute seizin, he has no seizin. However, if he produces witnesses to the effect that the original owner admitted to his father that he had sold the field to him or had given it to him by way of gift, he is to be confirmed in his possession of the field.

4. If the son of the robber produces proof to the effect that the original owner admitted to his father that he had sold his property to him, it is not good proof, as we have stated. But the son of the robber's son has seizin, even if he claims through his father. However, if he claims through his father's father, he has no seizin.

5. The taking of profits by a heathen, even for many years, does not constitute proof, and if the heathen does not produce a writing, the field is to be restored to the original owner without any oath on his part, because the informal oath was instituted only with respect to Israelites. An Israelite who claims through a heathen is like the heathen, whose taking of profits does not constitute proof.

6. If the Israelite who claims through a heathen says, "The heathen who sold the property to me had purchased it in my presence from this Israelite who is challenging my title," he is believed and is to swear the informal oath in support of his assertion. Since he could say, "I purchased the property from you and took the profits therefrom for the number of years required to constitute seizin," he is believed when he says, "I purchased it from such a one, who had purchased it from you in my presence."

7. No seizin may be acquired in the property of a minor, even after he has reached majority. How is this to be understood? If

the party in possession of the property took the profits therefrom for one year during the original owner's minority, and for two years after he had reached majority, and made a claim saying, "You sold it to me," or "You gave it to me by way of gift," it is not accounted for anything unless the party in possession of the property took the profits therefrom for three consecutive years after the original owner had reached majority.

8. If a man who had been in possession of a minor's property for many years made a claim saying, "This property is in my hands as a gage, and so much is owing to me on it," seeing that if he had wished he could have said, "It is mine by purchase"—since the property was not reputed to have belonged to the minor's father—he is believed. The party in possession collects from the rental of the property what he claims is owing to him, and the property is then restored to the orphans. But if the property was reputed to belong to the orphans, he is not believed, since no seizin may be acquired in the property of a minor. The property, together with all the profits which the party in possession has taken, must therefore be restored to the orphans, and the party in possession must wait until the orphans have reached majority, when he will be able to litigate the matter with them.

9. If he took the profits therefrom during the lifetime of the orphans' father for the number of years required to constitute seizin, he is believed when he says, "There is a debt owing to me from their father," since he could say, "The property came to me by way of purchase." He collects the debt from the profits of the field, and collects it without an oath, since he could say, "They are mine."

10. If a man escaped by reason of danger to his life, as where the king was seeking to put him to death, no seizin may be acquired in his property. Even if the party in possession took the profits from the property for many years and claimed that he had purchased it, the taking of the profits by him does not constitute proof and we do not say to the original owner of the field, "Why

did you not make formal protest?" because he is preoccupied with saving his life. But he who escapes by reason of matters pecuniary is like all other men, and if he fails to make formal protest, seizin may be acquired in his property.

11. Seizin may be acquired in the property of a married woman. How is this to be understood? If the party in possession of the property took the profits therefrom for part of the period required to constitute seizin during the lifetime of the husband and for three full years after his death, and made a claim saying, "You and your husband, jointly, sold the property to me," seeing that he could have said, "I purchased it from you after your husband's death"—since he took the profits from the property after the husband's death for the full period required to constitute seizin, without formal protest on the part of the wife—he is confirmed in his possession thereof. But if he took the profits of the property in the husband's lifetime, even for many years, but did not take such profits after the husband's death for the period required to constitute seizin, he has no seizin therein.

12. Every seizin that is not coupled with a claim of rightful ownership is not good seizin. How is this to be understood? If the party in possession of a field took the profits therefrom for many years and the challenger of his title came and said to him, "How do you come to this field? It is mine," and he made answer saying, "I do not know to whom the field belongs, but since no one ever told me anything I took possession thereof," it is not good seizin, since the party in possession does not claim that the challenger of his title sold it to him or gave it to him by way of gift or that it came to him by inheritance.

But the field is not to be taken away from the party in possession, even though he made no claim of rightful ownership thereof, unless the challenger of his title produces witnesses to the effect that the field is his. If the challenger of the title produces witnesses to the effect that the field is his, it is to be restored to him, and the party in possession is to make to him restitution of the profits he has taken therefrom. The court may not, at the outset, ask the party in possession a leading question, such as, "Did you perhaps at one time have a writing which you later lost?" The party in possession must make claim of rightful ownership of his own accord, and if he does not make such claim, he must make restitution of all the profits he has taken.

Similarly, if the party in possession of a field took the profits therefrom for the period of years required to constitute seizin on the basis of a writing which he holds in his hands, and the writing is found to be void, his seizin is also void, and he must restore the field to its original owner and make to him restitution of the profits he has taken.

13. He who claims by inheritance must produce proof that his father was in possession of the field, or made use thereof, at least for one day, and once the son took the profits from the field for three years, under claim through his father, he is confirmed in possession thereof. But if he fails to produce such proof, the field, together with all the profits therefrom, must be restored to the challenger who produces witnesses that the field is his, since the party in possession does not claim that the challenger sold it to him or gave it to him, and since the property is not known to have belonged to his ancestors.

If he produces proof that his father was seen on the property, it is of no avail, since it is possible that the father came to examine the property but did not purchase it. He must produce proof that his father was in possession at least for one day.

14. If the party in possession of a field took the profits therefrom for many years and the challenger of his title came and said, "How do you come to this field?" and the party in possession made an admission saying, "I know that this field once belonged to you, but such a one sold it to me after having purchased it from you," and the challenger said, "Such a one, who sold it to you, is a robber," seeing that the person in possession admitted that the field once belonged to the challenger and that he did not purchase it from him, the field, together with the profits therefrom, must be restored to the challenger, even though he produced no witnesses

to the effect that the field once belonged to him. And so it is in all similar cases. If, however, the party in possession produced witnesses to the effect that such a one, who sold the field to him, had been in possession thereof even for one day or if he said to the challenger, "Such a one purchased the field from you in my presence and subsequently sold it to me," he is to be confirmed in possession of the field, since his seizin is coupled with a claim of rightful ownership and since, having been in possession of the property for the number of years required to constitute seizin, he could have made a claim saying, "I purchased the property from you."

CHAPTER XV

1. If a man was in possession of a field and another who challenged his title thereto produced witnesses to the effect that the field was known to have belonged to him, and the party in possession produced a writing to the effect that he had purchased the field from the challenger, and he also produced witnesses to the effect that he had taken the profits therefrom for the number of years required to constitute seizin, we say to him first, "Confirm your writing," and if the writing is confirmed, he may rest his case thereon, and if he is unable to confirm the writing, reliance may be had upon the witnesses to the seizin, and the party in possession is to swear the informal oath to the effect that he purchased the field.

2. If one of the witnesses to the seizin testified that the party in possession of the field had taken the profits therefrom in wheat for the number of years required to constitute seizin, while the other witness testified that he had taken the profits in barley, the testimony is valid, because the witnesses do not pay particular attention to this matter.

If one of the witnesses testified that the party in possession had taken the profits from the field for the first, third, and fifth years, while the second witness testified that he had taken the profits for the second, fourth, and sixth years, their testimony is not to be combined, because the years comprised within the testimony of the one are not comprised within the testimony of the other. The land, together with the profits, must therefore be restored to the original owner.

3. If a man took possession of a field and took the profits therefrom upon the presumption that he was an heir to the deceased owner, and thereafter it was discovered that there was another heir who was a nearer kin to the deceased than the one who was in possession of the field and that he was entitled to the inheritance—whether the heirship of the other heir was established through the testimony of witnesses or through the admission of the party who was in possession of the field—the party in possession must restore all the profits he has taken from the field.

4. If two persons are contesting the ownership of a field each one saying, "The field is mine," and neither having any proof, or if each one of them produces witnesses to the effect that the field is his or that it belonged to his ancestors, or if each one produces witnesses to the effect that he took the profits from the field for the number of years required to constitute seizin, and the testimony of each set of witnesses relates to the same years, the field is left in the hands of both of them; the one who overpowers the other takes possession of the field, and the other one thus becomes a claimant against the party in possession and therefore has the burden of proof. But if a third person comes and overpowers both of them and takes possession of the field, he is to be removed therefrom.

5. If one of the contestants produces witnesses to the effect that the field is known to have belonged to his ancestors and that he took the profits therefrom for the number of years required to constitute seizin, and the field is in his hands, and the other contestant produces witnesses that he took the profits from the field during the same years, and the field is also in his hands—with the result that the seizin testimony offered by each of the two contestants is contradicted by that offered by the other—the field is to be confirmed in the hands of the one whose seizin witnesses also testify that the field is known to have belonged to his ancestors, and he is

to be placed in full possession thereof. However, if afterward the second contestant also produces witnesses to the effect that the field is known to have belonged to his ancestors, with the result that the testimony of the two sets of witnesses is mutually contradictory with regard to this matter also, the first contestant is to be removed by the court from full possession, the field is to be left in the hands of both contestants, and he who overpowers the other will take full possession thereof.

6. If one of the litigants said, "The field belonged to my ancestors," while the other one said, "It belonged to my ancestors," and one of them produced witnesses to the effect that the field had belonged to his ancestors, while the other one produced witnesses to the effect that he had taken the profits therefrom for the number of years required to constitute seizin, the field is to be restored to the one who produced witnesses that it had belonged to his ancestors, and the other one is to make restitution of the profits he has taken, since he made no valid claim against his adversary, and since the taking of profits by him does not constitute proof, the rule being that seizin which is not coupled with a claim against the original owner is of no avail. However, if afterward the one who was in possession said, "It is true that the field belonged to your ancestors but you sold it to me, and when I first claimed that the field had belonged to my ancestors I meant to say thereby that it was surely mine, as though it had belonged to my ancestors," or if he said, "It belonged to my ancestors by reason of purchase from your ancestors," it is a good plea, since he gave a good explanation of his first plea, and he is confirmed in the possession of the field. But if he first pleaded saying, "It belonged to my ancestors, and not to yours," he will not be heard to make a different plea, such as the one just mentioned. And so it is in all similar cases.

7. If Reuben was in possession of a field and Simeon came and challenged his title thereto, and Reuben said, "I purchased this field from Levi and took the profits therefrom for years of seizin," whereupon Simeon said to him, "But I have a confirmed writing

to the effect that I purchased the field from Levi four years ago to the day," and Reuben replied, "Does it occur to you that it is only three years since I purchased the field? It really is many years since I purchased it, so that I preceded you," Reuben's plea is a good plea, because a man is likely to refer to "many years" as "years of seizin." If, therefore, Reuben produced witnesses to the effect that he had taken the profits from the field for seven years and, consequently, that he had taken such profits for the number of years required to constitute seizin before Simeon purchased it, he is to be confirmed in the possession of the field; but if he took the profits for less than seven years, the field is to be restored to Simeon, because Levi sold the field to Simeon before Reuben acquired seizin therein, and there is no greater protest than that.

8. If one of the litigants says, "The field belonged to my ancestors," and produces witnesses to that effect, while the other one says, "It belonged to my ancestors," but he has no witnesses to testify thereto, the field is to be restored to the party who produces the witnesses, and all the profits, admitted by the other party to have been taken by him from the field, are to be restored by him, even if there be no witnesses to the taking of such profits, since he says that he took the profits by a right derived from his ancestors, while the witnesses testify that the field belonged to the ancestors of his adversary. And so it is in all similar cases.

9. If the challenger produces witnesses to the effect that the field belonged to him and the party in possession thereof pleads, "I purchased it from you, and here is my writing," producing a confirmed writing, and the challenger pleads that the writing is forged, and the holder of the writing makes an admission saying, "This is so, but I had a valid writing which I lost and I took this one in order to frighten him into an admission that he sold the property to me, as in truth he did," he is believed, and the field is not to be taken away from him—but he is required only to swear the informal oath—since he could rely on the writing which was confirmed.

10. If the challenger produces witnesses that the field belonged to him and the party in possession pleads, "I purchased it from you and took the profits therefrom for the number of years required to constitute seizin," producing witnesses to the effect that he took the profits from the field for the number of years required to constitute seizin, and the challenger pleads saying, "How can you claim that you purchased the field from me three years ago today, when I was not present in this locality at that time?" the party in possession is required to produce proof that the challenger was present in the locality at the time when he claims to have purchased the field from him. Even proof of the challenger's presence during one day, which would have enabled him to make the sale, is sufficient. But if the party in possession fails to produce such proof, he is to be removed from the field.

11. If a man went beyond the sea and his right of way to his field was lost, whether the four fields surrounding his field belonged to four different persons at the time when he went beyond the sea or to one person who later sold them to four other persons, the owner of each of the adjoining fields may deny the right of way to the party claiming such right, saying to him, "It is possible that you have your right of way against my fellow." He must therefore buy another right of way, even if it should cost him 100 minas, or fly through the air.

Similarly, if the four fields belong to one person who purchased them from four different persons after the right of way had been lost, the party claiming the right of way may not claim it against him, since he may say to him, "If I were to return the deed of purchase to each one of my vendors you would not be able to pass through the field of any one of them, and I purchased from each one of them all the rights he had in the field."

But if the four surrounding fields belonged to one person who was the owner of these fields from the beginning to the end, the party claiming the right of way may say to him, "In any event, my right of way is against you," and he has the right to use the shortest way in any field which the adjoining owner may choose. And so it is in all similar cases. But if he took possession of the right of way and said, "This is my right of way," he may not be removed therefrom without clear proof.

CHAPTER XVI

1. If Reuben sold a field to Simeon and Levi was one of the witnesses to the writing, and thereafter Levi came and challenged Simeon's title to the field claiming that Reuben had taken it away from him by robbery, no heed will be paid to him. He has lost all his rights to the field, and all the proofs which he may produce with regard thereto will be disregarded, because we say to him, "How can one be a witness to a sale and then come and challenge the vendee's title?"

Similarly, if Levi was a witness to a writing in which it was written, "Bordering in the easterly or westerly direction is the field belonging to Reuben," seeing that the field in question is mentioned in the writing as marking one of the boundaries of the field conveyed by the writing to which the challenger was a witness, he has lost his right to the field and cannot come back and challenge the title of Reuben or Reuben's transferee, because we say to him, "How can one be a witness to a writing in which the field in question is mentioned as marking one of the boundaries of the field conveyed by the writing, and is described therein as belonging to Reuben, and then come back and challenge Reuben's title?"

2. If the witness pleads, "It was only one strip of the field, and not the whole field that I designated as the boundary, and that strip alone immediately adjacent to the boundary line of the field conveyed by the writing belongs to Reuben," it is an acceptable plea and he may make a challenge with regard to the whole field except that strip.

All of the above has reference only to one of the witnesses to the writing who comes and presents a challenge. But the judge who confirmed the writing may present a challenge, because, a judge being permitted to confirm a writing without reading it, he may say, "I did not know what was written in the writing." But a witness may not sign a writing unless he has read it carefully.

3. If Simeon came to take counsel with Levi saying to him, "I am about to buy such a field from Reuben, and it is upon your advice that I will buy it," and Levi said to him, "It is a good field, go and buy it," Levi may nevertheless present a challenge to Simeon's title and has not lost his right to the field. Since he did not perform any deed he may say, "It was my desire to have the field come out of the hands of Reuben who is a man of violence, in order that I might be able to sue at law and obtain my field."

4. If Reuben challenged Simeon's title to a field and Simeon said, "I do not know whereof you are speaking; I purchased this field from Levi and I have witnesses that I took the profits therefrom for the number of years required to constitute seizin," and Reuben said to him, "But I have witnesses that last evening you came to me and said, 'Sell me this field,' it is not good proof, and Simeon may make a plea saying, "I wished to buy the field from you in order to prevent you from challenging my title and molesting me with a lawsuit, although I did not know whether the field belonged to you or to him," or he may make a similar plea. But if Simeon did not make such a plea, we do not plead for him.

5. If Reuben challenged Simeon's title to a field, producing witnesses that the field was his, and Simeon, who was in possession of the field, pleaded, "You sold it to me and I took the profits therefrom for the number of years required to constitute seizin," and Reuben said, "You took the profits by robbery"—whether there were no witnesses at all testifying to the taking of the profits, or there was one witness who testified that Simeon had taken the profits for three years—Simeon is not liable to make restitution of the profits he took, because he said in effect, "What I took was mine," and there were no witnesses whose testimony would have subjected him to liability for the profits, his taking thereof having been established only by his own admission. And as to the one witness who testified that Simeon had taken the profits of the

field for three years, his testimony was intended to support Simeon's position, and if there had been another witness with him, Simeon would have been confirmed in the possession of the field. Therefore, Reuben swears the informal oath that he did not sell the field to Simeon, and the field is to be restored to him, and Simeon swears the informal oath that he is not liable for the profits he has taken and is quit.

6. If two witnesses testified against Simeon that he had taken the profits of the field for a number of years less than that required to constitute seizin, he must make restitution of all the profits he has taken, and even if there be only one witness he must make restitution by the mouth of the one witness, since he does not contradict his testimony but, rather, says, "What he testifies to is true; I took the profits for three years, but what I took was mine." The result, then, is that he is liable to an oath but is unable to swear and must therefore pay.

7. Wherever one becomes liable to make restitution of profits, and the value thereof is unknown—and the court is unable to make an appraisal, such as they would make in the case of the rental for a house or the like, which is known—the profits having been taken from the fruit of trees or of a field, and the extent thereof being unknown, seeing that the plaintiff does not assert a claim for a sum certain, the defendant is to pay only what he admits to have taken, and the general anathema is to be proclaimed against him who took more than he would admit.

8. Wherever a party in possession of land is required to restore the land to its original owner, his tenants—if he let the land to others who are still living—are required to pay the rent a second time to the original owner, and they, in turn, may demand restitution of the rent from the party in possession, because he let to them a place which did not belong to him.

9. One is forbidden to make a false plea in order to pervert justice or to delay it. How is this to be understood? If a man has a debt of one mina owing to him from his fellow, he must not

claim two minas in order to have his adversary make an admission with respect to one mina and subject himself to liability to an oath.

If a man owed a mina to another and the creditor claimed two minas, the debtor must not say to himself, "I will deny everything in court and make an admission privately with respect to the one mina in order not to become liable to an oath."

10. If three persons had a debt of one mina outstanding against another who denied everything, it is not permissible for one to sue and have the other two appear as witnesses and divide the proceeds of the recovery. It is with respect to such matters and the like that Scripture has admonished us *Keep thee far from a false matter* (Exod. 23: 7).

TREATISE V

LAWS CONCERNING INHERITANCE

Involving One

Affirmative Commandment

To Wit

To administer the Law with respect to the order of inheritance.

An exposition of this commandment
is contained in the following chapters.

CHAPTER I

1. The order of inheritance is as follows: if a person died, his children shall inherit him, and they are prior to everyone else, and males are prior to females.

2. A female never shares in the inheritance with a male.

If the decedent left no children, his father shall inherit him; but by a rule derived from Tradition a mother does not inherit her children.

3. Whoever is prior in the order of inheritance, his issue is also prior. Therefore, if a person, whether man or woman, died leaving a son, the son shall inherit everything. If there be no son living, we look to the son's issue. If there be a son's issue, whether male or female, even a son's daughter's daughter's daughter, to the end of time, they shall inherit everything. If there be no son's issue, we resort to the daughter. If there be no daughter living, we look to the daughter's issue. If there be a daughter's issue, whether male or female, to the end of time, such issue shall inherit everything. If there be no daughter's issue, the inheritance resorts to the decedent's father. If the father is not living, we look to the father's issue, that is to the decedent's brothers. If there be a brother of the decedent or a brother's issue, he, or they, shall inherit everything, and if there be none, we resort to the decedent's sister. If there be a sister or a sister's issue, she, or they, shall inherit everything. If there be no issue of a brother or of a sister, seeing that there is no issue of the decedent's father, the inheritance resorts to the father's father. If the father's father is not living, we look to the issue of the father's father, that is to the decedent's father's brothers. The males are prior to the females, and the issue of the males are also prior to the females, just as is the rule in the case of the issue of the decedent himself. If there be no brothers of the decedent's father nor issue of such brothers, the inheritance shall resort to the father's father's father. And in this manner the inheritance continues to ascend up to Reuben.

It follows therefore that the son is prior to the daughter, and all of the son's issue are also prior to the daughter; the daughter is prior to her father's father, and all of her issue are also prior to her father's father; the decedent's father is prior to the decedent's brothers, because they are the father's issue; and the decedent's brother is prior to his sister, and all of the brother's issue are also prior to the decedent's sister. The decedent's sister is prior to her father's father, and all of her issue are also prior to her father's father; the decedent's father's father is prior to the decedent's father's brothers; the decedent's father's brothers are prior to his father's sister, and all of the issue of the father's brothers are also prior to the father's sister. The decedent's father's sister is prior to the decedent's father's father's father, and her issue are also prior to the decedent's father's father's father. And in this manner the inheritance continues to ascend to the beginning of the generations. Therefore, there is no man in Israel who has no heirs.

4. If a man died leaving a daughter and a son's daughter, nay, even a son's daughter's daughter's daughter, to the end of many generations, the latter is prior and shall inherit everything and the decedent's daughter shall not have anything. The same rule applies to the decedent's brother's daughter as against the decedent's sister, and to the decedent's father's brother's son's daughter as against the decedent's father's sister. And so it is in all similar cases.

5. If a man had two sons and they died in his lifetime, one of them leaving three sons and the other leaving one daughter, and thereafter the grandfather died, the three grandsons take one half of the inheritance and the granddaughter takes the other half, because the granddaughter takes the share to which her father would be entitled if he were living, and the three grandsons take the share to which their father would be entitled if he were living. And in similar manner the inheritance is divided between the decedent's brother's children and also between the decedent's father's brother's children to the beginning of the generations.

6. Maternal kin is not deemed kin with respect to inheritance; only paternal kin succeeds to the inheritance. Therefore, brothers by the same mother do not inherit each other, but brothers by the same father do inherit each other, and there is no difference between a brother by the same father only and a brother by the same father and the same mother.

7. All relatives tracing their relationship to the decedent through a prohibited union are, with respect to inheritance, on a par with those tracing it through a legitimate union. How is this to be understood? Where the decedent had a son or a brother who was a *mamzer,* such son or brother is like any other son or brother with respect to the inheritance. But the decedent's son by a bondwoman or by an alien woman is not deemed a son in any respect and does not inherit at all.

8. The wife does not inherit her husband at all, but, by enactment of the Scribes, the husband inherits all the property of his wife, and he is prior to everyone else with respect to her inheritance. Even though the marriage was one prohibited by law, such as that of a widow to a high priest, or of a divorced woman, or of a woman released from leviratical marriage, to a common priest, and even though the wife was a minor, or the husband a deaf-mute, the husband inherits his wife.

9. We have already stated in the Laws Concerning Marriage that a husband does not inherit his wife unless she entered his domain before she died, and that a hearing husband does not inherit a deaf-mute wife if he married her while she was a deaf-mute, even though she was later cured. We have also stated there that a husband inherits the property which came to his wife by way of inheritance and was vested in her, whether or not she brought such property as her dowry at the time of the marriage. We have also stated that if the wife was divorced by the husband by a bill of divorce of doubtful validity, the husband does not inherit her.

10. If a man married a minor girl of such tender age that no disaffirmance by her is required in order to render the marriage

null, he does not inherit her, since there is no marital relationship at all here. Similarly, a mentally incompetent man who married a mentally incompetent woman does not inherit her, since the Sages have not enacted that the mentally incompetent man or woman should have marital capacity.

11. If a man's wife died and thereafter her father or her brother or some other relative, to whose inheritance the wife would be entitled to succeed if she were living, died, it is not the husband who inherits them but the wife's issue, if there be any issue, and if there be none, the inheritance is to resort to her paternal kin, because the husband does not inherit property which was in expectancy at the time of the wife's death but only such property as had already come to the wife by inheritance when she died.

12. Nor does the husband inherit his wife while he is in the grave, as do the heirs who are the decedent's paternal kin. How is this to be understood? If the husband died and thereafter his wife died, we do not say, "Since the husband would have been prior to every other person in the order of inheritance, his heirs should also be prior to the wife's heirs," but it is the wife's heirs, who are her kin through her father, that inherit her if she died after her husband.

13. Similarly, a son does not inherit his mother while he is in the grave so as to transmit the inheritance to his brothers by his father. How is this to be understood? If a man died and thereafter his mother died, we do not say, "Since the son would have been prior in the order of inheritance if he had survived his mother, his heirs should also be prior to the heirs of this woman"—with the result that the son's brothers by his father would inherit from his mother who died after him—but it is the issue of the son who inherits the mother if there be such issue, and if there be none the inheritance resorts to the mother's paternal kin.

But if the mother died first and then the son died, even though he was an infant less than one day old and was born prematurely, so long as he lived one instant after his mother's death, he inherits his mother and transmits the inheritance to his heirs who are his paternal kin.

CHAPTER II

1. The first-born takes a double portion in his father's property. For it is written *To give him a double portion* (Deut. 21:17). How is this to be understood? If the decedent left five sons, one of them a first-born, the first-born takes one third of the property and each one of the four *plain* sons takes one sixth thereof; if he left nine sons, the first-born takes one fifth and each one of the eight plain sons takes one tenth; and according to this ratio they always divide the property among themselves.

2. The first-born son who was born after his father's death does not take a double portion. For it is written *It shall be in the day that he causeth his sons to inherit . . . But he shall acknowledge the first-born* (Deut. 21:16–17). But if his forehead emerged in his father's lifetime, even though his whole head did not emerge into the world until after his father's death, he takes a double portion.

3. A first-born who was operated upon by section and found to be a male does not take a double portion, and a plain son who was similarly operated upon and discovered to be a male does not cause a diminution in the primogeniture portion. For it is written *And they have borne him sons* (Deut. 21:15)—he must be a son from the moment of his birth.

4. What do we mean by saying that he does not cause a diminution in the primogeniture portion? If the decedent, at the time of his death, had a first-born son, two plain sons, and this *ṭumṭum* who was later operated upon and found to be a male, the first-born takes one quarter of the property for his primogeniture portion, as though the two plain sons alone were there to share with him, and the remaining three quarters are divided among the two plain sons, the ṭumṭum who was operated upon, and the first-born equally.

5. A one-day-old minor causes a diminution of the primogeniture portion, but an embryo does not cause such diminution. Thus, a son who was born after his father's death does not cause a diminution of the primogeniture portion.

6. If a doubt has arisen with respect to the identity of the decedent's first-born son, as where the first-born was confused with another son, he does not take a double portion.

What do the two sons do if their identity was at one time known and later they became confused? They write a power of attorney to each other and take the primogeniture portion when dividing the inheritance with their brothers. But if their identity was never known, as where they were born together in a hiding place, they may not execute a power of attorney to each other, and there is no primogeniture portion.

7. If a man had two sons, a first-born and a plain son, and both of them died in his lifetime leaving children, the first-born leaving a daughter, and the plain son leaving a son, the son of the plain son inherits one third of the grandfather's property, which is his father's share, and the daughter of the first-born inherits two thirds, which is her father's share. The same rule applies to the decedent's brother's children and to his father's brother's children and to all other heirs: if the father of one of the heirs who takes through his father was a first-born, the heir takes his father's primogeniture portion.

8. The first-born does not take a double portion in the property of his mother. How is this to be understood? If the first-born and a plain son succeed to their mother's inheritance, they divide the inheritance equally, whether the first-born be a first-born with respect to inheritance or a firstling.

9. A first-born with respect to inheritance is he who was born to his father first. For it is written *For he is the first fruits of his strength* (Deut. 21:17). No regard is had to the mother and even if she had previously given birth to several sons, the one who was born first to his father inherits a double portion.

10. He who comes after a prematurely born child, even though the head of the prematurely born child emerged while the child was still alive, is a first-born with respect to inheritance.

Similarly, if a child was born in the ninth month of the mother's pregnancy but when its head emerged it was dead, he who is born after that child is a first-born with respect to inheritance, because what is meant by *the first fruits of his strength* is that no other child, who emerged into the world alive, was previously born to him. Therefore, if a child born in the ninth month of the mother's pregnancy protruded the greater part of its head while it was still alive, he who comes after it is not a first-born.

11. Neither the child that emerged from the mother's side nor the child that came after such a child is a first-born—the former, because he was not *born,* and it is written *And they have borne him children* (Deut. 21:15), and the latter, because he was preceded by another child.

12. If a man had children while he was a heathen and then became a proselyte, he has no first-born with respect to inheritance. But if an Israelite father had a son by a bondwoman or by a heathen woman, seeing that he is not deemed a son, he who was born to the father by an Israelite woman after him is a first-born with respect to inheritance and takes the double portion.

13. If the first-born was a mamzer he takes the double portion. For it is written *But he shall acknowledge the first-born, the son of the hateful* (Deut. 21:15), that is of her whose union is hateful. And it is needless to say that if the first-born was the son of a divorced woman or of a woman released from leviratical marriage, he takes the double portion.

14. Three persons are believed with respect to the first-born: a. the midwife; b. the mother; c. the father. The midwife is believed, if immediately upon the birth she says, "This one emerged first"; the mother is believed, if within seven days after the birth she says, "This one is the first-born"; the father is believed forever. Even if the father said about one who had not been reputed to be

his son at all, "He is my son and my first-born," he is believed. Similarly, if he said about one who had been reputed to be his first-born, "He is not my first-born," he is believed.

15. If the father became mute he is examined in the same manner in which he would be examined with respect to a divorce. If he indicated by gesture or writing that *this one* is his first-born son, that son takes the double portion.

16. If witnesses testified that they had heard the father say certain things from which it was to be inferred that *this one* was his first-born son, that son takes the double portion, even though the father did not say explicitly, "This one is my first-born."

17. If the witnesses heard the father say, "This son of mine is a first-born," that son does not take the double portion by such testimony—since it is possible that he is first-born to his mother and that this was what the father had in mind—unless the father said, "He is *my* first-born son."

CHAPTER III

1. The first-born does not take the double portion in property in which the father had only an expectancy at the time of his death, but only in property which was vested in the father, having come into his possession. For it is written *Of all that he hath* (Deut. 21:17).

How is this to be understood? If one of those who, by the rules of inheritance, transmit their inheritance to the father died after the father's death, the first-born son and the plain son take equal shares. Similarly, if the father had a debt owing to him, or if he had a ship on the sea, they take equal shares.

2. If the father left a cow which was hired out for hire or on shares or was grazing in the pasture ground, and after the father's death the cow bore young, the first-born takes the double portion in the cow and her offspring.

3. If one of the father's friends slaughtered an animal and there-after the father died, the first-born takes the double portion in the priestly gifts due from the owner of that animal.

4. The first-born does not take the double portion in the improvement of the property which occurred after the father's death, but must reckon the value of such improvement in money and give the excess to the plain son, provided a change occurred in the property, as where green ears of corn or dates became ripe. But if the property improved of itself and no change occurred therein, as where a small tree grew thick or land was covered with alluvium, the first-born takes the double portion in the improvement. If, however, the improvement occurred through expenditures, he does not take the double portion therein.

5. The first-born does not take the double portion in a debt owing to his father, even if the debt be on a writing and even if land be recovered therefor.

If the father had a debt owing to him from his first-born son, it is doubtful whether the first-born son should take the double portion therein, because it is in his hand, or he should not take the double portion, because he succeeds to the debt through his father into whose hands it had not yet come when he died. Therefore, he takes therein one half of the primogeniture portion.

6. If the first-born sold his primogeniture portion before division of the inheritance was made, the sale is valid, because the first-born is deemed to have the primogeniture portion before division is made. Therefore, if the first-born divided with his brothers some of the property, whether landed or movable, and took a share equal to that of a plain son, he thereby relinquished his primogeniture portion in all of the property and takes in the balance thereof only a share equal to that of a plain son.

All this applies only if the first-born did not make protest. But if he made protest against his brothers, saying in the presence of two witnesses, "While I am dividing these grapes with my brothers equally, it is not because I have relinquished my primogeniture portion," it is a valid protest, and no relinquishment of the double portion in the balance of the property results from the division. Even if he made protest with respect to grapes while they were still attached to the vine and thereafter they were cut off and divided between the brothers equally, no relinquishment of the double portion in the balance of the property results from the division. But if the grapes were pressed after the first-born made protest and he divided the wine with his brothers equally, without making protest anew when the grapes were changed into wine, he has relinquished his double portion in the balance of the property. To what may this case be likened? To one who made protest with respect to grapes and thereafter divided olives with his brothers equally, thereby relinquishing his double portion in everything. And so it is in all similar cases.

7. He who marries his brother's wife by leviratical marriage inherits all of his brother's vested property. But with respect to the property which the deceased brother had in expectancy, he is like all the other brothers, since Scripture has called him first-born. For it is written *And it shall be that the first-born that she beareth shall succeed in the name of his brother that is dead, that his name be not blotted out of Israel* (Deut. 25:6). And just as he does not take the deceased brother's estate in expectancy, as he does his vested estate, so does he not take the deceased brother's share in the improvement which occurred in the father's property after the father's death between the time of the deceased brother's death and the time of the division of the father's property among the brothers. Even if the improvement occurred after he married his brother's wife and before they made division of the father's property, he is, with respect to the improvement, like all the other brothers—although he takes from the father's property two shares, his own and that of his deceased brother whose wife he married— seeing that the father died in the lifetime of all the brothers.

8. We have already stated in the Laws Concerning Neighbors that the first-born takes his two shares in one parcel, but that when the brother who has married his deceased brother's wife by levirati-

cal marriage makes division of his father's property with his brothers he takes his own share and that of his deceased brother by lot, and that if what falls to him as his lot happens to be in two different places, he takes in those places.

9. If a widow who had been waiting to be married by leviratical marriage to one of her deceased husband's brothers died, even though one of the brothers had betrothed her, her paternal kin succeed to her mĕlog property and to one half of the "iron sheep" property, and her husband's heirs succeed to her kĕṯubbah, together with one half of the "iron sheep" property. The husband's heirs, seeing that they succeed to her kĕṯubbah, are liable for her burial, as we have stated in the proper place.

CHAPTER IV

1. If a man said, "This is my son," or "This is my brother," or "This is my father's brother," or if he made a similar declaration with respect to other heirs, even though his declaration was made with respect to persons who had not been reputed to be his relatives, he is believed, and the person named by him is to inherit him, whether he made the declaration while in health or while lying sick. Even if, after having lost the power of speech, he wrote in his handwriting that this one is his heir, he is examined in the same manner as he would be examined with respect to a divorce.

2. If a man was reputed to be another man's brother or his uncle's son, and the other man said, "He is not my brother," or "He is not my uncle's son," he is not believed. But if he said with respect to a man who was reputed to be his son, "He is not my son," he is believed, and that man shall not inherit him. And it seems to me that even if the son had children—although with respect to pedigree the father is not believed when he says, "He is not my son," and the son is not established by the mouth of the father to be the issue of an adulterous union—the father is believed with respect to inheritance, and that son shall not inherit him.

3. If a man said, "This is my son," and then retracted and said, "He is my bondman," and then again retracted and said, "He is my son," he is believed, even though he waits upon him like a bondman, because it is assumed that when he said, "He is my bondman," he meant thereby that he was unto him like a bondman. But if they were wont to call him a hundred-zuz bondman, and similar appellations which are applied to bondmen only, the would-be father is not believed.

4. If, while passing through the customhouse, a man said, "This is my son," and thereafter he retracted and said, "This is my bondman," he is believed, because when he said, "He is my son," it was only for the purpose of avoiding the payment of duty. If he said in the customhouse, "He is my bondman," and then retracted and said, "He is my son," he is not believed.

5. Bondmen and bondwomen may not be called *father of such a one* and *mother of such a one,* lest a misunderstanding arise and *this son* be tainted as a result thereof. Therefore, if the bondmen and bondwomen are particularly important, have a reputation, and the entire community know them, as well as the sons and the bondmen of their master, as in the case of the bondmen of the prince, they may be called *father* and *mother.*

6. If a man had a bondwoman and he begot a son by her and was behaving toward him in the manner in which one behaves toward his sons or said, "He is my son and his mother has been emancipated," the son shall inherit him, if the father was a scholar or a worthy man of proven strictness in the observance of the religious precepts. Nevertheless, the son may not marry an Israelite woman unless he produces proof that his mother was emancipated before she gave birth to him, since the mother was reputed to be a bondwoman. But if the father was one of the common people— and needless to say if he was one of those who abandon themselves in such things—the son is presumed to be a bondman in every respect and his brothers by his father may sell him; and if his father left no other son but him, his father's wife is subject to the

Law of Leviratical Marriage. This is the rule which seems to me to go back to the principles of the tradition. There is, however, one authority who makes no distinction between worthy men and other people except with respect to the brothers' power of sale, and there is another authority who holds that even with respect to inheritance no distinction should be made among Israelites. However, it is not proper to rely on this opinion.

7. All heirs may succeed to the inheritance by reputation (ḥăzaḳah). How is this to be understood? If witnesses testified, "This man is known to us by reputation to be the son of such a one," or "his brother," he succeeds to the inheritance by their testimony, even though they are not witnesses of the pedigree and do not know the truth thereof.

8. If Jacob who had been reputed to have but two sons, Reuben and Simeon, died, and Reuben took hold of Levi, a man from the market, and said, "This one is also our brother," while Simeon said, "I do not know," Simeon takes one half of the property, Reuben takes one third—since he admitted that there were three brothers— and Levi takes one sixth.

If thereafter Levi died, the one sixth is to revert to Reuben. If other property had fallen to Levi as his inheritance, Reuben and Simeon divide it between themselves, since Reuben admitted to Simeon that Levi was their brother.

If an improvement occurred automatically in the one sixth and thereafter Levi died, then, if the improvement is such that it may be readily converted into usable profit, as grapes which have reached the stage of being cut off, the improvement is deemed like property which Levi inherited from elsewhere and it shall be divided between Reuben and Simeon, and if the grapes have not reached the stage of being cut off, they belong to Reuben alone.

If Simeon said, "Levi is not my brother," and Levi took part of Reuben's share, as we have stated, and thereafter Levi died, Simeon shall not inherit anything from him, but Reuben alone shall inherit the one sixth, together with any other property which Levi may have left.

The above rules apply to all heirs when some of them admit and others deny the heirship of additional heirs.

CHAPTER V

1. This is the general rule with respect to heirs: wherever there are two heirs and the heirship of one of them is certain, while that of the other is doubtful, he whose heirship is doubtful does not take anything. If the heirship of both of them is doubtful, that is wherever it is unknown whether one or the other is the heir, they divide the inheritance equally.

Therefore, if a man died leaving a son and a ṭumṭum or a hermaphrodite, the son inherits everything, since the heirship of the ṭumṭum or of the hermaphrodite is doubtful. If he left daughters and a ṭumṭum or a hermaphrodite, they inherit equally, the ṭumṭum and the hermaphrodite being considered like one of the daughters.

2. We have already stated in the Law Concerning Marriage the rule concerning the rights of daughters, as against sons, to have their maintenance and dowry out of the decedent's estate. We have stated there that the daughters' right to maintenance is one of the conditions of the keṭubbah.

When the amount of property left by the father is large, the daughters are entitled to their maintenance and the sons inherit everything, except that the daughters are to be endowed with one tenth of the value of the property each, in order to enable them to wed. When the amount of the property is small the sons take nothing and everything goes for the maintenance of the daughters.

Therefore, if a man died leaving sons and daughters and a ṭumṭum or a hermaphrodite, then, if the amount of the property is large, the sons inherit it and they relegate the ṭumṭum to the position of the daughters and, like the daughters, he receives maintenance, and if the amount of the property is small, the daughters relegate the ṭumṭum to the position of the sons and say to him, "You are a male and you are not entitled to maintenance together with us."

3. If a woman remarried, without having waited three months after her husband's death, and gave birth to a son, and it is unknown whether she bore the son to the first husband after a nine-month pregnancy, or to the second husband after a seven-month pregnancy, the son does not inherit either of them, because his heirship is doubtful, and if the son died, both of them inherit him and share equally, because the heirship of both of them is doubtful, it being equally possible that either one or the other is his father.

4. If a *yĕḇamah* married by leviratical marriage, without having waited three months after her husband's death, and gave birth to a son, and it is unknown whether she bore the son to the first husband after a nine-month pregnancy, or to the second husband after a seven-month pregnancy, and the son whose filiation is in doubt says to the *yaḇam*, "Perhaps I am the decedent's son and I should inherit all of his property, and you were not supposed to marry my mother by leviratical marriage, because she was not subject to such marriage," while the yaḇam says, "Perhaps you are my son and your mother was subject to leviratical marriage, and you do not have anything in my brother's property"—seeing that this yaḇam is also of doubtful status, it being possible that he is or that he is not a yaḇam—they divide the property equally.

A similar rule applies when the question concerning the property of the decedent, whose wife was married by leviratical marriage, arises between the son whose filiation is in doubt and the other sons of the yaḇam: they divide the property equally, that is, the son whose filiation is in doubt takes one half thereof, and the other sons of the yaḇam take the other half.

If the yaḇam died after having divided his deceased brother's property with this son whose filiation is in doubt, and the yaḇam's other sons whose filiation is certain come to succeed to their father's property, the son whose filiation is in doubt takes nothing in the father's property, nor may he recover anything from the other sons, despite the fact that he could say to them, "If I am your brother give me a share in this inheritance, and if I am not your brother return to me the one half of the inheritance which your father received from his brother who predeceased him."

5. If the son whose filiation is in doubt and the yaḅam come to divide the property of the yaḅam's father, the yaḅam's heirship is certain, while that of the son whose filiation is in doubt is not. The latter would be entitled to one half of the property, if it were certain that he was the son of the decedent's deceased son— and the yaḅam would be entitled to the other half—and would not be entitled to anything, if it were certain that he was the son of the yaḅam. Therefore, the yaḅam inherits everything, superseding the son whose filiation is in doubt.

If the yaḅam left two sons whose filiation was certain, and thereafter the yaḅam's father died, and the son whose filiation is in doubt says, "I am the son of your father's deceased brother and I am entitled to one half of our grandfather's property, and both of you are entitled to the other half," while the two sons of the yaḅam say, "You are our brother, the son of the yaḅam, and you are entitled only to one third of the property of our grandfather," they take the one half to which they are entitled by his admission, while he takes the one third to which he is entitled by their admission, and the remaining one sixth is divided between them equally, that is, he takes one half thereof and the two take the other one half.

If the son whose filiation is in doubt died, and the yaḅam says, "Perhaps he was my son, and I am entitled to inherit him," while the father of the yaḅam says, "Perhaps he was the son of my deceased son and I am entitled to inherit him," they divide the inheritance equally.

6. If a house collapsed upon a man and his wife, and it is unknown whether the wife died first, so that the husband's heirs are entitled to inherit all of her property, what is the rule? The mĕlog property is presumed to belong to the wife's heirs, and the kĕtubbah, principal and additional, is presumed to belong to the husband's heirs, and the iron sheep property they divide equally, the

wife's heirs taking one half thereof and the husband's heirs taking the other half.

But if a house collapsed upon a man and his mother, the mother's property is presumed to belong to the mother's heirs, because their heirship of the mother is certain, whereas the son's heirs' heirship of the mother is doubtful, since, as we have stated, the son's brothers by his father have nothing in the mother's property if the son predeceases the mother.

7. If a house collapsed upon a man and his daughter's son, and it is unknown whether the grandfather died first, and his daughter's son succeeded to the inheritance, so that the grandfather's property belongs to the grandson's heirs, or his daughter's son died first, and —the rule being that a son does not succeed to his mother's inheritance while he is in the grave, as we have stated—the grandfather's property belongs to his heirs, the property is to be divided between the heirs of the grandfather and the heirs of his daughter's son.

Similarly, if the grandfather was taken captive and died in captivity and his daughter's son died in his home country, or if the grandson was taken captive and died in captivity and his mother's father died in his home country, the grandfather's property is to be divided between his own heirs and those of his daughter's son.

8. If a house collapsed upon a man and his father, or upon any other person to whose inheritance he would succeed if he were living, and there is outstanding against the son his wife's kĕṭubbah and other debts, and the father's heirs say, "The son died first and did not leave anything, so that the debts are lost," while the creditors say, "The father died first and the son acquired a right in his inheritance, so that we are entitled to collect from his share," the property is presumed to belong to the heirs, and the woman and the creditors must produce proof or go without anything.

9. The rule with regard to those who died under the ruins of a collapsed structure, or drowned in the sea or fell into a conflagration, or died on the same day while one was in one country and the

other in another country, is the same, because in all of these cases, and in similar cases, we do not know who it was that died first.

CHAPTER VI

1. One may not constitute as an heir him whom the Law does not constitute as his heir; nor may one remove the inheritance from an heir—although this is a matter pecuniary—because in the division of Scripture treating of inheritances it is said *And it shall be unto the children of Israel a statute of judgment* (Num. 27: 11), that is to say: this Law is not subject to change and a condition qualifying it is not valid. Whether the decedent gave his instructions while he was in health or while he was lying sick, whether orally or in writing, they are not valid.

2. If, therefore, a man said, "Such a one, my son, my first-born, shall not take the double portion," or "Such a one, my son, shall not inherit me together with his brothers," his words are of no effect. If he said, "Such a one shall inherit me," when he had a daughter, or "My daughter shall inherit me," when he had a son, his words are likewise of no effect. And so it is in all similar cases.

But if he had many heirs, as where he had many sons or brothers or daughters, and while lying sick he said, "Such a one, my brother, of all my brothers, shall inherit me," or "Such a one, my daughter, of all my daughters, shall inherit me," his words shall stand, whether he uttered them orally or put them in writing.

But if he said, "Such a one, my son, alone shall inherit me," then, if he uttered these words orally, they shall stand, but if he wrote all his property to his son, he only made him guardian, as we have stated.

3. If he said, "Such a one, my son, shall inherit half of my property, and the other sons shall inherit the other half," his words shall stand. But if he said, "The first-born son shall inherit equally with the plain sons," or if he said, "He shall not inherit a double portion," his words are of no effect. For it is said *He may not make*

the son of the beloved the first-born before the son of the hated,
who is the first-born; but he shall acknowledge the first-born, the
son of the hated (Deut. 21 : 16, 17).

4. While he is in health he may not add anything to, or detract
anything from, either the portion of the first-born or that of any
other of his heirs.

5. All this applies only if he uttered his words in the language
of inheritance, but if he gave by way of gift, his words shall stand.
Therefore, if one divided his property among his sons by the word
of his mouth while he was lying sick, giving more to one and less
to another, or giving to the first-born a share equal to that of the
other brothers, his words shall stand. But if he uttered his words in
the language of inheritance, they are of no effect.

6. If he wrote words of gift either at the beginning, or in the
middle, or at the end, even though he mentioned language of inheritance at the beginning and at the end, his words shall stand.
How is this to be understood? If he said, "Such a field shall be
given to such a one, my son, and he shall inherit it," or if he said,
"He shall inherit it, and it shall be given to him, and he shall inherit
it," or "He shall inherit it, and it shall be given to him," seeing
that there is language of gift there, even though he mentioned
language of inheritance at the beginning and at the end, his words
shall stand.

Similarly, if he left three fields to three heirs saying, "Such a one
shall inherit such a field, and such a field shall be given to such a
one, and such a one shall inherit such a field," they all acquired title
to their respective fields, even though the one with respect to whom
he used the language of inheritance was not the one with respect to
whom he used the language of gift, provided he did not tarry between one phrase and another as much time as is needed for an utterance. But if he did tarry, it is necessary that language of gift be
contained in all of the three dispositions.

7. How is this to be understood? If he uses language of gift in the
middle, he must say, "Such a one and such a one shall inherit

such a field and such a field, which I have given to them by way of gift, and they shall inherit them." And if he uses language of gift at the beginning he must say, "Such a field and such a field shall be given to such a one and such a one and they shall inherit it." And if he uses language of gift at the end he must say, "Such a one and such a one shall inherit such a field and such a field, which I have given to them by way of gift."

8. The rule that the husband shall inherit his wife, although first introduced by the Sages, has been accorded by them the force of Pentateuchal Law, so that a stipulation with respect thereto is of no avail unless made during the period of betrothal, as we have stated in the Laws Concerning Marriage.

9. A heathen inherits his father by Pentateuchal Law, but in all other cases of inheritance he is allowed to follow his own customs.

10. A proselyte does not inherit his heathen father. However, because of apprehension that the proselyte might return to his rebellious ways if he was not accorded the right of inheritance, the Sages have enacted that he should inherit his heathen father, just as he would if he was not a proselyte. And it seems to me that a stipulation with respect to such inheritance is valid, since the heathen is not bound to abide by the enactment of the Sages.

A heathen does not inherit his proselyte father, nor does a proselyte inherit a proselyte, either by Pentateuchal or Rabbinical Law.

11. He who gives away his property to a stranger, leaving out his heirs, incurs the displeasure of the Sages, even though his heirs do not behave properly towards him. But such strangers acquire title to all the property given to them.

It is of the quality of piety that a pious man should not be a witness to a will by which a transfer of the inheritance from an heir is effected, even if it be from a son who is not of good behavior to his brother who is a wise man and of good behavior.

12. An apostate Israelite inherits his Israelite relatives. But if the court see fit, in order not to lend encouragement to him, to deprive him of his property right and penalize him that he should not inherit, they may do so. And if he has children in Israel, their apostate father's inheritance shall be given to them. Such is always the custom in the West.

13. The Sages have ordained that a man, during his lifetime, should not make any distinction between his sons, even with respect to small matters, in order that they might not come to rivalry and jealousy even as Joseph and his brothers.

CHAPTER VII

1. The heirs do not succeed to the inheritance until they have produced clear proof that their ancestor is dead. But if it was rumored that he had died or if a heathen came and in casual conversation told about his death—although his wife may be permitted to remarry and is entitled to collect her kĕṭubbah relying upon the statement of the heathen—the heirs may not take the inheritance in reliance thereon.

2. If a woman came and said, "My husband died," although she is believed in so far as her capacity to remarry and her right to collect her kĕṭubbah are concerned, the heirs may not enter upon the inheritance in reliance upon her statement. But if she said, "My husband died," and thereafter she married by leviratical marriage, her leviratical husband enters upon the inheritance in reliance upon her statement. For it is said *He shall succeed in the name of his brother* (Deut. 25:6)—and he has succeeded.

3. If a man drowned in endless waters and witnesses came and testified that he had drowned in their presence—and all trace of him was lost—the heirs may take the inheritance in reliance upon the testimony of the witnesses, although *at the outset* we may not permit his wife to remarry in reliance thereon.

Similarly, if witnesses came and testified that they had seen a man fall into a den of lions or leopards, or that they had seen him hanging and the birds eating his flesh, or that he had been murdered and that they did not recognize his face, but that he had distinctive marks on his body which they recognized—in all of these cases and the like, if thereafter all trace of him was lost, the heirs take the inheritance in reliance upon the testimony, even though his wife may not be permitted to remarry in reliance thereon. For we say that the strictness of the rule making such testimony ineffective in so far as the capacity of the man's wife to remarry is concerned is due to the fact that a prohibition entailing the penalty of extirpation is involved therein, but with respect to matters pecuniary, if the witnesses testified to things which raise a presumption of death, asserting that they had seen all those things—and all trace of the man was lost and it was rumored that he had died—the heirs may take the inheritance in reliance upon such testimony. Such is the daily practice of all the courts and we have heard of no dissent in the matter.

4. If a man was taken captive and it was rumored that he had died, and his heirs entered upon the inheritance dividing it among themselves, it shall not be taken away from them. Such is also the rule in the case of one who escaped because of danger. But if a man departed voluntarily and it was rumored that he had died, and his heirs entered upon his property dividing it among themselves, it shall be taken away from them unless they produce proof that their ancestor is dead.

5. It is incumbent upon the court to occupy itself with the property of a captive or of one who escaped because of danger. How shall it proceed? All the movable property is to be deposited in the hands of a trustworthy person, and possession of the landed property is to be delivered to the relatives who would be entitled to inherit the captive, or the one who escaped, if he died, in order that they may cultivate the land and occupy themselves with it either until it has become known that he is dead or until he has returned.

And when the captive or the one who escaped returns, the relatives in possession of the land make an appraisal, in accordance with the custom prevailing among all the tenants on shares in the locality, of the work they have done and of the profits they have taken.

And why does not the court always appoint a guardian, whether over the movables or over the landed property, until the owner has returned or until it has become known with certainty that he is dead? Because it is not incumbent upon the court to appoint a guardian for adults who are mentally competent.

6. If a man was taken captive or escaped because of danger, leaving behind him standing crops to be harvested, grapes to be cut, and dates or olives to be plucked, the court takes possession of his property and appoints a guardian over it who harvests, cuts, plucks, and sells the produce, depositing the money with the court to be kept together with all the other movables, and thereafter a relative of the captive, or of the man who escaped, is put in possession of the property. For if the relative were to be put in possession at first, he might remove the produce which is ready to be removed and consume it. The same rule applies to houses, inns, and shops which are designed to be rented out, do not require work and labor, and are not let on shares; a relative who would be entitled to inherit the absent man if he was dead is not put in possession of these, because he would be collecting the rent and consuming it.

What, then, is to be done? The court appoints a receiver and the rent remains on deposit with the court until the heir produces proof that the absent man is dead or until the man returns and takes what is his.

7. The relative is never put in possession except when the property consists of fields, gardens, vineyards, and the like, in which he is to act as a tenant on shares, in order that the property should not deteriorate and turn into wasteland.

8. If a man departed voluntarily, leaving his property behind, and it is not known where he went or what happened to him, the court does not put a relative of his in possession of his property;

but if the relative took possession it does not remove him. The court is not required to occupy itself with the owner's property and to appoint a guardian, either over the landed property or over the movables, since he departed voluntarily, leaving his property behind.

And what is the rule governing such property? Movables are to remain in the hands of him who has possession thereof until the owner comes and claims them or until he dies and his heir claims them.

9. As to landed property: if he left a tenant in a house, the tenant is to pay no rent; if his field or vineyard was in possession of a tenant on shares, it is to remain as he left it until he returns; and if he left a field or a vineyard uncultivated, it is to remain uncultivated, since he voluntarily caused a loss to himself, and a loss incurred voluntarily does not come within the commandment requiring us to restore lost property to its owner.

10. If it was rumored that he had died all the movables are recovered by the court and, by its order, are placed in the hands of a trustworthy person, and the fields and vineyards are delivered into the possession of a relative who is to hold them as a tenant on shares until he produces clear proof that the owner died or until the owner returns.

CHAPTER VIII

1. When a relative is put in possession of the property of a captive, or of one who escaped, or of one who departed voluntarily, and about whom it was rumored that he had died, it must not be a minor who is so put in possession, lest he cause the property to deteriorate.

A relative may not be put in possession of the property of a minor, lest the relative make a claim saying, "This is my share of the inheritance." Even a relative through a relative may not be put in possession. How is this to be understood? If there were two brothers, one adult and one minor, and the minor brother was taken captive or escaped, the adult is not to be put in possession of his field, because, the minor being unable to make formal protest, it is possible that his brother will hold on to the property and after the lapse of several years will say, "This is my share which came to me as my inheritance, and it was by right of inheritance that I entered upon the property." Even the captive minor's brother's son is not to be put into possession of his property, lest he say, "I inherited this share through my father."

2. A relative is never to be put in possession of a minor's property, even a relative through the minor's mother's brothers, who would not be entitled to inherit the minor if he died, this being an extraordinary precaution. And even if there be a writing of division between them, whether of houses or of fields, the relative shall not take possession; even if he says, "Write against me a writing of tenancy on shares," he shall not take possession, since it is possible that the writing will be lost and in the course of time the relative will claim that the property came to him from his ancestor by right of inheritance.

It once happened that a woman, who had three daughters, was taken captive together with one of her daughters, and her second daughter died, leaving a minor son. The Sages said: the remaining daughter shall not be put in possession of the property, since it is possible that the grandmother is dead and, consequently, one third of the property belongs to the minor, and a relative is not to be put in possession of a minor's property; nor is the minor to be put in possession of the property, since it is possible that the grandmother is still alive, and a minor is not to be put in possession of a captive's property. What, then, is to be done? Since it is necessary to appoint a guardian over the one half of the property belonging to the minor, the guardian is to be appointed over the entire property of the grandmother.

After some time it was rumored that the grandmother had died and the Sages said, "Let the remaining daughter take possession of the one third of the property which is her share of the inheritance, and let the minor take possession of the one third which is his share of the inheritance of the grandmother, and as to the one third belonging to the captive daughter, a guardian shall be appointed over it, because it is possible that the minor has a share therein, since if the captive daughter is dead, one half of her one third belongs to the minor. And so it is in all similar cases.

CHAPTER IX

1. Brothers, who have not yet divided their father's inheritance, but are using, all of them together, what their father left to them, are like partners in every respect. Other heirs are likewise partners in the property of their ancestor, and whenever one of them engages in a business transaction with the money left to them, the profits are shared in common.

2. If there were adults and minors among the heirs and the adult heirs improved the property, the improvement is shared in common; but if they said, "Take note of what our father left to us, as we are going to work upon it and take the profits," the improvement belongs to the improver, provided it resulted from expenditures made by him. But if the improvement occurred of itself, it is shared in common.

3. Similarly, if the wife of the decedent was one of his heirs, together with her sisters or together with her uncles' daughters, and she improved the property, the improvement is shared in common. But if she said, "Take note of what my husband left to me, as I am going to work upon it and take the profits," and she improved the property through expenditures, the improvement belongs to her.

4. If a man received property by inheritance from his father and improved it, planted, and built thereon, and thereafter he learned that he had brothers in another locality, then, if the brothers are minors, the improvement is shared in common, and if they are

adults, seeing that it was unknown that he had brothers, an appraisal, as in the case of a tenant on shares, is made for his benefit.

Similarly, if a brother entered upon a minor's property and made improvements thereon, no appraisal, as in the case of a tenant on shares, is made for his benefit and the improvement is shared in common, since he entered upon the property without the minor's consent.

5. If one of the brothers, who was a great scholar always engaged in the study of the Torah without even an hour's interruption, took of the money left by the father and engaged in business therewith, the profits belong to him alone, because a man in his position would not leave his studies and engage in business for the benefit of his brothers.

6. If one of the brothers was appointed by the king to the office of collector or of scribe in charge of revenues and expenditures, or to similar royal service, then, if the appointment was made on account of the father, as where the father had been known as an expert in the matter and the king said, "Let us appoint his son in his place in order to perform an act of kindness toward the orphans," the salary he receives and all his earnings in connection with the service belong to all of the brothers—even if he happens to be a particularly wise man and qualified for the appointment—and if he was appointed on his own merits, everything belongs to him alone.

7. If one of the brothers, who was carrying on business in the household, purchased bondmen in his own name, or made a loan, and the bond was written in his own name, and thereafter he said, "This money which I loaned," or "with which I purchased the bondmen belonged to me alone, I having received it by way of inheritance from my mother's father," or "found it," or "received it by way of gift," he must produce proof that he received another inheritance, or that he found the money, or that he received it as a gift.

Similarly, if a married woman who was carrying on business in the household had 'onot, that is, deeds of sale of bondmen, and bonds outstanding in her name, and she said, "They are mine, the money having come to me by way of inheritance from my ancestors," she must produce proof that she received the money by way of inheritance.

Similarly, if a widow who was carrying on business with the property of the orphans had 'onot and bonds outstanding in her name, and she said, "The money I loaned," or "with which I purchased the bondmen, I received by way of inheritance," or "found it," or "it was given to me by way of gift," she must produce proof. And if she had a dowry and said, "I took some of my dowry," she is believed. But if she had no dowry and failed to produce proof, everything is presumed to belong to the heirs.

8. All this applies to brothers and to a widow who were not receiving separate allowances for food. But if they were receiving separate allowances for food, it is possible that they saved up the money from their allowances, and the other brothers must therefore produce proof that the money came from the common fund. Also, if the brother who was carrying on business within the household died, the other brothers must produce proof, even though they were not receiving separate allowances for food.

9. If one of the brothers holds a bond, he must produce proof that his father gave it to him by writing and delivery, or that the father made a disposition of it in his favor while lying sick, and if he fails to produce such proof, it is shared in common.

10. All this applies to brothers, because they are presumed to slip things away from each other, but a stranger who claims that the decedent gave him the bond, or that he purchased it from the decedent, collects thereon and is not required to produce proof.

11. If one of the brothers took 200 zuz out of the common fund and went to study the Torah, or to learn a trade, the other brothers may say to him, "If you are not with us you will only receive an allowance for food in accordance with the blessing of the house-

hold, because the expenses for food for one person when he takes his food separately are not the same as when he takes it together with many other people.

12. If a man died leaving older and younger sons, the older sons do not get their clothing at the expense of the younger ones, nor do the younger ones get their food at the expense of the older ones, but they share equally.

If the older sons married after their father died, drawing upon the common fund for expenditures, the younger sons may marry in the same style, taking the expenditures out of the common fund, and thereafter a division of the property is to be made.

If the older sons married in the lifetime of their father and, after the father's death, the younger sons said, "We are going to marry in the same style as you married," no heed is to be paid to them, because what the father gave to the older sons he gave.

13. If the father married off his son, making a wedding feast at his expense, and wedding gifts were sent to the son in the lifetime of the father, reciprocation of the wedding gifts, after the father's death, is made out of the common fund. But if the feast was made at the son's own expense, reciprocation is made only out of the share of the son to whom the wedding gifts were sent.

14. If the father sent wedding gifts in the name of one of his sons, and the gifts were reciprocated to that son, they belong to him alone. But if the father sent the gifts in the name of his sons, without specification, the reciprocal gifts go into the common fund.

He to whom the gifts were sent is not bound to reciprocate unless all of the sons participated in the wedding festivities, since they were all bridegroom's friends, the gifts having been sent in the names of all of them. Therefore, if only some of them participated in the festivities he reciprocates only to the extent of the share of those who participated in the festivities, and this goes into the common fund.

15. If the oldest of the brothers dresses in handsome attire, he may draw the expenses of his attire from the common fund, provided the other brothers benefit by his being so dressed, in that he is listened to with respect.

CHAPTER X

1. If two brothers made a division of the inheritance and another brother came from overseas, or if three brothers made a division and a creditor came and took the share of one of them—even if one of the brothers took landed property and the other took money—the division is null, and they make another division of the balance into equal shares.

2. If a man while dying directed that a date tree or a field out of his property be given to such a one, and the brothers made a division without giving anything to the person named, the division is null. And how are they to proceed? They are to make the gift, as directed by their ancestor, and then they are to make a division anew.

3. When the brothers make a division, an appraisal is made of that which they are wearing; but that which their sons and daughters are wearing and which they purchased from the common fund is not appraised, nor is that which is worn by their wives, who have already acquired title therein for themselves. This applies only to garments worn on weekdays, but the Sabbath and festival clothes which they are wearing are to be appraised.

4. If a man left orphans, some of them adults and others minors, and they wished to make a division of their father's property in order that the adults might take their share, the court appoints a guardian for the minors, and the guardian selects for them the fairest share; and when they have reached majority, they cannot protest, since the division was made by order of the court. But if the court erred in the appraisal, assigning to the minors one sixth less

than their due, they may protest, and another division is to be made after they have reached majority.

5. A man, who is about to die and leave adult and minor heirs, must appoint a guardian who shall occupy himself with the share of the minors until they have reached majority, and if he failed to appoint such a guardian, the court is bound to appoint one to serve until the minors have reached majority, because the court is the father of orphans.

6. If the ancestor directed saying, "The share of the minor shall be given to him to do with it as he pleases," it is a permissible exercise of his power.

Similarly, if the ancestor appointed a minor, a woman, or a bondman as guardian, it is a permissible exercise of his power. But the court may not appoint as a guardian a woman, a bondman, a minor, or an ignorant person who is presumed to be suspect of transgressing the Law. It is to seek out a trustworthy and reputable man who knows how to assert the rights of the orphans and to plead their cause and is versed in the affairs of the world, knowing how to preserve property and to make profits therewith, and appoint him over the minors, whether he be a stranger or related to the minors, except that if he is related he may not take possession of landed property.

7. If the court appointed a guardian and thereafter it was reported that he was eating and drinking and spending more than his reputation for wealth would warrant, it must take into account the possibility that he is consuming the orphans' property, and he is to be removed and another one appointed in his place.

But if the father of the orphans appointed him, he is not to be removed, and the doubt is to be resolved in his favor by saying, "It is possible that he found a treasure-trove." However, if witnesses came and testified that he was wasting the orphans' property, he is to be removed, and it is the consensus of the Geonim that he is to be subjected to an oath, since he was committing waste.

The same rule applies if the father of the orphans appointed a guardian who had a good reputation, was honest, and ever anxious to do pious deeds, and who later turned glutton and drunkard and walker in the ways of darkness, or became lax with respect to vows or quasi robbery: the court is bound to remove him, subjecting him to an oath, and to appoint a guardian who is a worthy man. And all these matters are within the discretion of the judge, because every court is the father of orphans.

8. After a minor has reached majority the court may not withhold his property from him and may not appoint a guardian over him, even though he is eating and drinking extravagantly, committing waste and walking in the ways of the wicked, unless his father or other ancestor directed that the property should not be given to him unless he was a worthy and successful man, or that it should not be given to him before the lapse of a certain time.

A mentally incompetent and a deaf-mute are like minors, and a guardian is to be appointed over them.

CHAPTER XI

1. If money was left to orphans by their father, it is not necessary to appoint a guardian. What, then, is to be done? A man is to be sought out who has landed property of the fairest quality, is trustworthy, versed in the Torah, and has never been subjected to excommunication, and the money is to be turned over to him by order of the court for the purpose of doing business therewith on condition that the orphans share in the profits but not in the losses, so that the orphans may benefit from the use of the money; if he has no landed property, he must give a pledge of broken lumps of gold which have no distinctive marks, and the court takes the pledge and gives him the money on condition that the orphans share in the profits but not in the losses.

And why should the court not take a pledge of gold utensils or of a gold bar? Because it may be that the utensils or the gold belongs to others, who, after the death of the pledgor, would come, name the distinctive marks, and take the utensils or the bar, if the judge should happen to have knowledge that the pledgor was not reputed to be wealthy enough to own such a utensil or bar.

And at what ratio of the total profit shall the orphans' share be fixed? In accordance with the discretion of the judge; either one third of the profits, or one half thereof, or even one quarter, if the judge deems it to be to the advantage of the orphans.

If no man can be found who is willing to take the money on condition that the orphans do not share in the losses but only in the profits, some of the money may be spent to provide food for the orphans, until landed property shall have been purchased for the balance of the money and delivered to the guardian whom the court shall have appointed.

2. All the movables belonging to orphans must be appraised and sold in court, and if there is a market place near the locality, the movables must be brought there and sold, and the money realized from the sale is to be added to the other money belonging to the orphans.

3. If a man has in his possession beer belonging to orphans which, if he should leave where it is until it is sold there, might turn sour, or, if he should take to the market place, might be lost through accident on the way, he may do with it what he is accustomed to do with his own beer. And so it is in all similar cases.

4. When the court appoints a guardian over the orphans, it delivers to him all of the orphans' landed property and the unsold movables, and he makes disbursements and receives income, builds and takes apart, breaks and plants, sows, and does everything else as to him may seem best for the interests of the orphans, and he provides them with food and drink and gives to them all other expenditures in accordance with the amount of money they own and with what is fitting for them, without too much largess or too much stringency.

5. When the orphans have reached majority the guardian turns over to them the property of their ancestor, and he is not required

to render an account of receipts and disbursements. He may say to them, "This is what is left over," but he must swear while holding a sacred object that he did not rob them of anything.

This applies only to a guardian appointed by the court, but one appointed by the father of the orphans or by another ancestor is not required to swear with respect to a claim doubtful.

The guardian may purchase his attire out of the property belonging to the orphans in order that he be respected and listened to, provided the orphans derive a benefit from the respect which the guardian commands.

6. The guardian may sell domestic animals, bondmen and bondwomen, fields, and vineyards in order to provide food for the orphans; but he may not sell these and let the money lie, nor may he sell fields in order to purchase bondmen, nor bondmen in order to purchase fields, because it is possible that what he will have purchased will not succeed. But he may sell a field in order to buy oxen for the cultivation of other fields, because oxen are essential to all field property.

7. A guardian may not sell that which is distant in order to redeem that which is near, nor that which is of poor quality in order to redeem that which is of good quality, because it is possible that what he will have acquired will not succeed; nor may he litigate at law to incur a liability in order to acquire a right, because it is possible that he will not acquire any right and that, as a result, only a liability will remain.

8. A guardian may not emancipate a bondman, even if he receives money from the bondman for his emancipation; but he may sell him to others and take the money from them on condition that they emancipate him, and these others are the ones who may emancipate the bondman.

9. A guardian may set aside tĕrumah and tithes from the orphans' property in order to make it fit for consumption by them, because it is not proper to make the orphan eat food which is prohibited; but he may not set aside tithes and tĕrumah in order to

have produce fit for consumption stored away for future sale. Let him sell it in the state of ṭebel, and whosoever may wish to make it fit for consumption may do so.

10. A guardian may procure for the minor a *lulaḇ,* a *sukkah,* fringes, a shophar, a scroll of the Law, phylacteries, mĕzuzah scrolls, and a *megillah.* Whenever the expenditure of a fixed amount is necessary in connection with the fulfillment of an affirmative commandment, whether Pentateuchal or Rabbinical, the guardian may make such expenditure, although the minors are not obligated to fulfill any of these commandments, and when they are made to fulfill them it is only for the purpose of training them. But no contribution to charity, even for the redemption of captives, may be made on behalf of the orphans, because fulfillment of these commandments entails expenditures which have no fixed limitation.

11. If a man has become a mentally incompetent or a deaf-mute, the court, in the proper case, may make a contribution to charity on his behalf.

12. Although the guardian is not required to render an account, as we have stated, he must make reckoning to himself privately with great care and beware of the Father of these orphans who rideth upon the skies, as it is written *Extol Him that rideth upon the skies . . . A father of the fatherless* (Ps. 68:5–6).

NOTES

References consisting of numbers only indicate passages found in the Code outside the present volume, the numbers referring, respectively, to the Book, the Treatise, the Chapter and the Section where the passage in question occurs.

Treatise I: Hiring

Chapter I

1. BM 7: 8; B. *ibid.*, 93a.
2. *Ibid.*
   "or lost." The word lost is used here, and elsewhere in this Book, in the sense of a disappearance or destruction of the object bailed under circumstances not amounting to negligence on the bailee's part but not constituting force majeure.
   "as hereinafter stated." See below II, ii, 1.
3. BM 8: 1; B. *ibid.*, 94b–95a.
   "and the bailee borrowed or hired the services of the owner." The idea underlying the bailee's exemption from liability in the case of a bailment *with the owner* is perhaps similar to that underlying the doctrine of contributory negligence in Anglo-American law.
4. B. BM 29b, 36a.
   "recently." Literally, "last night."
5. Cf. above Sec. 4.
6. BM 3: 2; B. *ibid.*, 36b; B. Giṭ 14a.

Chapter II

1. BM 4: 9; B. *ibid.*, 57b, 58a.
   "Ḳinyan." Literally, acquisition. A formality, simulating an exchange, wherein the party to whom a transfer of property is made, or toward whom an obligation is assumed (or the witnesses to the transaction on his behalf) delivers to the party making the transfer, or assuming the obligation, some object, such as a scarf or a handkerchief, to make the transaction binding and enforceable.
2. B. BM 58a.
4. Shebu 6: 6.
5. Mek, *Mišpaṭim* (ed. Horowitz), Sec. 15, p. 302.
6. Cf. BḲ 1: 3, and B. *ibid.*, 15a.
7. "A positive assertion by the defendant's adversary." In the ordinary case, a litigant is required to take an oath only in support of a denial of a positive assertion of fact by his adversary, while an assertion of fact by a minor is not given sufficient weight to warrant an oath by his adversary. However, in the case of a bailment, no positive assertion by the bailor, of negligence on the bailee's part, is necessary in order to subject the bailee to an oath, an assertion by the bailor of

lack of knowledge in this respect being sufficient. Therefore, there is no difference, so far as the bailee's liability to an oath is concerned, between a bailment in which the bailor is an adult and one in which he is a minor.

8. "except by a drawing to himself." B. BM 99a.

" 'Keep this for me.' " BM 6: 6.

" 'Leave it where you please.' " B. BM 81b.

" 'Why, the house is at your disposal.' " B. BM 49b.

"may have the anathema proclaimed generally." There is no Talmudic authority for this rule, which originated with the Geonim.

"The inference of credibility." This rule of evidence, known under the name of *miggo*, is to the effect that a defendant's plea is to be believed, if a more convenient or more advantageous plea was available to him. See below Sec. 12.

"the requirement of a partial admission." See below iv, iii, 1.

9. BM 7: 10; B. *ibid.*, 94a.

10. "by accumulation." See Shebu 7: 8.

"that there was a stipulation." Imposing upon the bailee a more strict liability than that imposed upon him by law.

"by accumulation." Wherever, by the rules pertaining to oaths, a party is required to take an oath with respect to a certain allegation, his adversary may demand that he include in the oath other matters in dispute between them, for which matters he would otherwise not be subject to an oath. See below iv, i, 12.

11. Cf. Shebu 6: 3.

12. B. BB 70a–70b.

"as hereinafter stated." See below iii, 1.

Chapter III

1. B. BM 83a.

2. "the Sages have established the rule." See B. BM 83a, and Alf, *ibid.*
"Another rule." *Ibid.*

3. B. BM 99b, in accordance with the reading of Alf, *ibid.* See gloss. of R. Elijah of Vilna, *a. l.*

4. BM 7: 9; B. *ibid.*, 93b.

5. B. BM 94a.

6. B. BM 93a.

7. Cf. Ket 8: 5.

8. B. BM 93a.

9. BM 7: 9; B. *ibid.*, 36b.

10. B. BM 36b.

Chapter IV

1. BM 6: 3–4; B. *ibid.*, 80a.

2. B. BM 80a.

3. BM 6: 4; B. *ibid.*, 81b.
"the inference of credibility." See above note to ii, 8.

4. BM 6: 5; B. *ibid.*, 80a.

5. B. BM 79b.

6. BM 6: 5; B. *ibid.*, 80a–80b.
7. B. BM 80b.
8. B. BM 79b.

Chapter V

1. BM 6: 3; B. *ibid.*, 78b–79a.
2. *Ibid.*
3. B. BM 79a–79b.
6. BM 8: 9; B. *ibid.*, 103a.
7. *Ibid.*

Chapter VI

1. B. BB 6a–6b.
2. B. BM 102a.
3. BM 8: 7; B. *ibid.*, 101b–102a.
4. BM 10: 2; B. *ibid.*, 116b–117a.
5. BM 8: 7; B. *ibid.*, 101b–102a.
   "a man's courtyard acquires property for him." See XI, iii, ii, 8.
6. Alf, BM 101b.
7. BM 8: 6; B. *ibid.*, 101b.
8. B. BM 101b.
9. *Ibid.*
10. *Ibid.*
11. B. BM 101b.

Chapter VII

1. "hiring is but a sale for a specified time." Cf. B. BM 56b.
2. BM 8: 8; B. *ibid.*, 102b.
3. B. BM 102b; Alf, *ibid*. See gloss. of R. Elijah of Vilna, *a. l.*
   "by a writing or without witnesses." So ed. Rome (?), before 1480; ed. Soncino (1490); ed. Constantinople (1509); MSS Enelow Memorial Collection, Nos. 354, 398, 405 and Codex Adler (1692), in the Library of the Jewish Theological Seminary of America.
   "if the lessor made demand within 30 days." I.e., within the 30 days of notice in the case of a lease for an indefinite term.
   "present a separate claim." The rule being what it is, that only a defendant may be subjected to the informal oath, the lessee may not have the lessor subjected to such an oath unless he assumes the position of a plaintiff. See below iv, i, 6.
4. B. BM 103a.
5. B. BM 109b.
6. B. BM 110a.
7. B. BM 101b.
8. B. Ket 103a.

Chapter VIII

1. Tos Dem 6: 2.
2. B. BM 103b.
3. BM 9: 9–10.
4. BM 9: 2; B. *ibid.*, 103b–104a.
5. BM 9: 6; B. *ibid.*, 105b–106b.
6. BM 9: 1; B. *ibid.*, 103b.
7. BM 9: 7; B. *ibid.*, 106b.
8. BM 9: 4.
10. BM 9: 1, 9; B. *ibid.*, 109a; Tos *ibid.*, 9: 1.
11. B. BB 95a.
12. BM 9: 5; B. *ibid.*, 105.
13. BM 9: 3; B. *ibid.*, 104b.

"'out of the fairest of my property.'" Cf. Exod. 22: 4. See Herbert Danby, *The Mishnah* (Oxford, Clarendon Press, 1933), BM 9: 3, p. 362.

"'asmakta." Literally, "reliance." This is the technical name for a Talmudic doctrine relating to the invalidity of certain conditional transfers of property and conditional obligations. Maimonides was apparently of the opinion that a transfer of property made, or an obligation assumed, upon a condition precedent comes within the doctrine of 'asmakta. See XII, 1, xi. Other authorities were of the opinion that only a conditional transfer of property, or a conditional obligation, which is in the nature of a penalty or forfeiture comes within this doctrine. See *Responsa* of R. Solomon b. Adret No. 933 (Lemberg, 1811). The rather lengthy argumentation, which is unusual in the Code, seems to represent an attempt on the author's part to reconcile the rule concerning the lessee's liability with his view of the doctrine of 'asmakta. The distinction which he seems to make between the ordinary case of an obligation assumed upon a condition precedent and that of the lessee who undertook to compensate the lessor if he failed to cultivate the land is that in the latter case the lessee would have been under a moral obligation to compensate the lessor, even if he had not specifically undertaken to do so.

14. B. BM 104b.

Chapter IX

1. BM 7: 1.
2. B. BM 87a.
3. B. BM 76a.
4. BM 6: 1; B. *ibid.*, 76a–78a.
5. Tos BM 7: 8.
6. B. BM 77a.

"But if it was the way of the river to cease flowing." That is, to cease flowing into the employer's field. See MM, *a. l.*

7. B. BM 77a.
8. Tos BM 7: 2.
9. B. BM 76a.
10. BM 10: 5.
11. B. BM 12b.

Chapter X

1. BM 6: 7; B. *ibid.*, 82a.
2. B. BM 81a.
   "a keeping with the owner." Cf. above, i, 3.
3. BM 6: 6; B. *ibid.*, 80b–81a.
4. BK 9: 3–4; B. *ibid.*, 98b, 101a.
   "I do not wish to avail myself of this enactment." That is, that he should pay to the craftsman either the value of the improvement or the expenditure, whichever is smaller.
5. B. BK 99b; Alf, *ibid.*
   "because they are receivers of hire." And a receiver of hire is liable for loss under circumstances not amounting to force majeure. See above i, 2.
6. B. BM 109a–109b.
   " 'asmakta." See above note to viii, 13.
7. B. BM 109a–109b.

Chapter XI

1. BM 9: 12; B. Mak 16a.
2. B. BM 110b–111a.
3. B. BM 112a.
4. BM 9: 12; B. *ibid.*, 110b–111a, 112a.
5. B. BM 110b.
6. BM 9: 12; B. Shebu 45b; B. BM 113a; P. Shebu 7: 1.
   " 'No such thing ever occurred.' " I.e., a general denial.
7. B. Shebu 46a.
8. B. Shebu 46a.
   "Seizin (ḥazaḳah)." Possession under circumstances giving rise to a presumption of rightful ownership. Cf. below iv, ix, 1–3.
9. B. Shebu 48b–49a.

Chapter XII

1. BM 7: 2; B. *ibid.*, 87b.
   "has not been completely processed." For ḥallah and tithes. See below Sec. 6.
2. BM 7: 4.
3. Sif Deut. (ed. Friedmann), Sec. 267, p. 122a.
4. B. BM 89a.
5. *Ibid.*
   "ḥallah." Dough offering. See Ḥal 1: 1.
6. B. BM 89a.
   "ṭebel." Untithed produce, the eating of which is forbidden.
7. BM 7: 6.
   "fourth-year plantings." See Lev. 19: 24.
   "he must first redeem the fruit." See Ma'aser Sheni 5: 4.
8. B. BM 89a.
9. BM 7: 3; B. *ibid.*, 93a.

10. BM 7: 4; B. *ibid.*, 87b, 89b, 91b.
11. "is forbidden to overeat." B. BM 87b.
   "even to a denar's worth." BM 7: 5.
   "was guarding four or five stacks." B. BM 93a.
   "was guarding four or five stacks." Belonging to four or five persons.
12. B. BM 91b.
13. *Ibid.*, 92a.
14. BM 7: 6.

Chapter XIII

1. "Whether attached to the soil or severed from it." B. BM 88b.
   "of the burden on its back." B. BM 92a.
2. BḲ 5: 7; B. BM 88b, 90b, 91a.
   "from the moment he drew it to himself." The liability to payment for the animal's food thus attaches before the liability to lashes attaches; hence the rule that a liability to payment is canceled by a liability to lashes which attaches simultaneously therewith does not apply. See XI, II, iii, 1.
3. B. BM 90a, 90b.
4. B. BM 89b–90a.
   "*tĕrumah.*" Heave offering. See VII, III, ii, 1.
5. B. BM 90a.
   "*dĕmai.*" Produce originating from a grower who is suspected of nonobservance of the Laws relating to heave offering and tithes.
6. B. BM 89a, 90b.
7. "the fourth benediction of grace." See II, v, iv, 2.

Treatise II: Borrowing and Depositing

Chapter I

1. BM 7: 8; B. *ibid.*, 96b, 97a.
2. See above I, iii, 1.
3. B. BḲ 11a.
4. B. BM 91a, 96b.
   "from the moment he draws it to himself." Cf. above I, xiii, 2.
5. "without specifying the time." Cf. Tos BM 8: 11.
   "for a specified time." B. BM 99a.
   "Even if the borrower died." B. Ket 34b.
6. B. BM 103a.
7. *Ibid.*
8. *Ibid.*
9. *Ibid.*
10. Tos BM 8: 11.

Chapter II

1. BM 8: 1; B. *ibid.*, 95a, 97a.
"as hereinabove stated." See above 1, i, 3.
"it is a case of borrowing with the owner." There is discernible here a tendency to limit the strict rule of the commodatary's absolute liability by resort to a legal fiction.
2. B. BM 97a.
3. *Ibid.*
4. *Ibid.*
5. B. BM 96a.
"to his messenger." I.e., to his agent.
6. B. BM 96b.
7. B. BM 96b; *ibid.*, 81a.
8. B. BM 96a.
"If the borrower was negligent." A bailee who causes damage through negligence is presumed to be liable unless he can show that he comes within the exception of a bailment *with the owner* exempting him from liability. The applicability of this exception being in doubt, the bailee's liability remains unaffected. Cf. above 1, ii, 3.
9. B. BM 96a.
10. *Ibid.*, 98b.
11. *Ibid.*, 96b.

Chapter III

1. BM 8: 3; B. *ibid.*, 99a.
2. B. BM 99a; *ibid.*, 80b.
3. BM 8: 2; B. *ibid.*, 97a–98b.
4. B. BM 98a.
"will be stated in the Laws Concerning Pleading." See IV, iv, 7–8.

Chapter IV

1. BM 7: 8; B. BK 107b.
2. B. BM 41a; *ibid.*, 42a.
3. B. BM 42a; P. *ibid.*, 3: 11.
4. B. BM 42a.
5. *Ibid.*
6. BM 3: 10; B. *ibid.*, 42a.
7. B. BM 42a.
8. B. BM 36a–36b; BM 3: 10; B. *ibid.*, 42a–42b.
"as hereinabove stated." See 1, i, 5.
9. B. BM 42b.

Chapter V

1. B. BḲ 117b; *ibid.*, 93a.
2. B. BḲ 117b.
3. B. BM 93b.
4. BM 3: 4–5; B. *ibid.*, 37a–37b.
5. BM 3: 7–8; B. *ibid.*, 40a.
6. B. BM 98a.
   "as hereinafter stated." See IV, iv, 7.
7. P. BḲ 6: 7.
   "the bailee would have been subjected only to the informal oath," which is not considered an oath for the purpose of the above rule.

Chapter VI

1. B. BM 34b; *ibid.*, 35a; B. BḲ 107b.
2. Cf. above I, ii, 9.
   "even though the deposit was made in the presence of witnesses," and, consequently, the bailee could not deny receipt of the deposit.
3. B. BM 83a.
4. B. BB 45b; B. Ket 85b; B. Yeb 115b.
   "as will be stated in the Laws Concerning The Sanhedrin." See XIV, i, xxiv, 1.
   "as hereinabove stated." See above I, ii, 8.
5. Shebu 6: 3; B. *ibid.*, 40b.

Chapter VII

1. BM 3: 6; B. *ibid.*, 38a.
   "tĕrumah." Heave offering, the eating of which by non-priests is forbidden.
2. B. BM 38a.
3. B. Pes 13a.
   "the fourteenth day of the month of Nisan." I.e., the eve of the Feast of Passover.
4. B. BM 29b.
5. B. BM 38a; cf. BM 3: 11.
6. BM 3: 11; Alf, *ibid.*, 43a.
7. Alf, BM 43a.
8. BM 3: 11.
   "with a householder." I.e., one who is neither a money-changer nor a shopkeeper.
9. BM 3: 9; B. *ibid.*, 41a.
10. B. BB 51b–52a.
11. B. BḲ 118a; BḲ 10: 6.
12. There is no direct Talmudic authority for the propositions contained in this section.

Chapter VIII

1. BM 3: 1; B. *ibid.*, 34a.
"We have already stated." See XI, II, i, 11.
"abandonment." Resignation by the owner to the permanent loss of a stolen or lost object.
2. B. BḴ 34a.
3. B. BM 35a.
4. B. BḴ.
5. B. BM 34a–34b.
"even outside of the Land." I.e., outside of the Land of Israel. The courts outside of Palestine were without jurisdiction to render a judgment imposing a penalty, such as twofold payment, for example, upon a defendant who was liable thereto under the Law. However, if the party entitled to the penalty seized some of the defendant's property, up to the amount of the penalty, the defendant could not reclaim it from him. See below XIV, I, v, 8, 13, 17.
6. B. BḴ 108b.
"and, consequently, the bailee is quit of payment," on the principle that he who claims aught from his fellow has the burden of proving that he is entitled to what he claims.

Treatise III: Creditor and Debtor

Chapter I

1. Mek Mišpaṭim (ed. Horowitz), Sec. 19, p. 313.
2. B. BM 75b; Sif Deut. (ed. Friedmann), Sec. 113, p. 97b.
3. B. BM 75b, 110b.
4. "even though it is bound." B. Ket 90a.
"kĕṭubbah." I.e., dower.
"to seize the property." The word *seizure* or *seize* is used here, and elsewhere in this Book, in the sense of a taking by the creditor from the debtor's transferees, by virtue of a prior lien, of landed property bound for the payment of the debt.
5. Ar 6: 5; B. BḴ 11b; P. Ḳid 1: 4.
6. Alf, *Responsa*, No. 209 (Leghorn, 1780).
7. Ar 6: 3–4; B. BM 113b–114a.
"a vow of valuation." See VI, IV, i, 1.
8. There seems to be no specific Talmudic authority for this proposition, which is, however, deducible from the general principles laid down in this chapter.

Chapter II

1. Cf. above, 1: 7.
6. B. Ḳid 15a; B. Ket 19a; B. BḴ 40b; Ket 9: 7–8.
"to seize his debtor's property," which is in the hands of a third party. See above note to i, 4.

7. B. BM 75b.
8. B. BB 51a.

Chapter III

1. BM 9: 13; B. Mak 16a.
2. BM 9: 13.
3. B. BM 116a.
4. BM 9: 13; B. *ibid.*, 113a–113b.
"the court's representative." Literally, the court's messenger.
"because the negative commandment is coupled with an affirmative one."
The transgression of a negative commandment which is coupled with an affirmative one does not subject the transgressor to lashes, provided the circumstances are such that the affirmative commandment may still be fulfilled. See XIV, 1, xviii, 2.
5. BM 9: 13; B. *ibid.*, 114b–115a.
"canceled by the advent of the Sabbatical year." See Shebi 10: 2.
"movables in the hands of the debtor's children." Such movables were not subject to levy by a decedent's creditor. See below xi, 7.
6. BM 9: 13; B. *ibid.*, 113b, 114b.
7. B. BM 115a.
8. BM 6: 7; B. *ibid.*, 82b.

Chapter IV

1. B. BM 60b–61a.
2. BM 5: 11; B. *ibid.*, 75b.
3. B. BM 62a.
"if it was *directly stipulated* usury." See below vi, 1.
4. B. BM 62a.
5. B. BK 94b.
6. B. BM 72a; *ibid.*, 61b.
7. B. BM 71a; *ibid.*, 61b.
8. B. BM 75a.
10. B. BM 63b–64a.
11. B. BK 97b–98a.
12. BK 97a–97b.
13. "the Sages have expressly said." See above Sec. 5.
14. B. BM 70a.

Chapter V

1. BM 5: 6; Sif Deut. (ed. Friedmann), Sec. 26, p. 121b.
2. B. BM 70b–71a.
3. B. BM 71b.
4. *Ibid.*
5. *Ibid.*
6. B. BM 72a.
7. B. BM 71a.

8. B. BM 70a.

9. BM 5: 4.

"at an assessed valuation." The party receiving the animals being answerable for each animal to the extent of one half of the assessed value thereof.

"as we have stated in the matter of partnership." See XII, iv, viii.

10. B. BM 68a.

"who will collect interest by means thereof." If the partnership, or the joint venture, should result in a loss, the heir would nevertheless collect on the writing the full amount of his father's investment, without deducting his father's share of the loss. The difference between this amount and the amount to which he would be entitled would constitute interest.

11. BM 5: 10.

12. B. BM 75b.

13. BM 5: 10.

14. Tos BM 4: 2; B. BM 69b.

15. B. BM 62b; *ibid.*, 68a.

16. B. BM 69b.

17. B. BM 73b.

Chapter VI

1. BM 5: 1–2.

"which is recoverable in a court of law." That is, by the borrower who has paid it.

2. B. BM 65a.

4. BM 5: 3; B. *ibid.*, 65b.

5. B. BM 65b.

6. BM 5: 3; B. *ibid.*, 65a.

Chapter VII

1. B. BM 67a.

2. B. BM 67a; *ibid.*, 68a.

3. B. BM 67b.

4. *Ibid.*

"the first-born does not take." The gagee's tenancy being terminable at the will of the gagor, it is not considered an interest in land.

"Lifted up the fruit." Lifting up is a mode of acquiring title to chattels. Cf. XII, i, ii, 5.

6. B. BM 73b.

7. B. BM 65b.

8. BM 5: 2.

9. B. BM 69b.

10. BM 5: 10.

11. *Ibid.*

12. B. BB 86b–87a.

Chapter VIII

1. BM 5: 2; B. *ibid.*, 65a.
2. Tos BM 6: 4.
3. B. BM 65a.
4. P. BM 5: 8.
5. B. BM 73a.
6. *Ibid.*
7. *Ibid.*
8. *Ibid.*
9. B. BM 73b.
10. B. BM 64a; *ibid.*, 73b.
11. B. BM 69b–70a.
12. BM 5: 6; B. *ibid.*, 70b.

   "iron sheep." Wherever one party delivers property to another on condition that the party accepting the property be responsible for any loss or damage thereto, the property is referred to as iron sheep, that is to say, the party accepting the property on such terms in effect guarantees its indestructibility. Cf., IV, 1, xvi, 1.

13. B. BM 69b.
14. B. BM 68b.
15. B. BM 65a.

Chapter IX

1. BM 5: 7; B. *ibid.*, 74a.
2. B. BM 74b.
3. B. BM 64a.
4. B. BM 72b, according to the version of Alf, *ibid.*

   "mixed wheat." I.e., wheat collected from various sources, such wheat being of poorer quality than the uniform "householder's wheat."

5. BM 5: 6.

   "subjects himself to the malediction of 'He who punished.'" A malediction pronounced by the court, under certain circumstances, against a retracting party in an agreement for the purchase and sale of chattels. The formula of the malediction begins with the words "He who punished." See XII, 1, vii, 1–2.

   "as we have stated." See XII, iv, i, 2.

6. B. BM 63b.
7. B. BM 73a.
8. *Ibid.*
9. B. BM 72b–73a.
10. B. BM 64a.

Chapter X

1. B. BM 72b.
2. B. BM 75a.
3. BM 5: 9.
4. The proposition stated in this section follows from the rule that it is for-

bidden to lend a se'ah for a se'ah. See above Sec. 2. The transaction being a quasi-usurious one, the borrower may refuse to pay the excess.

5. BM 5: 8; B. *ibid.*, 74b.

"wheat for wheat." I.e., a given quantity of wheat to be repaid in kind in the same quantity.

"since the tenant when he takes possession." The loan agreement may therefore be considered part of the consideration for the tenancy agreement.

6. B. BM 62b.

Chapter XI

1. "the borrower is not required to pay it in the presence of witnesses." B. Shebu 41b.

"he swears the informal oath." B. Shebu 40b.

"he is not believed." *Ibid.*, 41a.

"they must consult him." B. Ket 55a.

"is designed to be reduced to writing." B. BB 40a.

2. B. Giṭ 86b.

3. BB 10: 8; B. *ibid.*, 175b–176a.

4. B. BB 175b.

5. B. BB 41b.

6. B. BB 174a–174b.

7. "that he is concealing his movables." B. Ket 86a.

"from the debtor's heir." Ket 9: 3.

8. "under a moral duty." B. Ket 91b.

"If the creditor seized." B. Ket 84b.

"consist of writings obligatory." B. Ket 85b; Alf, *ibid*.

9. B. Ket 92a.

10. B. Ket 92a.

"the indebtedness is not bound." Cf. above Sec. 7.

"and seize it from them." Cf. above Sec. 9.

11. "rather than by reason of the enactment." The text reads *yoter min hattakkanah*. Some of the older commentators understood this phrase as meaning "more than under the enactment" and found it difficult to explain why the creditor should collect more (See KM, *a. l.*). LM, *a. l.*, suggests "in addition to the enactment." However, the word *min*, "from," would seem to exclude this interpretation, which would require *'al*, "upon," instead of *min*. Cf. *yeter 'al* above iv, 9, and Ket 4: 10.

Chapter XII

1. B. Ar 22a.

2. Cf. below xv, 4.

3. B. Ar 22a.

5. B. Ar 22b.

6. "which is not theirs." B. Ar 22b.

"which is not theirs." Which is not known to have belonged to their ancestor.

"descended upon a field." B. BK 112b.

7. "If landed property is in the possession." B. BḲ 112a.

"If landed property is in the possession (ḥăzaḳah) of orphans." And is known to have at one time belonged to their ancestor, which raises a presumption of rightful ownership.

"if the claimant produces a writing." B. BḲ 112b.

8. Ar 6: 1; B. *ibid.*, 21b–22a.

9. B. Ket 104b.

10. B. Ket 100a–100b.

"as though they erred about a matter stated in the Mishnah." That is, about a well-established rule of Law. An error of this nature renders the action of the court void. See XIV, 1, vi, 1.

11. Ket 11: 5; B. *ibid.*, 100a–100b.

Chapter XIII

1. B. Ket 88a.

"the door would be closed to would-be borrowers." That is, people would be discouraged from lending money to others.

2. "That the writing is authentic." Literally, "to confirm the writing."

3. The text seems to be corrupt, as noted by RABD, *a. l.* When the matter placed by us in parentheses is excluded, the text becomes intelligible. The point is that the creditor, because he is not making a claim to the pledge itself as belonging to him, is not in the position of a defendant who, under similar circumstances, would be required to swear the informal oath only; rather, the creditor is in the position of a plaintiff, and as such he must swear the formal oath before he may be allowed to take what he claims, notwithstanding the inference of credibility, which he has in his favor. Cf. above 1, ii, 8.

It is not unlikely that the passage we have placed in parentheses is a gloss which was added by Maimonides himself, in consequence of an actual case, sometime after the section had been written, and which was later incorporated in the text. In one of his *Responsa*, No. 336 (ed. Freimann), which was penned by him after the completion of the Code, there is a report of a case which involved the point dealt with in our section, and in which the controversy was between the heirs of the pledgor and the heirs of the pledgee. There is no mention of our section in this *Responsum*, although there is reference there, on an incidental point, to another section of the Code. This would seem to indicate that the passage under discussion was not in the text of the Code at the time the *Responsum* was written; for if it had been there, our section would have furnished a complete and direct answer to the question, and Maimonides would hardly have failed to refer the questioner to our section which is so pertinent to the question.

4. "If a man lent money." Shebu 6: 7.

"that the pledge is not in his possession." B. BM 34b.

"having made a partial admission." Shebu 6: 7.

" 'I lent you a sela' on it and it was worth a sela'.' " B. BM 35a.

"as hereinabove stated." See above 1, x, 1.

"as hereinafter stated." See below iv, iv, 7.

5. B. Mak 3b.

8. B. BḲ 118a.

Chapter XIV

1. Ket 9: 7–8; B. BB 5b.
2. B. Shebu 41a.
   "the court will not subject him to an oath." And will render no judgment against the defendant. See B. Shebu 41a.
3. "a confirmed writing." A writing bearing a certification by the court that the signatures of the witnesses appearing thereon have been authenticated.
4. B. BB 128b.
   "out of the borrower's *free* property." The debtor's property, which is subject to execution for his debts, falls into two classes: *free* property and *alienated* property. By the former term is meant property which has not been transferred by the debtor to others by way of sale, gift, or in discharge of an indebtedness; by the latter term is meant property which has been so transferred by the debtor.
6. B. BB 32b.
7. B. BM 17a.
8. B. BB 32b.
9. B. Shebu 42a.
10. Cf. B. BB 33b–34a.
    "as hereinabove stated." See above Sec. 2.
11. "he is liable to an oath but is unable to swear." Wherever the testimony of two witnesses subjects a defendant to liability to pay, the testimony of one witness subjects him to liability to take an oath. The defendant in this case is therefore liable to an oath. He is, however, unable to swear, because the oath must be taken in support of an allegation contradicting the testimony of the witness, but here the defendant does not contradict the testimony. See below IV, i, 1 and XI, III, iv, 13–14.
14. B. BM 7a.
15. Cf. BM 35a.

Chapter XV

1. B. Shebu 41b.
2. *Ibid.*
   "written on parchments, as they were wont to write approximately 500 years ago." The word *gĕwilin*, rendered here as "parchments," may also mean "rolls." (Marcus Jastrow, *A Dictionary of the Targumim, the Talmud Babli and Yerushalmi and the Mishradic Literature* [New York, 1926] s.v., *gĕwil*.) There is possibly a reference here to a copy of the Gemara written on rolls of papyrus about the seventh century.
3. B. Shebu 42a.
4. *Ibid.*
   "two witnesses being like 100 witnesses." Since two witnesses are the standard required to establish a fact in a court of law, it is assumed that the borrower merely meant testimony which would be conclusive of the fact of payment, using the phrase "two witnesses" in the sense of conclusive testimony.
   "since the borrower referred to a specific number of witnesses." Other than the standard number of two witnesses.
6. Alf, Ket 87a.

7. *Ibid.*

"from the *best* of the borrower's property." See below xix, 1.

Chapter XVI

1. B. Giṭ 78b.

"as though it were a bill of divorce." That is, the rules applicable to bills of divorce should apply. Cf. Giṭ 8: 2.

2. B. Giṭ 14a.

"he may not do so." Because Simeon acquired a right in the money on the principle of *zĕḳiyah,* which is to the effect that a right may be validly conferred upon a person through the mediation of another, even without the knowledge of the recipient of the right. See XII, II, iv, 2. This principle played an important part in the development of the negotiable promissory note, payable to N. or to bearer, among the Jews in the Middle Ages.

4. XII, I, vi, 9.

"even though the order was given in the presence of all three parties," and Simeon accepted.

5. Shebu 7: 5; B. *ibid.,* 47b.

"because it is an oath taken in support of a demand." See below IV, i, 1.

6. Shebu 7: 5.

7. "by writing and delivery." An instrument of indebtedness may be validly transferred by a deed of transfer and the delivery of the instrument to the transferee. See XII, I, vi, 10–11.

"transfer adjunct to a transfer of land." Wherever a party transfers land to another by one of the valid modes of transfer applicable to land, and simultaneously therewith declares that he is also transferring to the same transferee chattels, or bonds, the transferee acquires title to the chattels, or bonds, by a transfer adjunct to the transfer of land. See XII, I, vi, 14.

8. B. San 31a–31b; B. BM 20b.

9. B. BM 20b–21a.

10. *Ibid.*

11. BM 1: 8.

"and does not know what its status is." That is, he does not know by whom and on what terms it was deposited with him.

12. BB 10: 7; B. *ibid.,* 173a.

Chapter XVII

1. Shebu 7: 7; B. *ibid.,* 48a.

2. Shebu 7: 7.

3. B. Shebu 48a–48b.

4. B. Shebu 48b.

5. *Ibid.*

6. B. Ket 88a.

7. Alf, Ket 87a.

"the condition of credence is the very essence of the bond." So that the heirs succeeded to the obligation as qualified by the condition.

8. B. BB 7b.

9. B. Ket 110b.

"testimony incapable of refutation by *alibi testimony*." In criminal suits the witnesses are to be subjected by the court to an examination with respect to the time and place of the commission of the offense. This rule is designed to afford the accused an opportunity to refute the testimony by alibi testimony, that is, by testimony of other witnesses to the effect that at the time specified by the accusing witnesses the latter were in a place other than that in which, according to their testimony, the accused committed the offense. See XIV, 11, i, 4–5.

"as will be stated in the proper place." See below xxiii, 2.

Chapter XVIII

1. "without specification as to security for the loan." BM 1: 6; B. *ibid.*, 14a.

"stands back of, and is surety for, the debt." B. BB 173a; B. Ket 82a.

"he makes demand upon the debtor in the first instance." B. BB 173a.

"If the property in the possession of the debtor does not suffice." Like the surety, the debtor's property in the hands of third parties is only secondarily liable for the debt.

"all the property which the debtor should ever acquire." B. BB 157b. Cf. B. Ket 82b.

2. B. BB 44b.

"conveyed to the creditor a security title to all of his movables." Literally, "conveyed to the creditor all of his movables." What is meant is a conveyance of title for the purpose of securing the debt, and not an outright conveyance.

"transfer adjunct." See above note to xvi, 7.

"'asmaḳta." See above note to 1, viii, 13.

3. B. Giṭ 41a.

"If a man hypothecated his field." That is, designated the field specifically, though not exclusively, as security for the debt.

4. P. Yeb 7: 1.

5. B. BB 44b.

6. Giṭ 4: 4; B. *ibid.*, 40b–41a.

"because leavened matter, emancipation, and dedication to the sanctuary break an obligation resting upon a person's property." This terse statement contains three separate rules of law: 1. if a Jew pledged to a heathen for a loan property containing leavened matter, and the Feast of Passover supervened, the pledge is deemed to belong to the Jew and, accordingly, he may not use or sell it when the Feast of Passover is over, because the law concerning leavened matter supersedes the creditor's lien; 2. dedication to the sanctuary likewise supersedes the creditor's lien, as stated in the next section; 3. the rule about emancipation is stated in this section.

7. Ar 6: 2.

"as we have stated in the Laws Concerning Valuations." See VI, IV, vii, 16.

8. B. Ket 91b; B. BM 15b.

9. B. Ket 91b.

10. *Ibid.*

Chapter XIX

1. Giṭ 5: 1–2; B. BḲ 8a.
2. Giṭ 5: 2; B. Ket 95b.
3. B. BḲ 8a–8b.
4. B. BḲ 7b–8a.
5. *Ibid.*, 8a.
"they all effect seizure." That is, the tortfeasee, the creditor, and the woman for her kĕṭubbah.
6. B. BḲ 8a–8b.
7. *Ibid.*
8. B. Ket 95a–95b.

Chapter XX

1. "he is to restore what he took." B. Ket 90a.
"which he acquired after he borrowed." B. BB 157b.
2. "the field is obligated to the first creditor." *Ibid.*
"There is no right of priority in movables." Alf, Ket 90a.
"If a person other than a creditor." B. Ket 84b.
"Also, if the debtor said." Cf. above xvi, 2.
3. Ket 10: 5; Alf, *ibid.,* 93b.
4. Ket 10: 4; Alf, *ibid.,* 93a.
"and still another of 700 zuz." In all of the printed editions the reading is "and still another of 300 zuz." The reading adopted in this translation is based upon three manuscripts from Yemen (Enelow Memorial Collection, Nos. 354, 398, 405), and one from Spain (Codex Adler, 1692), in the Library of the Jewish Theological Seminary of America.

The reading in the printed editions is palpably impossible. This is evident from the last illustration given by the author: "If 600 zuz is available, etc." If the debts of the three creditors amounted to 100, 200 and 300 zuz, respectively, the available money, 600 zuz, would be sufficient to pay each of the three creditors in full, and there would be no problem at all. The complicated method of distribution, which the author seeks to illustrate, would therefore be entirely unnecessary. Furthermore, the word "only" in the phrase "so that in the end he obtains 300 zuz only," is meaningless under the reading of the printed editions. Why "300 zuz only," when his debt does not amount to more than that?

It is to be noted that R. Joseph Caro in *Šulḥan 'Aruḵ,* HM 104: 10, in quoting this section of the Code, left out, apparently deliberately, the word "only" in the above phrase. However, the fundamental difficulty, namely, that the whole complicated procedure is pointless when the amount of the debtor's assets is 600 zuz and the total of his liabilities is also 600 zuz, still remains.

It should also be noted that the error is apparently of very long standing, as it appears in a quotation from this section in the *Sefer hat-tĕrumot,* chap. 66, by R. Samuel has-Sardi, a thirteenth-century authority from Spain.

5. B. Ket 94b.

NOTES

313

Chapter XXI

1. "A creditor may obtain satisfaction out of the improvements of the property." B. BB 15a.

"in the case of improvements which accrued through expenditures." B. BB 157b.

"though he has the lower hand." That is, he takes whichever is smaller, the amount of his expenditures or the value of the improvements. Cf. XI, iii, x, 9.

The matter placed by the translator in parentheses would appear to have been inserted in the text of the original after the entire section had been written. It is remarkable that the illustration given by the author in the conclusion ("Therefore, if Reuben borrowed," etc.) accords with the rule stated by the author at the beginning of the section, but not with the dissenting opinion of the "great Sages," of which he allegedly approved. Whether the insertion was made by Maimonides himself or by someone else, is difficult to determine with certainty. The indications, however, are that the insertion did not emanate from the author himself. In the first place, Maimonides was not in the habit of using characterizations such as "great" with respect to the authorities which he cited. Secondly, if the author had changed his opinion after having written a first draft of the section, he would have rewritten the entire section, together with the illustration given by him at the end thereof, instead of just adding a passage which is out of context with the rest of the section and at variance with the illustration. Finally, in the earliest editions of the Code (Rome [?], before 1480; Soncino [1490]; and Constantinople [1509]), the passage in question is missing.

"But the value of the improvements." Giṭ 5: 3; B. ibid., 50b; B. BM 14b.

"profits taken by a disseizor." Even the profits which were taken by the disseizor after judgment had been rendered against him are collectible only from his *free* property, and not from his *alienated* property, although a judgment is attended by publicity.

"one of the rules of leniency applicable to dower." Bek 8: 9.

2. B. BM 15a; Alf, *ibid.*
3. B. BM 15a.
4. Cf. *ibid.*
5. Alf, BM 15b.
6. Cf. B. BM 15b.
7. B. BM 110a–110b; Alf, *ibid.*

Chapter XXII

1. "and when it is confirmed." B. Ket 19a.

"If the judge erred." B. BB 174a.

"the court gives him 30 days." Alf, *Responsa,* cited by MM, *a. l.*

"the court issues a writ of execution against his property immediately." B. BḲ 112b.

"in the case of an oral debt." Cf. above xi, 4.

3. B. BḲ 112b.
4. *Ibid.*
5. B. BḲ 112b.

6. "three appraisers assess." Cf. B. BB 169a.
"causing proclamation to be made." Cf. Ar 6: 1; B. BM 35b.
"is torn up." Cf. B. BB 169a.
7. "the writ of execution is then torn up." Cf. *ibid.*
8. "having torn up the writ of execution." Cf. *ibid.*
9. "three experienced men." Cf. B. BḲ 107a.
"for a period of 30 days." Cf. Ar 6: 1.
10. "the seizor is also subjected to an oath." Cf. Ket 9: 7.
12. B. BM 35b.
13. B. BB 169a.
14. B. BB 107a.
15. Alf, *Responsa,* cited by MM, *a. l.*
16. B. BM 35a.
17. *Ibid.*

Chapter XXIII

1. Shebi 10: 5; B. BM 72a.
2. Shebi 10: 5.
3. Giṭ 2: 2; B. *ibid.,* 18a.
4. B. BB 171a.
5. BB 10: 3; B. BM 13a.
6. B. BB 172a.
7. B. BB 171b–172a.
8. B. BM 72a–72b.
9. B. BB 169a.
10. B. BB 168b–169a.
"on one of the deeds of purchase." The obligation of the warranty, which is usually contained in the instrument of conveyance—and which is implied in every conveyance for a valuable consideration—constitutes an *in rem* charge on the property remaining in the hands of the vendor. Consequently, a vendee, whose property was seized in satisfaction of a prior obligation of his vendor, may, upon producing his deed of purchase containing the warranty and a certificate of the court to the effect that his property was seized in satisfaction of his vendor's obligation, effect seizure out of other property which at one time belonged to his vendor and which is in the hands of other vendees, whose deeds of purchase are dated subsequently to his.
11. B. BB 168a.
"the falsity of the plea is deemed established." See below iv, vi, 2.
12. BB 10: 6.
13. B. BB 168b.
"and if they wrote in addition." If it was the witnesses who had attested the instrument that were invited by the holder thereof to bear witness to its contents, and these witnesses were examined by the court.
14. B. BB 168b.
"which was torn." In a manner different from that customarily employed by the court for the cancelation of judicial instruments.
15. B. BB 170b; *ibid.,* 171b.

16. B. BB 171b.

"a *claim certain.*" I.e., a claim made with certainty as of the claimant's knowledge, as distinguished from a claim doubtful, i.e., a claim asserted as a possibility only.

17. B. BB 172a.

"holding an impaired bond." Cf. above xiv, 1.

18. B. BB 172a.

Chapter XXIV

1. BB 10: 3–4; B. BM 13a.
2. BB 10: 3–4.
3. Cf. BB 10: 3.
4. B. BB 167b.
5. B. BB 138b; *ibid.*, 155a.
6. B. Giṭ 19a–19b.
7. *Ibid.*, 19b.
8. BB 10: 7; B. *ibid.*, 173a.
9. B. BB 172a–172b.
10. Ket 13: 9; B. *ibid.*, 110a.
11. Ket 13: 8; B. *ibid.*, 110a.

Chapter XXV

1. B. BB 176a–176b.
2. *Ibid.*, 176b.
3. BB 10: 7; B. *ibid.*, 173b.
4. B. BB 173b.
5. *Ibid.*, 174a.

"ḳabbĕlan." One who assumes an obligation. The word is used in the technical sense of a surety who assumes a primary liability similar to that of the principal debtor.

6. B. BB 174b.

"and since he did not occasion a pecuniary loss." The woman not having parted with money in reliance upon the guarantee.

7–8. "'asmaḳta." See above note to 1, viii, 13. The obligation of a warranty is conditional by its very nature, since it does not become operative unless the vendee's title is challenged.

9. P. Shebu 5: 1.

Chapter XXVI

1. BB 10: 8; B. *ibid.*, 176a.
2. Cf. above xxii, 1.

"the power of the guarantor." To ask for an extension of time.

3. B. BB 174b.
4. "in accordance with the enactment of the later Sages." See above ii, 2.
6. "collects from the creditor." B. BB 174b.

"if he became a guarantor or a ḳabbĕlan of his own accord." Cf. B. Ket 108a.
"if a man paid another's bond." *Ibid.*
"If the debtor died." B. BB 174a–174b.
"If the creditor was a heathen." B. BB 174b.
7. B. BB 174b.
9. Cf. BḲ 8: 4.
12. B. BB 139a.

Chapter XXVII

1. "An instrument that is written in any language." B. Giṭ 19b.
"But instruments which are signed by heathen." B. Giṭ 10b–11a; Alf, *ibid.*
"their." The heathen are usually referred to as "they."
"If the Israelite judges do not know." B. Giṭ 19b.
"Collection on such an instrument." Giṭ 19b, in accordance with the author's version, which is at variance with that of the printed editions.
2. B. Giṭ 11a.
3. B. BB 161b–162a.
4. "by a space sufficient to write two lines." B. BB 162a.
"In measuring the two-line space." B. BB 163a.
"does not use a hand like that of a scribe." I.e., does not use a professional hand. The scribe, occupying a position of trust, would not be a party to a forgery. The forger must therefore have recourse to a nonprofessional hand.
"filled with ink scratches." *Ibid.*, 163a.
"was contained in one line." *Ibid.*, 163b.
5. B. BB 163b.
6. *Ibid.*
"The judicial confirmation of an instrument." A notation by the court to the effect that the signatures of the witnesses appearing on the instrument are genuine. Cf. XIV, II, vi, 2.
7. B. BB 163a.
8. "erasures must be confirmed at the end of the instrument." *Ibid.*, 161b.
"where the phrase *firm and valid* usually appears." *Ibid.*, 161a.
"the phrase *firm and valid.*" Which is the closing phrase of all legal documents, except the bill of divorce which has a different closing formula.
9. B. BB 163b–164a.
10. *Ibid.*, 163a–163b.
"the instrument is not to be confirmed through the confirmation witnesses." That is, the confirmation may not be relied upon, and a new confirmation is required. The phrase "confirmation witnesses" apparently refers to the three individuals who, sitting as a court, confirmed the instrument. Cf., *Šulḥan 'Aruḳ*, ḤM 46: 33, where the section is quoted verbatim and where the phrase "confirmation judges" appears, instead of "confirmation witnesses." There is, however, no doubt that the reading *'eḏe haḳḳiyyum*, "confirmation witnesses," is correct. It occurs in all of the printed editions, in all of the manuscripts we have examined, and, most importantly, in the fragments of the Code in Maimonides' own handwriting, published by Luzki, *Mišneh Torah* (New York, 1947), App. to Vol. V.

11. B. BB 164a.
12. *Ibid.; ibid.*, 167a.
13. *Ibid.*, 167a.
14. "If the instrument contains the sum." BB 10:2.
"If the instrument contains one name." B. BB 166b.
"two letters in the later name." P. BB 10:3.
15. "If the instrument contains the word seṗel." B. BB 166b.
"It once happened." *Ibid.*, 166b–167a.
"has the lower hand." Cf. above note to xxi, 1.
16. B. BB 105b.
17. *Ibid.*, 165b.

Treatise IV: Pleading

Chapter I

1. "makes a partial admission." Shebu 6:1.
"the testimony of one witness." B. Shebu 40a.
2. "in the Laws Concerning Hiring." See above i, i, 1.
"swears and is quit of payment." Shebu 7:1–8.
"he who impaired his writing." Cf. above iii, xiv, 1.
"a claim doubtful." See above note to iii, xxiii, 16.
3. "and the defendant denies everything." Shebu 6:1.
"tenders to the plaintiff." B. BM 4a.
"or 'I returned it to you.'" Shebu 6:2.
"that the defendant owes him wheat." Shebu 6:3.
"But the Sages of the Gemara." B. Shebu 40b.
"in the Laws Concerning Oaths." VI, i, xi, 8 and 13.
4. "resort is had to his property." B. Shebu 41a.
"may not shift the oath." *Ibid.*, in accordance with the interpretation of Alf, *ibid.*
"'I do not wish to avail myself of the enactment of the Sages.'" That he swear and take what he claims.
5. B. Shebu 41a.
"lashes of disobedience." As distinguished from lashes provided for in certain cases by the Law. Cf. Deut. 25:2–3.
6. B. Shebu 41a.
7. Cf. B. Shebu 40a.
8. Cf. B. Ket 12b.
9. BḲ 10:7; B. *ibid.*, 118a.
12. "has become liable to an oath." B. Ḳid 27b.
"or Rabbinical." B. Shebu 48b.
"to the extent that." B. Ḳid 28a.
"does not apply to a hired man." See above i, xi, 9.
13. P. Shebu 7:10.
14. Rab Hai Gaon in *Šaʿăre Šĕḇuʿoṭ*.

16. Cf. Shebu 8: 4; XI, ɪv, v, 6.
"in a place where the courts are authorized to impose penalties." As distinguished from compensatory damages. See above note to ɪɪ, viii, 5.
17. Cf. Ket 42a.

Chapter II

1. Shebu 7: 1; B. *ibid.*, 41a.
2. Shebu 7: 4; B. *ibid.*, 46b–47a.
"*oath of utterance.*" See VI, ɪ, i, 1.
3. Cf. B. San 9b.
"*at the outset.*" He is disqualified to the extent that one ought not to constitute him a witness to a legal document, for example. However, if he did attest a legal document, the attestation is not void.
4. Shebu 7: 4.
6. "because the suspect is not liable to the oath by virtue of a rule of the Law." Cf. above, Sec. 4.
7. B. Shebu 41a.
10. Cf. Mak 3: 15.
11. "he must pay." B. BḲ 106a.
"an addition of one fifth." Cf. VI, ɪ, i, 9.
12. Cf. B. BḲ 106a.

Chapter III

1. "unless the admission is with respect to one pĕruṭah." Shebu 6: 1.
3. Shebu 6: 1; B. *ibid.*, 39b.
5. B. Shebu 40a.
6. *Ibid.*
8. Shebu 6: 3; B. *ibid.*, 40a.
9. B. Shebu 43a.
10. B. BḲ 35b.
11. B. Shebu 40a–40b.
12. Cf. B. Shebu 40b.
13. Ket 13: 4; B. *ibid.*, 108b.
15. Cf. B. BM 4a.

Chapter IV

1. Shebu 6: 6; B. *ibid.*, 43a.
2. Shebu 6: 6.
3. *Ibid.*
4. Cf. B. BM 4a.
5. "a writing referring to sela'." B. BM 4b.
"Similarly, if a man said." Shebu 6: 1.
"But if an heir made a claim." Cf. B. Shebu 42a–42b.
6. Cf. above ɪɪɪ, xiii, 3.
7. B. BM 98a.

8. B. Shebu 32b. See above note to III, xiv, 11.
9. Cf. below vi, 3.
10. B. BM 3a.

Chapter V

1. "According to the rule of the Law." Shebu 6: 5; B. *ibid.*, 42b–43a.
"Only the informal oath." B. Shebu 40b.
"property belonging to the sanctuary." B. BM 58a.
2. Cf. B. BM 5a.
3. Shebu 6: 3.
4. Shebu 6: 6.
9. Cf. above I, ii, 7.
11. "from which the minor derived a benefit." Cf. Giṭ 5: 7.
"claims arising out of torts." BḲ 8: 4.
"a shopkeeper." Cf. III, xvi, 5.
12. Cf. B. Giṭ 71a.

Chapter VI

1. Cf. San 3: 6.
"since we always apply the inference of credibility." Cf. above note to I, i, 8.
"his dishonesty is deemed established." B. BM 17a.
2. B. Shebu 34a–34b.
3. B. Shebu 41b.
4. "witnesses remember only that which they are called upon to witness." B. Shebu 41b.
"near that pillar." *Ibid.*, 34b.
5. B. BB 170a–170b.
6. B. San 29a–29b.
"what is not done by attestation a man might not remember." That is, a man's memory may not be relied upon in these matters, if he was not originally called upon to bear witness to the fact to which he now testifies.
7. B. San 29a–29b.
8. B. San 29a.

Chapter VII

1. B. San 29b.
"cognizor" and "cognizee." The party who makes a recognizance and the party in whose favor a recognizance is made, respectively.
2. B. San 29b. Cf. above III, xi, 1, and below Sec. 3.
"in the presence of three persons." Three laymen may be constituted by a party as a lay court for the purpose of taking a recognizance from him and for various other purposes. Cf. Giṭ 4: 2; San 3: 2; B. San 29b.
3. B. San 29b.
4. "because there is a presumption." *Ibid.*
"a doubt may be entertained." B. San 29b–30a.

5. B. BM 16b–17a.
6. *Ibid.*
8. B. BB 31a.

Chapter VIII

1. Cf. B. BB 45a–45b.
"seizin (ḥāzakah)." See above note to 1, xi, 8.
2. Cf. above III, xiii, 3.
3. B. Shebu 46b.
4. *Ibid.*, 46a–46b.
5. BḴ 10:3.
6. *Ibid.;* B. *ibid.*, 114b–115a.
8. Cf. above Sec. 5.
10. B. BM 116a.
"Support for our view." See above Sec. 9.
"But all other scissors and books," which are not proved by the testimony of witnesses to have been used by the owner for lending and renting out, do not come within the rule. The author's inference that in the case cited in B. BM 116a in the name of Raba witnesses were produced who testified that the book and the scissors had been used by the owner for lending and renting out seems to be based upon the fact that the Talmud specifies the kind of book and the kind of scissors that were involved. If the rule, referred to in Sec. 3, were applicable to any articles fit to be lent or rented out, there would be no point in specifying the kind of book and the kind of scissors that were involved, since all books and all scissors are fit to be lent or rented out. The author therefore concludes that Raba's was a special case in which witnesses testified that the owner had been using the particular kind of book and the particular kind of scissors for lending and renting out, and that where no such testimony is available the rule of Sec. 3 does not apply to articles (such as books and scissors) which, though *fit* to be lent or rented out, are not *designed* to be lent or rented out.

Chapter IX

1. BB 3:3; B. *ibid.*, 45a–46a.
2. B. BB 45b–46a; see above 1, xi, 8.
3. B. BB 47a.
4. B. Shebu 46a–46b.
5. Cf. B. BM 116a.
"We have already stated." See above Sec. 1.
6. B. BB 33b.
7. BM 1:1.
8. *Ibid.*
9. B. BM 7a.
10. *Ibid.*
11. B. BM 6a.
12. *Ibid.*
13. *Ibid.*

Chapter X

1. B. BB 36a.
2. *Ibid.*
3. Cf. above III, xiii, 3.
4. BB 3: 1; B. *ibid.*, 36a.
5. B. BB 31a.
6. *Ibid.*, 34b.

Chapter XI

1. Cf. B. BB 32b–33a.
"Reuben swears the informal oath." See above v, 1.
2. "for three years in succession." BB 3: 1; B. *ibid.*, 29a.
"it was a time of war." B. BB 38a.
3. B. BB 30a.
This section is to be read together with the last paragraph of the section immediately preceding it.
4. B. BB 29a.
5. *Ibid.*
6. B. BB 39a.
7. *Ibid.*, 38b–39a.
8. *Ibid.*, 39b–40a.
9. *Ibid.*, 35b.

Chapter XII

1. BB 3: 1; B. *ibid.*, 36b, 37b.
2. B. BB 29a.
"because this matter relates to an assertion made by themselves." The allegation of continual dwelling having been made by the lessees, and not by the party claiming seizin (ḥăzaḳah), it is necessary that witnesses other than the lessees themselves testify thereto.
3. B. BB 29b.
4. *Ibid.*, 29a.
5. *Ibid.*, 29b.
6. *Ibid.*, 41b.
7. *Ibid.*, 42a.
8. *Ibid.*
9. B. BB 36a–36b.
10. *Ibid.*, 36a.
11. *Ibid.*
12. *Ibid.*
" 'orlah." The fruit of young trees during the first three years of growth. See Lev. 19: 23.
"diverse kinds." See Lev. 19: 19.
13. B. BB 29b.
14. Cf. BB 3: 5; B. *ibid.*, 57b.

15. B. BB 36a.
16. *Ibid.*, 29b.
17. B. BB 37a.
18. *Ibid.*, 37b–38a.
19. *Ibid.*, 36a.
20. *Ibid.*, 37a.

Chapter XIII

1. ḄB 3:3. As to the informal oath, see above xi, 1.
2. "by the exilarchs." B. BB 36a.
   "by a robber." *Ibid.*, 47a.
   "by a heathen." *Ibid.*, 35b.
   "by a deaf-mute, a mentally incompetent, or a minor." There seems to be no direct authority for this proposition in the Talmud.
   "from the property of the deaf-mute, the mentally incompetent, or the minor." B. BM 39a–39b.
3. B. BB 47a.
4. *Ibid.*, 46b. See R. Samuel b. Meir (Rashbam), *a. l.*, who interprets the term *'aris batte 'aḅoṭ* as hereditary tenant.
5. *Ibid.*, 46b, 47a.
6. Cf. B. BM 39a–39b.
7. "a field to which the rule of compulsory partition does not apply." B. BB 42a.
   "to which the rule of compulsory partition applies." B. BB 42a.
   "the rule of compulsory partition." See XII, III, i, 1, 4.
   "if the husband took the profits." *Ibid.*, 49a–50a.
   "if the wife took the profits." *Ibid.*, 51a.
8. B. BB 52a.
10. *Ibid.*, 36a.
11. *Ibid.*, 47a.

Chapter XIV

1. "it is good proof." B. BB 47b.
   "with the exception of a robber." *Ibid.*
   "or of a husband." B. BB 49a–50a.
   "iron sheep." See above note to III, viii, 12.
   "mĕloḡ." Property of which the husband has the usufruct but for the depreciation of which he is not answerable.
   "as we have stated in the Laws Concerning Marriage." IV, 1, xxii, 17–18.
2. B. BB 47b.
   "as we have stated." XI, III, ix, 14–15.
3. B. BB 47a.
4. *Ibid.*
5. B. BB 35b.
6. *Ibid.*, 36a.
7. B. BM 39a–39b.
8. Cf. B. BB 32b–33a.

"from the rental." This rendering is based upon the reading (*miš-śeḵarah*) found in three manuscripts from Yemen (Enelow Memorial Collection, Nos. 354, 398, 405) and in one from Spain (Codex Adler, 1692), in the Library of The Jewish Theological Seminary of America. In the Venice edition of 1574, and in all of the later editions, the reading is *miš-šibḥah*, "from its improvement." However, this reading is entirely unsatisfactory, as there is no mention anywhere in this section that an improvement, either through expenditures or without expenditures, occurred in the property. Furthermore, what if there is no improvement? Shall the gagee go without recovery at all? In all of the editions prior to the Venice edition of 1574, the reading is *bišḇu'ah*, "by an oath." This reading is equally unsatisfactory, since neither the formal nor the informal oath may be imposed upon a party in a case, such as is dealt with in this section, where land is involved and where his adversary does not make a claim certain (see above i, 7 and v, 1).

On the other hand, the reading adopted in this translation presents no difficulty. The "rental" refers to the amount representing the rental for the gaged property which the gagee agreed with the gagor to deduct yearly from the amount of the loan. Since a gage without a deduction on account of the rental is quasi-usurious (see III, vi, 7–8), it must be assumed that there was an agreement between gagor and gagee for such a deduction. The rule of this section, therefore, is that the agreement, as alleged by the party in possession, shall stand, and that he shall remain in possession until the debt is extinguished by the annual deductions.

9. Cf. B. BB 32b–33a.

"from the profits of the field." In Sec. 8, above, it is stated that the creditor is to collect "from the rental." The difference seems to be due to the fact that in Sec. 8, the creditor claimed to hold the property as a gage from the father of the orphans, with an agreement for the deduction of a definite amount yearly as rental, whereas in this section the creditor merely claimed that there was "a debt owing" to him from the father, and not that the field had been gaged to him under an agreement of gage.

10. B. BB 38b.
11. *Ibid.*, 50b.
12. BB 3:3; B. *ibid.*, 41a; Tos *ibid.*, 2:1.
13. BB 3:3; B. *ibid.*, 41b.
14. B. BB 30a–30b; Alf, *ibid.*

Chapter XV

1. B. BB 169b.
2. *Ibid.*, 56b.
3. B. BB 33a.
4. *Ibid.*, 34b–35b.
6. *Ibid.*, 31a.
7. *Ibid.*, 30b–31a.
8. Cf. above Sec. 7.
9. B. BB 32a–32b.
10. *Ibid.*, 29b; Alf, *ibid.*
11. Ket 13:7; B. *ibid.*, 109b.

Chapter XVI

1. Ket 13: 6.
2. B. Ket 109a–109b.
3. B. BB 30b.
4. *Ibid.*
5. B. BB 33b–34a.
6. *Ibid.*
   "but is unable to swear." See above note to III, xiv, 11.
8. Cf. B. BB 29a.
9. B. Shebu 31a.
10. *Ibid.*

Treatise V: Inheritance

Chapter I

1. BB 8: 2.
2. *Ibid.*
   "A female never shares in the inheritance with a male." Unless it be by representation. If a man died leaving a son and a granddaughter, the daughter of a deceased son, the granddaughter shares in the inheritance equally with the son because she takes by representation through her father, that is, she takes the share to which her father would have been entitled if he had survived the decedent. See below, Sec. 5.
   "if there be no son living." Literally, "if there be no son in the world." In all of the printed editions there is here an obvious corruption of the text: *ba'olam*, "in the world," was misread as *lĕ'olam*, "always." As a result, a copyist connected it with the phrase that follows it and read the text as if it meant, "if there be no son, we always look to the son's issue."
   The reading *ba'olam* adopted in this translation is found in three manuscripts from Yemen (Enelow Memorial Collection, Nos. 354, 398, 405), and in one from Spain (Codex Adler, 1692), in the Library of the Jewish Theological Seminary of America. That this is the correct reading is apparent from the phrase "if there be no daughter living," which occurs but two or three lines further in this section and in which the printed editions agree with the manuscripts just mentioned.
   "the inheritance continues to ascend up to Reuben." B. BB 115a–115b.
3. "Whosoever is prior." BB 8: 2.
5. Cf. BB 8: 3.
6. BB 8: 1; B. *ibid.*, 110b.
7. Yeb 2: 5; B. *ibid.*, 22a–22b.
   "a *mamzer*." That is, the issue of an adulterous or incestuous union. See V, I, xvii, 1.
8. BB 8: 1; B. Ket 83b.
9. See IV, I, xxii.
10. Cf. Yeb 13: 2; B. *ibid.*, 112b.
11. B. BB 125b.

12. *Ibid.*, 114b.
13. B. BB 114b; B. Nid 44b.

Chapter II

1. BB 8: 4; B. *ibid.*, 112b.
2. B. BB 142b; B. Bek 46b.
3. B. BB 126b–127a.
5. *Ibid.*, 142b.
6. *Ibid.*, 127a.
7. BB 8: 3.
8. BB 8: 4.
9. Bek 8: 1.
10. *Ibid.;* B. *ibid.*, 46b.
11. Bek 8: 2.
12. B. Yeb 62a; Bek 8: 1.
13. Cf. Yeb 22a.
"a mamzer." See above note to i, 7.
"the son of the hateful." The Deuteronomy passage is usually rendered as *the son of the hated.*
"the son of a divorced woman or of a woman released from leviratical marriage." That is, the son born of a union between such a woman and a common priest. See V, i, xv, 1 and xvii, 1.
14. B. Ḳid 74a.
15. Giṭ 71a.
16. B. BB 126b.
17. *Ibid.*

Chapter III

1. "the father had only an expectancy." Bek 8: 9.
"a debt owing to him." B. BB 125b.
"a ship on the sea." Cf. Ar 4: 3.
2. B. BB 123b.
3. *Ibid.*
"If one of the father's friends." If the father was a priest and the friend had been accustomed to give to him the gifts due to the priests.
4. B. BB 124a.
5. *Ibid.*, 125b–126a.
6. *Ibid.*, 126a–126b.
7. Yeb 4: 7; Bek 8: 9.
8. See XII, iii, xii, 2.
9. See IV, i, xxii, 10.
"iron sheep," "mĕloḡ." See above notes to iv, xiv, 1.

Chapter IV

1. BB 8: 6; B. *ibid.*, 135a.
"as he would be examined with respect to a divorce." See Giṭ 7: 1.

2. Cf. B. BB 127b.
3. *Ibid.*
4. B. BB 127b.
5. B. Ber 16b.
7. Cf. B. Ḳid 80a.
8. BB 8: 6; B. *ibid.*, 135a–135b.

Chapter V

1. BB 9: 2; B. *ibid.*, 140b.
"ṭumṭum." One whose sex is doubtful.
2. BB 9: 1–2.
"in the Laws Concerning Marriage." See IV, 1, xix, 10.
3. Yeb 11: 6–7.
4. B. Yeb 37b.
"yĕḇamah." A widow who has married (by leviratical marriage) one of
her deceased husband's brothers.
"yaḇam." One who has married (by leviratical marriage) the widow of
his deceased brother who died without issue. The yaḇam succeeds to his deceased
brother's property. See above iii, 7.
"and the yaḇam's other sons, whose filiation is certain." The reading *banim
wadda'im* adopted here is found in Luzki, "Variae Lectiones," *Mišneh Torah*
(New York, 1947), App. to Vol. V, and is based on several manuscripts. Cf. below
Sec. 5, where the phrase banim wadda'im occurs in a similar context.
5. B. Yeb 37b.
"If the yaḇam left two sons whose filiation was certain and thereafter the
yaḇam's father died." In all of the printed editions the reading is *meṯ hay-yaḇam*
"the yaḇam died," instead of *meṯ 'aḇi hay-yaḇam,* "the yaḇam's father died."
This is clearly incongruous. The phrase "the yaḇam left two sons," implies that the
yaḇam is dead. How, then, could he die again "thereafter"? Furthermore, it is
obvious from the context that the dispute is not about the inheritance left by the
yaḇam but about that left by his father, that is, by the grandfather of the parties
to the dispute. The translator, therefore, did not hesitate to adopt the reading
meṯ 'aḇi hay-yaḇam found in three manuscripts from Yemen (Enelow Memorial
Collection, Nos. 354, 398, 405), and in one from Spain (Codex Adler, 1692), in
the Library of the Jewish Theological Seminary of America.
6. "upon a man and upon his wife." BB 9: 9; B. *ibid.*, 158b.
"upon a man and upon his mother." BB 9: 10; B. *ibid.*, 158b.
7. B. BB 159b.
8. BB 9: 8.

Chapter VI

1. Cf. BB 8: 5.
2. BB 8: 5; B. *ibid.*, 131b.
" 'Such a one, my son, alone shall inherit me.' " When the testator had other
sons.
3. BB 8: 5.

4. B. BB 131a.
5. BB 8: 5.
6. *Ibid.*; B. *ibid.*, 129a–129b.
8. Ket 9: 1; B. *ibid.*, 83a.
8. "as we have stated in the Laws Concerning Marriage." See IV, 1, xxiii, 6.
9. B. Ḳid 17b.
10. *Ibid.*
11. BB 8: 5; B. *ibid.*, 133b.
12. B. Ḳid 18a.
13. B. Shab 10b.

Chapter VII

1. Cf. Yeb 15: 3.
2. *Ibid.*; B. *ibid.*, 117a.
3. Cf. Yeb 16: 3–4.
4. Cf. B. BM 39a.
5. *Ibid.*
6. *Ibid.*
7. Cf. *ibid.*
8. Cf. B. BM 38b.
9. Cf. *ibid.*

Chapter IX

1. B. BM 39a.
   P. BB 9: 4.
2. B. BM 39a–39b.
   BB 9: 3; B. *ibid.*, 143b.
3. BB 9: 3; B. *ibid.*, 144a.
4. B. BM 39b.
5. B. BB 144a.
6. BB 9: 4; B. *ibid.*, 144b.
7. B. BB 52a–52b.
   " '*onot*, that is, deeds of sale of bondmen." The word '*onot* is the Hebrew plural of Greek *ōnē*, meaning a deed of sale. See A. Kohut, *Aruch Completum,* I, 134. The author apparently does not mean to imply that the word always has the restricted meaning of deeds of sale of bondmen only, but that in this context, where it is used with reference to objects of trade and commerce, it has that meaning. The word is often used in the Talmud in the sense of a deed of sale of land as well as of bondmen. See e.g., B. BB 154b.
8. B. BB 52b.
9. B. BB 173a.
   "by writing and delivery." A bond may be validly assigned only by a deed of assignment and delivery of the bond to the assignee, or, if the assignment is made by a sick person in contemplation of death, by mere word of mouth. See XII, 1, vi, 11; 11, x, 2.
10. B. BB 173b.

11. *Ibid.*, 144b.
12. BB 8:7.
13. B. BB 144b.
14. BB 9:4; B. *ibid.*, 144b.
15. B. BB 139a.

Chapter X

1. B. BB 106b.
2. B. Ket 109b.
3. B. BK 11b.
4. B. Kid 42a.
5. Cf. Git 5:4.
6. B. Git 52a.
7. *Ibid.*; Alf, *ibid.*
8. B. BM 39a; B. Ket 48a.

Chapter XI

1. B. BM 70a.
2. B. Ket 100b.
3. *Ibid.*
4. Cf. B. Git 52a.
5. "he is not required to render an account." B. Git 52a.
   "he must swear." Git 5:4.
   "may purchase his attire." B. *ibid.*, 52b.
6. B. Git 52a.
7. *Ibid.*
   "to incur a liability in order to acquire a right." That is, if the orphans are sued and the guardian wishes to appear for them and assert on their behalf a counterclaim against the plaintiff.
8. B. Git 52a.
9. *Ibid.*
10. *Ibid.*
11. Cf. B. Ket 48a.

LIST OF ABBREVIATIONS

Tractates of Mishnah and Talmud

Ab—'Aḅoṭ
Ar—'Ărakin
BB—Baḅa Baṭra
Bek—Bĕkoroṭ
Ber—Bĕrakoṭ
BK—Baḅa Ḳamma
BM—Baḅa Meṣi'a
Giṭ—Giṭṭin
Ḥal—Ḥallah
Ket—Kĕṭubboṭ

Ḳid—Ḳiddušin
Mak—Makkoṭ
MSh—Ma'ăśer Šeni
Pes—Pĕsaḥim
San—Sanhedrin
Shab—Šabbaṭ
Shebi—Šĕḅi'iṭ
Shebu—Šĕḅu'oṭ
Yeb—Yĕḅamoṭ

When the name of the tractate is preceded by B., the reference is to the Babylonian Talmud, and when preceded by P., the reference is to the Palestinian Talmud; otherwise, it is to the Mishnah.

Other Abbreviations

Alf—Alfasi
ḤM—Ḥošen Mišpaṭ
KM—Kesef Mišneh
LM—Leḥem Mišneh
MM—Maggid Mišneh

Mek—Mekilta
RABD—Rabbi Abraham b. David
Sif—Sifre
Tos—Tosefta

GLOSSARY *

Alibi testimony ('*eḏuṯ hazzamah*)
    testimony by one set of witnesses that another set of witnesses, who
    testified to a certain event as having occurred in their presence at a
    certain time and place, were at that time at another place
Alienated property (*nĕḵasim mĕšu'baḏim*)
    property which has been transferred by a debtor by way of sale, gift,
    or in discharge of an indebtedness
'*Asmaḵta*
    a Talmudic doctrine relating to the invalidity of certain conditional
    transfers of property and conditional obligations
Claim certain (*ṭa'ănaṯ wadday*)
    a claim made with certainty as of the claimant's knowledge
Claim doubtful (*ṭa'ănaṯ sāp̄eḵ*)
    a claim asserted as a possibility only
Cognizee
    the party in whose favor a recognizance is made
Cognizor
    the party who makes a recognizance
Confirmed writing (*šĕṭar mĕḵuyyam*)
    a writing bearing a certification by the court that the signatures of
    the witnesses appearing thereon have been authenticated
Credence (*ne'ĕmanuṯ*)
    a stipulation in which the parties to a legal transaction agree in
    advance as to which one of them shall be believed, if a dispute grow-
    ing out of such transaction and involving certain conflicting allega-
    tions should arise between them
Dĕmai
    produce originating from a grower who is suspected of nonobserv-
    ance of the laws relating to heave offering and tithes
Dust of usury ('*ăḇaḵ ribbiṯ*)
    quasi usury which is prohibited by Rabbinical law only
Free property (*nĕḵasim bĕne ḥorin*)

---

    * The terms representing weights, measures and monetary units (such as *ḵor,
sĕ'ah, ḵaḇ, loḡ, sela', zuz ma'ah, pĕruṭah*, etc.), which occur frequently in the
text, have not been listed here, since these terms may easily be found in the
standard dictionaries of the Talmud.

property which has not been transferred by a debtor by way of sale, gift, or in discharge of an indebtedness

Habdalah
a benediction recited over a cup of wine or similar beverage at the end of the Sabbath or of a festival day to mark the conclusion of the holy day and the beginning of the ordinary day

Hallah
dough offering (cf., Num. 15: 20 ff.)

Hăzakah
presumption; reputation; seizin. See Index under these topics; see also Introduction

Hypothec
specific property designated as security for a debt

Inference of credibility (*miggo*)
a rule of evidence that a defendant's plea is to be believed, if a more convenient or a more advantageous plea was available to him

Informal oath (*šěbu'at heset*)
an oath administered to a defendant under a special enactment ascribed by the Babylonian Talmud (*Šěbu'ot* 40b) to Rab Nahman. This oath is administered wherever, under the rules pertaining to oaths, the defendant, though denying a claim asserted against him with certainty, is not liable either to a Pentateuchal or to a quasi-Pentateuchal oath. It is of lesser solemnity than either the Pentateuchal or the quasi-Pentateuchal oath, the party taking it not being required to hold a sacred object, such as a scroll of the Law, while it is being administered

Iron sheep (*son barzel*)
property delivered by one party to another on condition that the party accepting the property be responsible for any loss or damage thereto regardless of the cause of such loss or damage

Judicial confirmation of instrument (*kiyyum šětarot*)
a notation by the court to the effect that the signatures of the witnesses appearing on the instrument are genuine

Kabbělan (literally: one who assumes)
a surety who assumes a primary liability similar to that of the principal debtor

Kětubbah
writ, especially marriage contract, containing, among other things,

the settlement of a certain amount due to the wife on her husband's death or on being divorced

Ḳinyan (literally: acquisition)
a formality, simulating an exchange, wherein the party to whom a transfer of property is made, or toward whom an obligation is assumed (or the witnesses to the transaction on his behalf), delivers to the party making the transfer, or assuming the obligation, some object, such as a scarf or a handkerchief, to make the transaction binding and enforceable

Law, the (*Torah*)
the Pentateuch

Mamzer
the issue of an adulterous or an incestuous union

Mĕloğ (literally: plucking)
that part of the wife's property of which the husband has the usufruct but for the depreciation of which he is not answerable

Oath by accumulation (*šĕbu'ah 'al yĕde gilgul*)
wherever, by the rules pertaining to oaths, a party is required to take an oath with respect only to a certain allegation, his adversary may demand that he also include in the oath other matters in dispute between them, as to which matters he would otherwise not be subject to an oath. An oath inclusive of such matters is an oath by accumulation

Oral tradition (*šĕmu'ah*, literally: hearing)
interpretation of the Written Law transmitted orally by tradition. The author uses this phrase whenever an interpretation put by the Talmud upon a certain passage of the Pentateuch is not apparent from the plain meaning of its words

'Orlah
the fruit of young trees during the first three years of growth

Pentateuchal oath (*šĕbu'ah min hat̞-torah*)
an oath administered to a defendant in cases in which it is either directly prescribed in the Law or derived therefrom by interpretation.

Quasi-Pentateuchal oath (*šĕbu'ah ḳĕ'en šel torah*)
an oath administered in certain cases to a party, plaintiff or defendant, who is not liable to a Pentateuchal oath. This oath was established by the Sages of the Mishnah and is attended by all the formalities of the Pentateuchal oath

Recognizance (*hoda'ah,* literally: admission)
a formal acknowledgment, before witnesses or before a court, of
an obligation by an obligor or of a conveyance by a grantor

Seizin (*hăzakah*)
possession under circumstances giving rise to a presumption of
rightful ownership. See Introduction

Seize, Seizure (*tirpa*)
a taking by a creditor from his debtor's transferees, by virtue of a
prior lien, of landed property bound for the payment of a debt

Tebel
untithed produce

Tĕrumah
heave offering

Transfer adjunct to the transfer of land (*kinyan 'aggab karka',* literally: acquisition by dint of land)
a transfer of chattels, bonds, intangible property, or property rights,
made simultaneously with, and merged in, a transfer of land

Tumtum
one whose sex is doubtful

Yabam (see Deut. 25: 5 ff.)
one who has married, by leviratical marriage, the widow of his deceased brother who died without issue

Yĕbamah
a woman who has married, by leviratical marriage, one of her deceased husband's brothers (see Deut. 25: 5 ff.)

INDEX

ANATHEMA, pronouncement of, 9, 79, 81, 119, 168, 193, 210

Animals, preventing animal from eating of that at which it is working, prohibited, 48 f.

'Asmakta (see Glossary), cases of, 97, 100, 175, 176, 269

BABYLONIA, 143

BAILMENT:

Bailee for hire, assessment of damages payable by porter for merchandise lost or destroyed, 13; craftsman deemed as, 37; pledgee deemed as, 37; rule of liability applicable to, 4

Bailee's oath, liability of bailee for hire to, 4; liability of gratuitous bailee to, 4; liability of hirer to, 4 f.; scope of, 68 f.

Bailment with owner, bailee's freedom from liability in case of, 5, 55; cases of, 37, 56; definition of, 5

Change of status of property during period of, 7

Commodatary, commencement and termination of borrower's responsibility for thing borrowed, 58; deviation by, from terms of borrowing, 52; duration of borrowing, 53 ff.; duty of, to feed borrowed animal, 53; likened to donee, 53; measure of damages payable by, in case of damage to thing borrowed, 53; rule of liability applicable to, 4, 52

Delivery of bailed object by bailee to another, prohibition of, 5 f.; resulting in lowering standard of care, 6; resulting in raising standard of care, 6 f.

Deposit, bailee claiming lack of knowledge as to value of, 66; care of, by bailee, 72; conflicting allegations with respect to identity of, 70; made with head of household, 62; may be delivered to court in case of bailor's absence abroad, 74; misappropriation of, by bailee, 71; of money dedicated to poor or to redemption of captives, 64; of money with householder, 73; of money with shopkeeper, 72 f.; place where demand for return of, may be made, 73 f.; plea of purchase of, by bailee, 69 f.; sale of deteriorating, by bailee, 71 f.

Deviation by bailee from terms of, 15 ff.

Election by bailee to pay for stolen deposit entitling him to collect penalty from thief, 74 f.

Enactment of Sages, with respect to porters, 12; with respect to property belonging to sanctuary, 7 f.

Exclusion of landed property, slaves, and bonds, and of property belonging to sanctuary or to heathen from rules applicable to, 7 f.

Formation of bailor-bailee relationship, 9 f.

Gratuitous bailee, commingling deposited produce with his own, 65 f.; election by, to pay rather than to take bailee's oath, 68, 74; reasonable care by, illustrated, 60 ff.; rule of liability applicable to, 4, 60

Hirer, object of hiring becoming unusable, 18 f.; rule of liability applicable to, 4 f.

Loss of bailed object through force majeure, examples of, 13; freedom from liability for: of bailee for hire, 4, of gratuitous bailee, 4, of hirer, 4; witnesses to, required, 11 f.

Minor as bailor, 9

Negligence of bailee, 64 f., liability for, only if negligent act *sine qua non* cause of loss, 15; liability for, with respect to property excluded from ordinary rules of bailment, 8; proof of, 69

Reimbursement of bailee for expenditures incurred in saving bailed object from violence, 14

Stipulations with respect to, conflicting allegations with respect to, 10, 69; *ḳinyan* not required for validity of, 10; validity of, 10, 69

Suit by bailee against thief, 76

Types of, 4

CAUSATION. *See* Bailment

Claim certain (*see* Glossary), 228

Claim doubtful (*see* Glossary), 190

Confirmed writing (*see* Glossary), 128 f.

Craftsman (*see also* Seizin), conflicting allegations with respect to amount of craftsman's pay, 43; deemed bailee for hire, 37; duty to pay craftsman on time, 40 f.; learners, 38 f.; liability of, for damage to thing given to him for repair or for failure to repair in manner agreed, 37 f.; mutual rights and liabilities of employer and craftsman, 38; mutual rights and liabilities of owner of land and tree planter, 39; public butcher, bloodletter, scribe, and teacher may be removed for malfeasance without warning, 39

CREDITOR:

Admission by, of invalidity of writing obligatory, 129 f.

Exemption from levy by, of food for 30 days and clothing for 12 months, 80; of garments of debtor's wife, 79; of tools and implements, 80, 87

May not enter debtor's house for purpose of making distraint, 81

Not to lend money without witnesses, 84

Oath by, in case of *seizure* of debtor's property, 84

Oath by heirs of, 140 f.

Predeceasing debtor, 141

Release by, produced for first time against his heirs, 142 f.

Required to take oath in certain cases, 127 f.

Stipulation by, that he be believed as to nonpayment, 135; with respect to proof of payment, 133

DEBT:

Exaction of, forbidden, 78

Novation of contract of, 137

On writing (*see* Writing Obligatory)

Oral, collectible from debtor's heirs only under certain conditions, 118; how contracted, 116 f.; not collectible from purchasers of debtor's property, 117 f.; plea of payment of, must be supported by informal oath, 116 f.; proof by witnesses of payment of, not required, 116 f.; testimony by one witness to, 131; unattested note of hand treated as, 117

Payment of, by draft on third party, 138

Remittance of, to creditor through third party, 137

Risk of loss of money representing payment of, 137 f.

Time and place of payment of, conflicting allegations with respect to date fixed for repayment, 127; demand may be made at any place, 127; loan without date fixed for repayment, 126 f.; no demand may be made before due date, 126

DEBTOR:

Concealment of movables by, 118 f.

Imprisonment of, for debt not to be allowed, 81

Insolvent, method of distribution of assets of, where priority not applicable, 152 f.; no priority in movables belonging to, 151 f.; oath of insolvency by: judge's discretion with regard to, 83, not required in certain cases, 82 f., required only once for all creditors, 82; order of priority of creditors, with respect to landed property belonging to, 150 f., 153

Movables in hands of heirs of, 119 f.

Plea by, of forgery, usury, or other ground for invalidity of confirmed writing, 128 f.; that witnesses to payment departed overseas or died, 133

Predeceasing creditor, 141 f.

Redemption by, of property taken in execution, 162 f.

Remedy of, in case of a writing containing stipulation of credence to creditor as to nonpayment, 135

Stipulation by, that he be believed as to payment, 136

Stipulation of credence to, binding upon creditor's heirs, 142

Suit by, who claims to have paid twice by reason of stipulation of credence, 135 f.

Writings of indebtedness belonging to, subject to *seizure* by creditor, 83 f.

Deposit. *See* Bailment

Discovery and inspection of documents, party holding document containing evidence of another party's rights may be compelled to produce same, 210

EGYPT, parchments of Gemara found in, 133 f.

EMPLOYER AND EMPLOYEE:

Conflicting allegations of, with respect to payment or amount of wages, 41 f.

Effect on employee's wages of supervening changes in work situation, 35 f.

Employee may not be compelled to work, 34

Employee reneging after he has begun to work, 33 f.

Employee's failure to come to work, 33

Employer hiring workers through agent, negative commandment with respect to delay of payment not applicable in case of, 40 f.; worker's rights in certain cases against employer and against agent, 32 f.

Employer's duty to pay worker's wages on time, 39 f.; affirmative and negative commandments applying to, 39 ff.; demand by worker necessary in order to make negative commandment with respect to, operative, 41

Employer's failure to provide work, 33

Local usage with respect to length of working day governing, 31 f.

Measure of damages payable by reneging employee, 33 f.

Special rule of leniency applicable to worker's oath, 43 f.

Worker's right to eat of that at which he is working, 44 ff.

ENFORCEMENT OF OBLIGATIONS:
Execution against debtor's property, appointment of 3 appraisers in case of, 160; by lender, against landed property of fairest quality, 147 f.; by tortfeasee, against landed property of medium quality, 147; by woman for her *kĕṭubbah*, against landed property of poorest quality, 148; demand upon debtor necessary prior to, 158; in debtor's absence: notice to debtor, 124, oath by creditor on writing required, 124, proof required of creditor on writing, 124; in hands of deceased debtor's minor heirs: not to be allowed except in certain cases after appointment of guardian, 121, procedure to be followed, 122 f., proclamation, investigation, and appraisal, 123 f., writ of execution, form of, 123; in hands of debtor's transferees: assessment of property by 3 experienced men, 161, oath by creditor, 161, proclamation for 30 days, 161, writ of execution, form of, 160, writ of seizure, form of, 161, writ of transfer of possession, form of, 161
Extension of time to debtor, to make good debt, 158; to produce proof of forgery, 158 f.; issuance of writ of excommunication against debtor upon his failure to appear after 3 court days, 159; issuance of writ of execution after waiting period of 90 days, 159

FORCE MAJEURE. *See* Bailment

GEONIM, 81, 92, 101, 120, 121, 131, 153, 176, 180, 225
GUARANTEE AND SURETYSHIP:
Guarantee, conditional, 175; for debtor's body, 176; for unspecified amount, 176; formation of obligation of, 173; given after attestation of bond by witnesses, 176 f.
Guarantor, bondman, married woman, or minor as, 179; conjoined with debtor in bond, 176 f.; creditor may not demand payment in first instance from, unless he so stipulated, 174; debtor to be subjected to oath of insolvency before creditor may collect from, 178; definition of, 174; demand in first instance upon, when debtor not available, 177; extension of 30 days to, 177; on *kĕṭubbah,* 174; on warranty in sale of landed property, 174; proof of payment by, seeking reimbursement, 179; recourse of, against debtor, 178 f.; stipulation by, waiving right to 30-day extension, 177; to guarantor, 175 f.
Joint debtors deemed guarantors for each other, 175
Ḳabbĕlan (*see* Glossary), creditor may demand payment in first instance from, 174; definition of, 174
Two guarantors for same debt, 175
GUARDIAN:
Ancestor may direct that minor's share be given to him without appointment of, 290
Appointment of, by ancestor, 290; by court, 289 f.; not necessary, if only money was left by ancestor, 289; over mentally incompetent and deaf-mute, 291
Court is father of orphans, 291
Court may not withhold property from heir after he has reached majority unless so directed by ancestor, 291
Court not required to appoint, over property of mentally competent adult, 282
Court's supervision of property belonging to person who has escaped because of danger, 282, 283 f.

Disposition of money belonging to orphans, 291 f.

Distinction between, appointed by court and one appointed by ancestor, with regard to court's power of removal, 290

Duty of court to appoint, upon failure of ancestor to appoint, 290

Duty of person about to die to appoint, 290

Not required to render account, but must take oath, if appointed by court, 292 f.

Not required to take oath, if appointed by orphans' ancestor, 293

Orphans' property to be managed by, until they reach majority, 292 f.

Powers of, and limitations thereof, 293 f.

Qualifications of, 290

HYPOTHEC:

Emancipation by debtor of bondman subject to, 145 f.

Hypothecation of specific property, exclusive of other property belonging to debtor, 145; without exclusion of other property belonging to debtor, 145

Property subject to, may not be redeemed by debtor's vendee, 146

Sale by debtor of property subject to, 146 f.

INHERITANCE:

Apostate Israelite's right of inheritance of property left by his Israelite relatives, 280

Death of ancestor, ascertainment of, 280 f.

Disposition of property, at variance with laws of inheritance, 277; by sick man, increasing share of some of heirs and decreasing share of others, 277 f.

Distinction between disposition using language of inheritance and one using language of gift, 278 f.

Distribution of, between issue of deceased heirs per stirpes, 261

Division of inheritance, double portion of first-born son: applies only to property vested in father, 267, applies only to son born to his father first, 265, does not apply to debt owing to father, 268, does not apply to improvements occuring after father's death, 268, does not apply to mother's inheritance, 265, does not apply to son born after father's death, 264, *mamzer* entitled to, 266, midwife's, mother's, or father's declaration with respect to identity of first-born son, 266 f., sale or relinquishment of additional portion by first-born son, 268 f., to be allotted contiguously, 269 f., *ṭumṭum* operated upon and found to be male not entitled to, 264

Division of inheritance, null if made under error, as to number or identity of heirs, 289; null if share of one of heirs *seized* by ancestor's creditor, 289; property to be included in, 289; when some of the heirs are adults and some are minors, 289 f.

Heirship, ascertainment of, 270 ff.; doubt arising with respect to, 273 ff.

Husband inherits only property which was vested in wife during her lifetime, 263

Husband inherits wife, 262

Husband's heirs do not inherit wife by representation, if he predeceased her, 263

Issue of deceased heir take his place in order of priority, 260 f.

Man's brothers by his father do not inherit his mother by representation, if
he predeceased her, 263 f.

Maternal kin not deemed kin with respect to, 262

Of widow who died while waiting to be married by leviratical marriage, 270

Order of, 260

Priority of males to females, 261

Proselyte's right of inheritance of property left by his heathen father, 279

Relatives tracing relationship to deceased through prohibited union on par
with those tracing it through legitimate union, 262

Wife does not inherit husband, 262

Iron sheep. *See* Usury

JOSEPH HALLEWI, Rabbi, 66

Judgment, deemed debt on writing, 219 f.; plea of payment of, 219 f.

LAND OF ISRAEL, 143

Law, the (*see* Glossary), 4, 7, 12

LEGAL DOCUMENT:

Attesting witnesses to, must know how to read and to sign, 171; presumed to
have had personal knowledge of parties thereto, 170; presumption that, will not
sign unless maker has legal capacity, 170; required to have personal knowledge of
the parties to, 170

Collection on writing obligatory prepared by heathen, 181

Construction of, 185 f.

Formal requirements of, 182 ff.

Invalidity of, except deed of purchase and sale and writing obligatory, if attested by heathen witnesses, 180 f.

May be signed by chief of court, if read to him by his scribe, 171

Method of identification of maker of, 171

Payment of the scribe's fee for, 169

Type of, which may be prepared at instance of one of the parties, 169; which
may not be prepared except in presence of both parties, 169

Validity of, if written in any language or script, 180

LETTING AND HIRING:

Accidental destruction of leased house, 21

Assignment of contract of hiring by hirer of ship, 20

Assignment of lease by tenant of house, 20 f.

Burden of proof in case of conflicting allegations with respect to duration of
lease or payment of rent, 24 f.

Crop of field under lease destroyed by locust or tempest, 28

Distinction between movables and landed property or ship with respect to
assignability of contract of hiring, 20 f.

Lessee may not sow field to crop less advantageous to lessor than that stipulated for, 29 f.

Lessee's duty to weed field, 29

Lessor's duty to keep house in habitable condition, 22

Local custom governs in certain matters, 28 f.

Manure in courtyard belongs to lessee, 22

Scope of, 22

Spring feeding irrigated field under lease drying up, 27 f.

Stipulations with respect to, 24

Substituted performance of terms of, 26

Tenancy, for definite term: lessor's right to compel lessee to vacate premises at end of term, 28; for indefinite term: increase or decrease in rent, 23, lessor, his heir, or transferee may not compel lessee to vacate premises during rainy season, 23, lessor's right to remove lessee in certain cases of hardship, 22 f., notice of 30 days by lessee to lessor, required during warm season, 23, notice of 30 days by lessor, his heir, or transferee, to lessee required during warm season, 23, 24; for specified amount of money, 27; for specified amount of produce, 27; on shares: duty of tenant on shares to cultivate field under lease, 30 f., measure of damages payable by tenant on shares who fails to cultivate field or sows it to crop other than that stipulated for, 31; per month: benefit of intercalation in case of, belongs to lessor, 24; per year: benefit of intercalation in case of, belongs to lessee, 24

Trees of orchard under lease drying up, 25

MINORS, DEAF-MUTES, AND INCOMPETENTS (*see also* Enforcement of Obligations, Guardian, Seizin), blind person treated as normal in every respect, 212; claim for tort or personal injury may not be asserted against minor, 212; claim may be asserted against minor only with respect to something from which he derived benefit, 211 f.; oath not to be administered on claim involving deaf-mute or mentally incompetent, 212; suit against minor allowed in certain cases after appointment of guardian, 122

NEGOTIABLE INSTRUMENTS, 310

OATH:

Bailee's, 4 f., 6, 10

By accumulation, 43, 60; extent of, 194; liability to, 194

In general, defendant liable to strict and light, to take strict which is to include all matters at issue, 194; person incompetent as witness deemed suspect with regard to, 196; person suspect with regard to, may not be subjected to, 196; repentance of person who was suspect with regard to, 198; status of suspect with regard to, how established, 196, 198; to be inclusive of all claims made by adversary, 194

Informal, 10, 11, 25, 42, 116, 132; as to lack of knowledge concerning plaintiff's claim, 192 f.; defendant liable to: is quit if he is suspect with regard to oath, 197, may not shift it to plaintiff who is suspect, 197 f.; defendant to be subjected to, only by reason of *claim certain* on part of plaintiff, 192; liability to, of defendant: on claim asserted against him by minor, 211, on claim of personal injury, 195, on claim touching landed property, bondmen, and bonds, and property belonging to sanctuary, 207 ff., 209 f., who is quit of Pentateuchal oath, 191

Of insolvency, 81 f.

Pentateuchal, claim for rental not deemed claim touching land, with respect to, 209; defendant liable to: refusing to swear, 191, suspect with regard to oath,

196 f., unable to swear, 206; defendant not to be subjected to, by reason of claim asserted by minor, except in case of bailment, 210; exemption from, when party making partial admission may be deemed restorer of lost property, 205; liability to, of defendant: if witnesses testify to part of plaintiff's claim, 207, making admission of at least 1 *pĕruṭah* and denial of at least 2 *ma'ah,* 199, making full denial against testimony of one witness, 190, making partial admission of claim touching movables, 190, on claim of utensils, not dependent upon value of what is admitted and what is denied, 200, only if admission relates to claim, 201 f., only when he admits something which he could deny, 204 f., only where plaintiff claims something measurable, weighable, or numerable, 203 f.; may not be shifted, 192; not to be imposed with respect to claim touching landed property, bondmen, and bonds and property belonging to sanctuary, 207 f.

Quasi-Pentateuchal or Rabbinical, defendant liable to, refusing to swear, 191 f.; liability to, 191; may not be shifted, 191, plaintiff subject to, suspect with regard to oath, 196
Oral tradition (*see* Glossary), 93, 190

PENALTY, admission of liability to, 195
PLEADING:
Burden of proof in case of conflicting allegations with regard to ownership of movables, 226 ff.
Change of plea, with explanation, 221, 232, 252; without explanation, 221
Defendant admitting that liability at one time existed but claiming lack of knowledge as to discharge thereof, 193
Nature of proof required to establish defendant's dishonesty under certain pleas, 214 f.
Ultimate facts and not conclusions of law to be pleaded, 212 ff.
PLEDGE:
Conflicting allegations of creditor and debtor with respect to value of lost, 125 f.
Court's representative must not enter debtor's house for purpose of taking, 86
For hire due, 88
From surety, 88
May be hired out by creditor in certain cases, 88
Not to be taken, against debtor's will except through court, 86; from widow, 85; of what is used in preparation of food, 85
Presumption (*ḥăzaḳah*) (*see* Glossary and Introduction), 64, 170, 219, 224, 228 f., 233, 250, 271, 276, 281
Purchase and sale, antedated or postdated deed of, invalid, 165; duplicate of deed of, containing special clause may be prepared in case of claim by vendee of loss of original, 166

RECOGNIZANCE (*see* Glossary), informal admission of indebtedness not deemed as, 216; made before court, 218 f.; made before witnesses, 217 f.; made in absence of cognizee, 217; made in presence of cognizee, 218; touching land, 219; touching movables, 219
Reputation (*ḥăzaḳah*) (*see* Glossary and Introduction), 223, 272
Right of way, loss of, 254

SAGES, the, 8, 12, 17

Scribes, the, 262

SEIZIN (*ḥăzaḳah*) (*see* Glossary and Introduction):

Of landed property, acquisition of, by possession coupled with taking of profits for 3 years, 233 f.; belonging to: married woman, 248, minor, 246 f., person who has escaped by reason of danger to his life, 247 f.; disagreement in testimony of witnesses to, with respect to kind of profits taken by party in possession, 250; each of 2 witnesses to, testifying to different years of possession, 250 f.; Joinder of times of possession: against ancestor and heir, 239, by ancestor and heir, 238, by tenants in common, 238, by vendor and vendee, 238; must be coupled with claim of rightful ownership, 248, 249 f., 352; not acquired through required period of possession by: craftsman, 242, deaf-mute, mentally incompetent, and minor, 242, exilarch in Talmudic times, 244, guardian, 243, heathen, or Israelite claiming through heathen, 246, husband of wife's property, 244, notorious robber, 245, tenant in common, 243 f., tenant on shares, 243; party relying upon, and upon writing required to produce writing, 250; period of possession must be consecutive, 237 f.; possession must be coupled with taking of profits, 239 f.; presumption of loss of deed of conveyance, 234; profits taken by party in possession upon erroneous presumption of heirship to deceased owner, 251; proof required of party claiming through ancestor, 249; protest by original owner preventing acquisition of, by party in possession, 234 f.; required period of possession must be complete in case of property producing profits continually, 236; restitution of profits by party in possession failing to produce proof of, 256; son of craftsman, of tenant on shares, or of guardian claiming by purchase or by inheritance from father, 246; son of notorious robber, claiming through his father, 246; sufficiency of reaping 3 harvests from unirrigated field to constitute, 236; tenants holding under party who is required to restore property to owner, 257; two parties contesting over field and neither, or both, producing witnesses to, 251 f.

Of movables, designed to be lent or rented out, 222; distinction between things designed to be lent or rented out and those fit to be lent or rented out, 224 f.; in hands of craftsman, 225 f.; not designed to be lent or rented out, 222; possession of bondman: able to walk, 231, coupled with enjoyment of his services for 3 years, 231 f., unable to walk, 232; possession of unguarded animal, 230 f.

Seize, seizure (*see* Glossary), 79, 84

Spain, 220

TEACHERS, my, 66, 98, 100, 131, 133, 168, 177, 181, 191, 193, 200, 203, 211

USURY:

Addition by vendor, of own accord, to measure of produce purchased at market price permissible, 107 f.

Advanced or delayed, prohibited, 95 f.

Advances by lessor to tenant on shares, 104

Agreement for future delivery of produce forbidden unless market price has been published, 109 f.

Augmentation or decrease of weight of coin stipulated for in writing obligatory, 91 f.

Borrower at, transgresses 2 negative commandments, 89
Children not bound to return usury money left by father, 90
Directly stipulated, recoverable from lender, 90
Evasions of, 96
Father not to borrow money from small children at, though intending excess payments as gift, 91
Gage, distinction between gage of field and gage of house, 100 f.; of field, 100 f.; of house, 100; sale of field or of house with condition of repurchase distinguished from, 99; stipulation by gagee that gagor sell property to him only, forbidden, 104; with deduction, 101; without deduction, 100
Iron sheep (*see* Glossary), acceptance of, from Israelite, forbidden, 108; definition of, 108 f.
Lender at, transgresses 6 negative commandments, 89
Lending to, or borrowing from, heathen or alien resident at, permissible, 93
Letting denar at hire, prohibited, 97
Offer of restitution of, not to be accepted, 90
Pardon of, by borrower to lender, 92
Pentateuchal, cases of, 98 f.; definition of, 97, 98 f.
Prohibition of, applicable to lender, borrower, surety, and witnesses, 89
Purchasing bonds at less than face value, permissible, 96
Quasi usury, deduction of, by borrower, from principal remaining unpaid, 102; definition of, 98; delivery of property to party for trading on shares with no participation in losses, prohibited as, except in case of property belonging to orphans, 92 f., 95; not recoverable from lender, 90; transfer of accounts with respect to, 102
Rules governing loans of produce, 104 ff.
Sale of property, with part payment of purchase price, 99 f.
Special enactment of the Sages prohibiting lending to heathen at, 93
Stipulation for increase, definition of, 102, 104, 105; exceptions to rule forbidding, 106; with respect to man's hire, prohibited, 105; with respect to rent of landed property, permissible, 104; with respect to sale, forbidden, 105 f.
Surety and witnesses to usurious transaction transgress one negative commandment, 89
Surreptitious transfer of money to heathen for purpose of lending it to Israelite at, forbidden, 94
Transfer of accounts, defined, 102
Trading on shares permitted only upon certain conditions, 95

WEST, the, 120, 280
WRITING OBLIGATORY:
Allegation by creditor that payment was made on account of another debt, 129 f.
Antedated, invalid, 163
Assignment of, by deed and delivery and by transfer adjunct, 139
Attested by one witness, 131
Circumstances under which witnesses may reduce oral acknowledgment of debt to, 116 f.
Coin in which collectible, 143

Collectible from, debtor's *alienated* property, if *free* property not available, 143 f., 147 f. *See also* Enforcement of Obligations; debtor's *free* property, in first instance, 143 f.; debtor's *free* property only, in certain cases, 129; purchasers of debtor's property, 117 f.

Creditor on, not entitled to *seize* debtor's after-acquired property unless included within scope of, 144; not entitled to *seize* property dedicated by debtor to Sanctuary, 146

Dated on the Sabbath or on *Yom Kippur,* 164

Dating of, on day when *ḳinyan* was performed, 164

Definition of judicial incision, 168

Duplicate of, may not be prepared in case of claim by creditor of loss of original, 167

Depositary of, believed with respect to discharge of, 139

Found among deceased creditor's effects with note of discharge, 140

Found among effects of deceased depositary, 139

In the form of "I, X, son of Y, owe you," valid, 171

May be written at debtor's instance, in absence of creditor, 164

Movables not subject to *seizure* by creditor on, unless included within scope of, 144

Once discharged, may not be used again, 130

Postdated, valid, 143, 163

Preparation of duplicate of, in case of decay of original, 167

Preparation of, for lesser amount in case of part payment of debt, 168

Proof by testimony of witnesses of payment of, 130

Recital of time and place of making of, not necessary to validity of, 143

Release by creditor on, claiming loss of, 168; to debtor's vendee, of right of enforcement of, 150

Seizure by creditor on, of improvements of debtor's property in hands of debtor's transferees or heirs, 154 ff.

Torn by judicial incision, 168

Written in debtor's own hand and delivered to creditor in presence of witnesses, 117